Garfield
loses his feet

BY JIM DAVIS

Ballantine Books • **New York**

A Ballantine Book
Published by The Random House Publishing Group
Copyright © 1984, 2004 by PAWS, Inc. All Rights Reserved.

All rights reserved under International and Pan-American Copyright Conventions. Published in the United States by The Random House Publishing Group, a division of Random House, Inc., New York, and simultaneously in Canada by Random House of Canada Limited, Toronto. Originally published in slightly different form by The Random House Publishing Group, a division of Random House, Inc., in 1984.

Ballantine and the Ballantine colophon are registered trademarks of Random House, Inc.

"GARFIELD" and the GARFIELD characters are registered and unregistered trademarks of PAWS, Inc.

www.ballantinebooks.com

Library of Congress Control Number: 2004092947

ISBN 0-345-46467-2

Manufactured in the United States of America

First Colorized Edition: September 2004

10 9 8 7 6 5 4 3 2 1

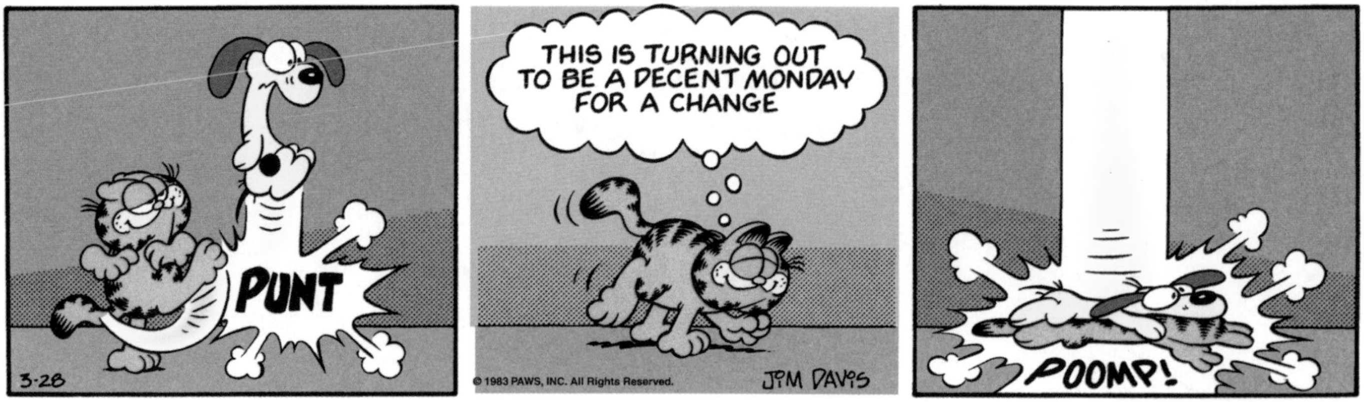
PUNT
3-28
THIS IS TURNING OUT TO BE A DECENT MONDAY FOR A CHANGE
© 1983 PAWS, INC. All Rights Reserved.
JIM DAVIS
POOMP!

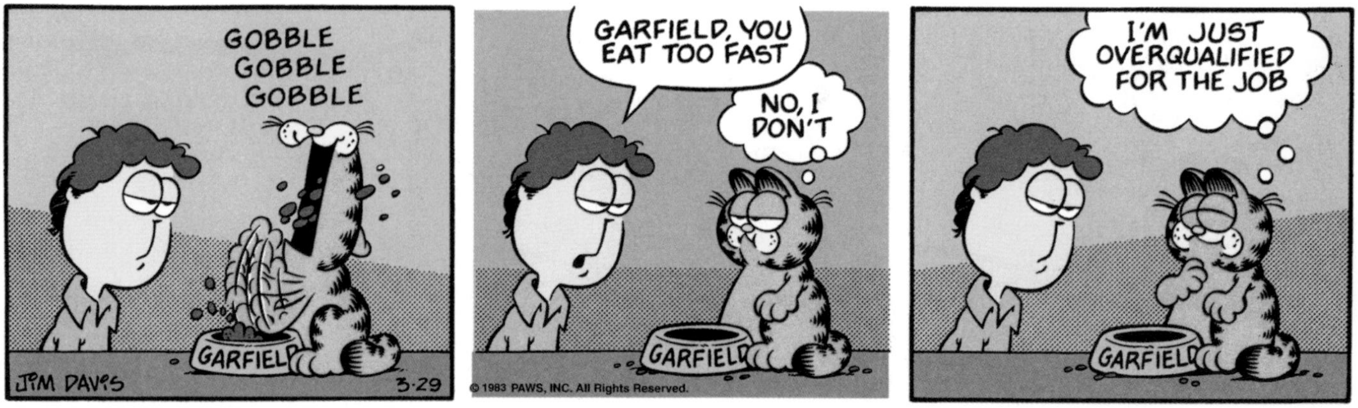
GOBBLE GOBBLE GOBBLE
GARFIELD
JIM DAVIS
3-29
GARFIELD, YOU EAT TOO FAST
NO, I DON'T
GARFIELD
© 1983 PAWS, INC. All Rights Reserved.
I'M JUST OVERQUALIFIED FOR THE JOB
GARFIELD

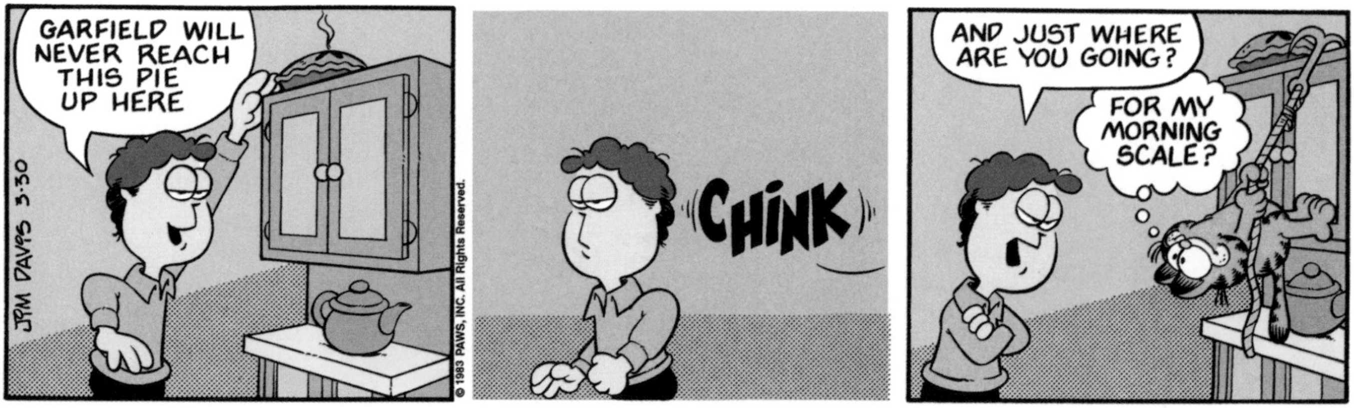
GARFIELD WILL NEVER REACH THIS PIE UP HERE
JIM DAVIS 3-30
© 1983 PAWS, INC. All Rights Reserved.
CHINK
AND JUST WHERE ARE YOU GOING?
FOR MY MORNING SCALE?

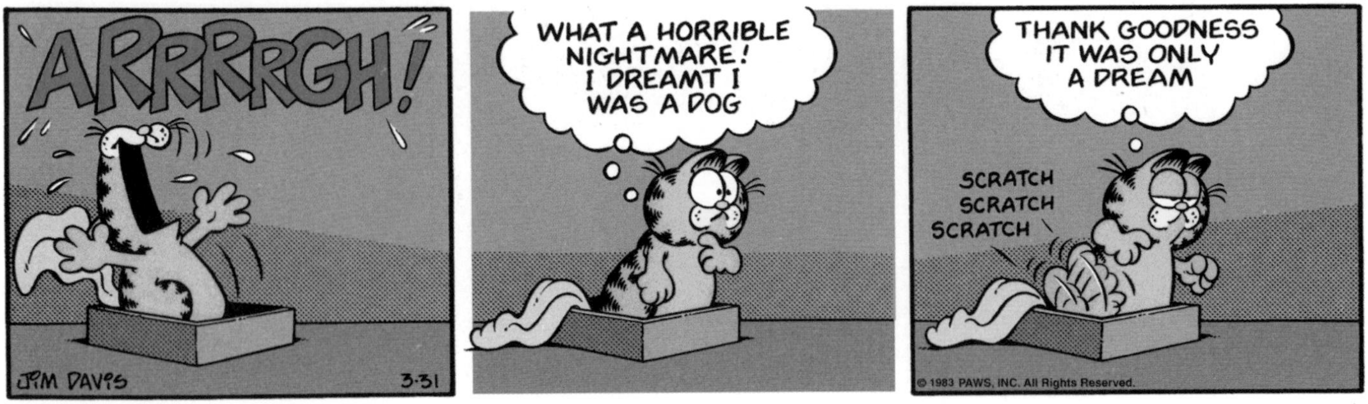
ARRRRGH!
JIM DAVIS
3·31
WHAT A HORRIBLE NIGHTMARE! I DREAMT I WAS A DOG
THANK GOODNESS IT WAS ONLY A DREAM
SCRATCH SCRATCH SCRATCH
© 1983 PAWS, INC. All Rights Reserved.

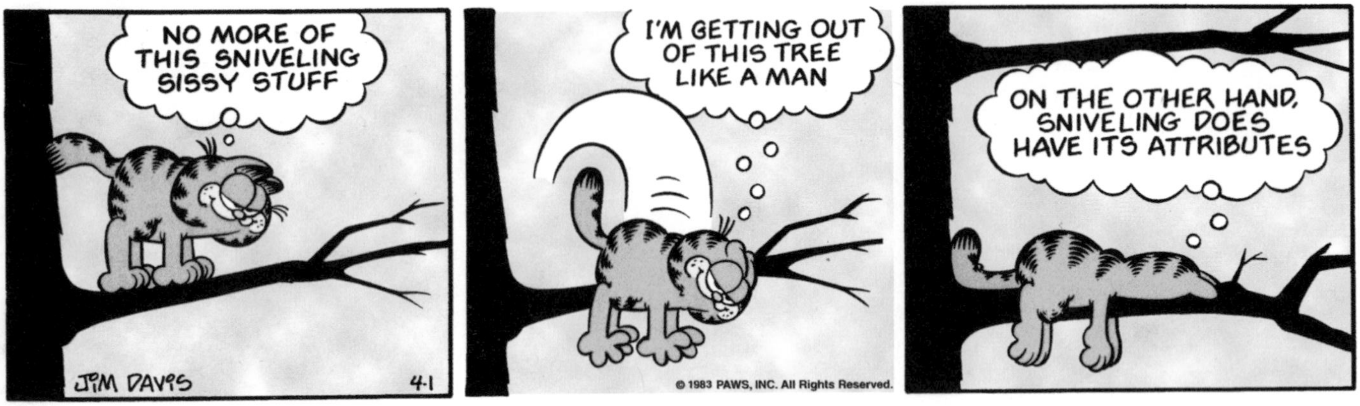
NO MORE OF THIS SNIVELING SISSY STUFF
JIM DAVIS
4·1
I'M GETTING OUT OF THIS TREE LIKE A MAN
© 1983 PAWS, INC. All Rights Reserved.
ON THE OTHER HAND, SNIVELING DOES HAVE ITS ATTRIBUTES

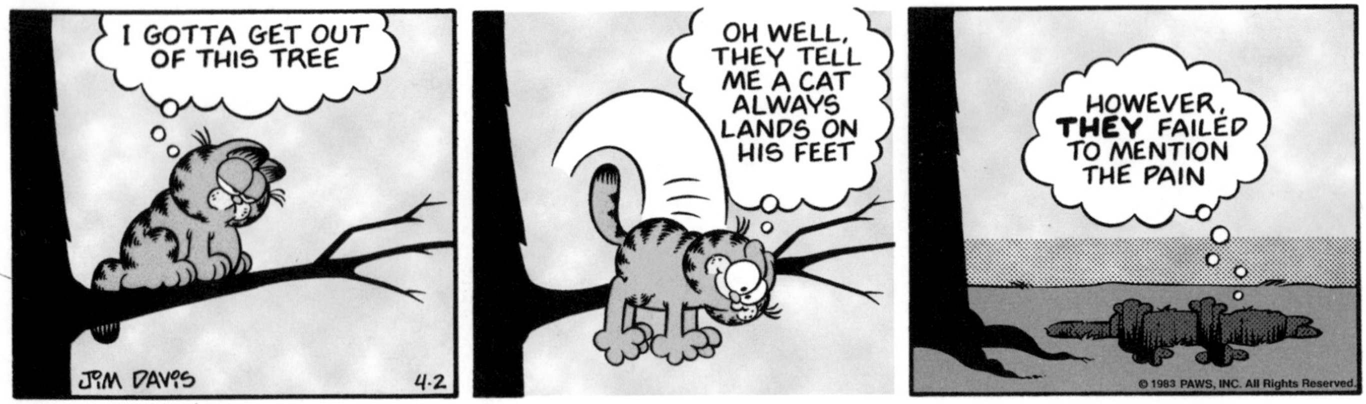
I GOTTA GET OUT OF THIS TREE
JIM DAVIS
4·2
OH WELL, THEY TELL ME A CAT ALWAYS LANDS ON HIS FEET
HOWEVER, **THEY** FAILED TO MENTION THE PAIN
© 1983 PAWS, INC. All Rights Reserved.

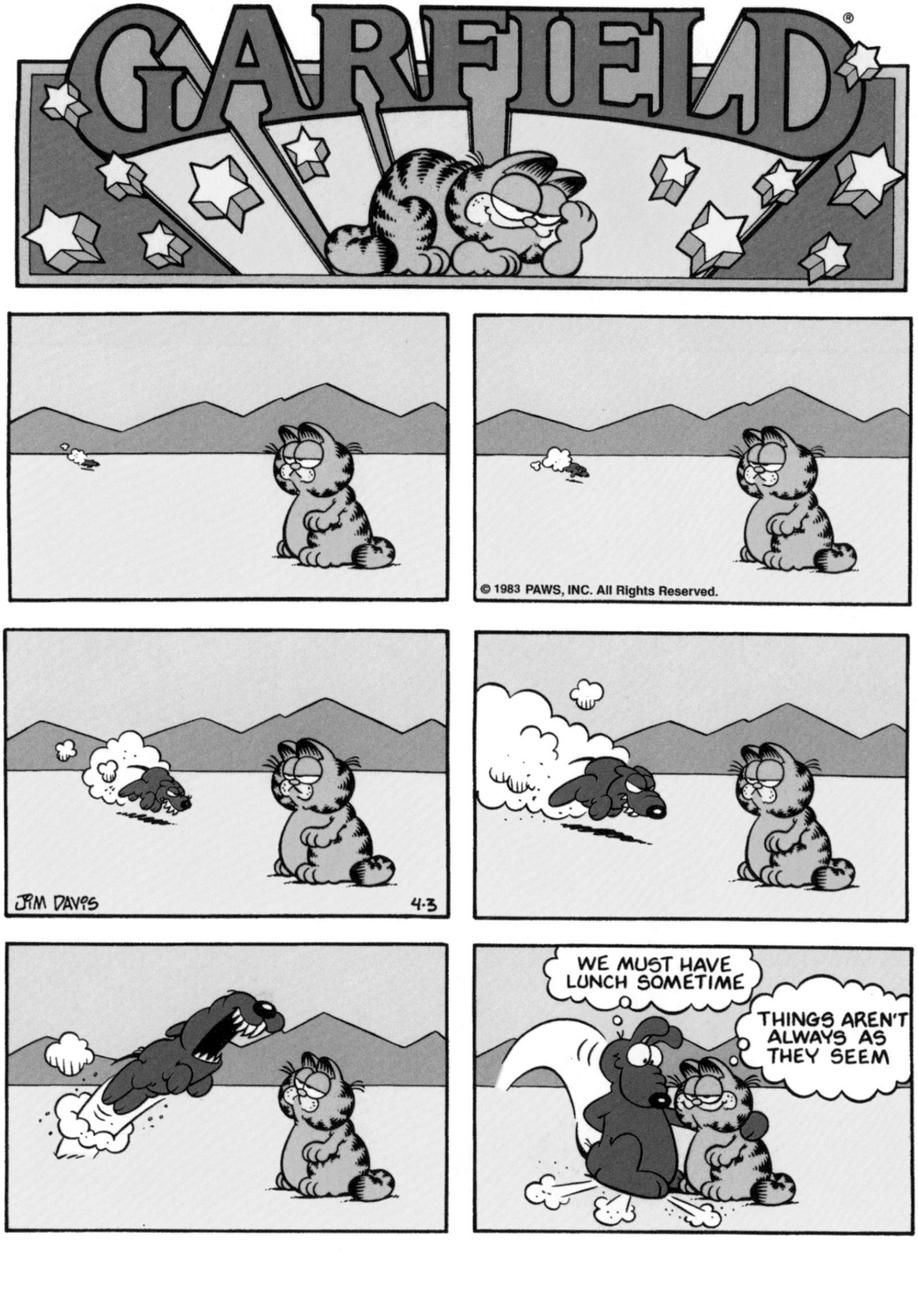
GARFIELD®
© 1983 PAWS, INC. All Rights Reserved.
JIM DAVIS
4-3
WE MUST HAVE LUNCH SOMETIME
THINGS AREN'T ALWAYS AS THEY SEEM

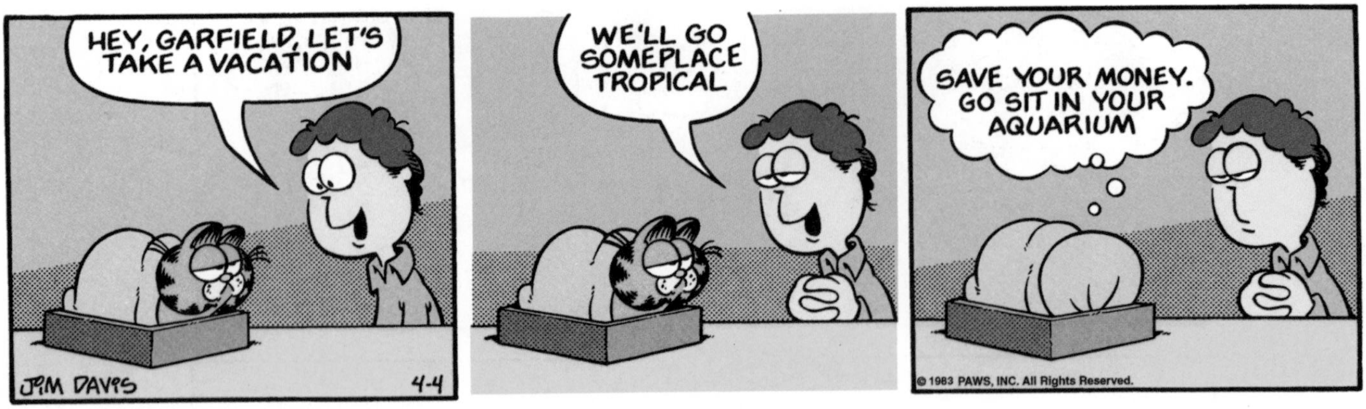
HEY, GARFIELD, LET'S TAKE A VACATION
JIM DAVIS
4-4
WE'LL GO SOMEPLACE TROPICAL
SAVE YOUR MONEY. GO SIT IN YOUR AQUARIUM
© 1983 PAWS, INC. All Rights Reserved.

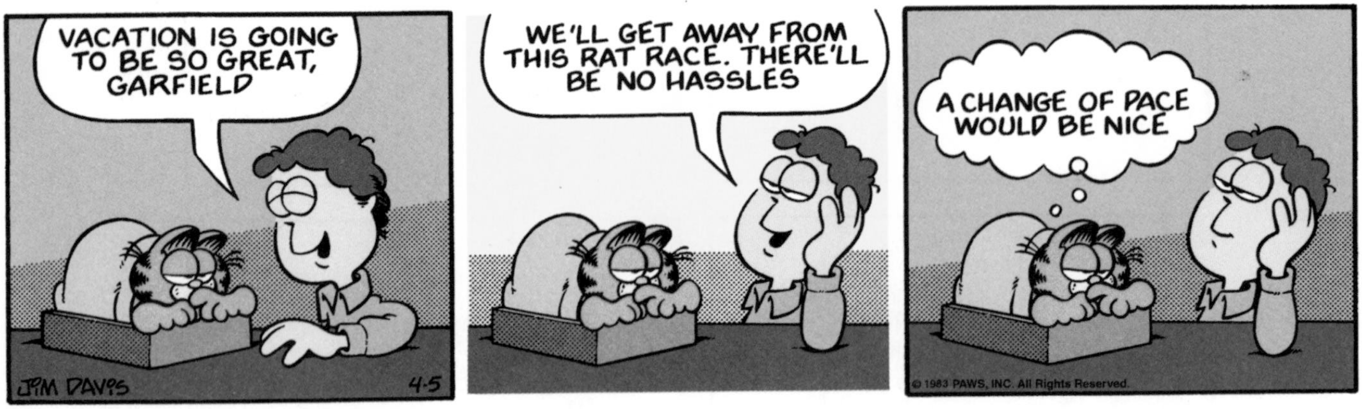
VACATION IS GOING TO BE SO GREAT, GARFIELD
JIM DAVIS
4-5
WE'LL GET AWAY FROM THIS RAT RACE. THERE'LL BE NO HASSLES
A CHANGE OF PACE WOULD BE NICE
© 1983 PAWS, INC. All Rights Reserved.

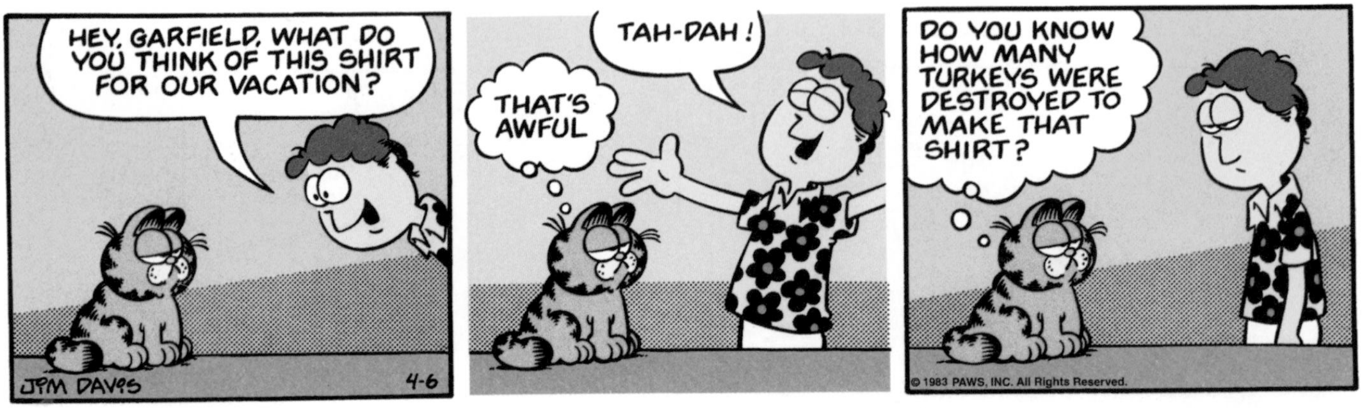
HEY, GARFIELD, WHAT DO YOU THINK OF THIS SHIRT FOR OUR VACATION?
JIM DAVIS
4-6
TAH-DAH!
THAT'S AWFUL
DO YOU KNOW HOW MANY TURKEYS WERE DESTROYED TO MAKE THAT SHIRT?
© 1983 PAWS, INC. All Rights Reserved.

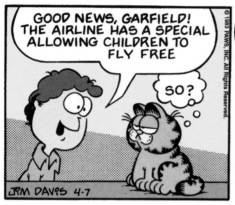

GOOD NEWS, GARFIELD! THE AIRLINE HAS A SPECIAL ALLOWING CHILDREN TO FLY FREE
SO?
JIM DAVIS 4-7
© 1983 PAWS, INC. All Rights Reserved.
SO WHEN WE LEAVE ON VACATION, YOU CAN POSE AS MY SON AND RIDE UP FRONT
I WILL NOT DEMEAN MYSELF BY DRESSING UP AS SOME STUPID KID
OTHERWISE, YOU'LL HAVE TO RIDE IN A KITTY CARRIER IN THE BAGGAGE COMPARTMENT
DADDY!

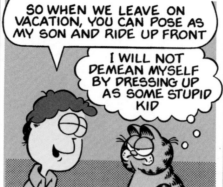

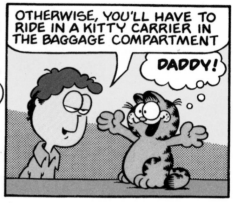

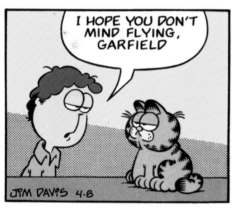

I HOPE YOU DON'T MIND FLYING, GARFIELD
JIM DAVIS 4-8
SOME ANIMALS DON'T TRAVEL WELL
NONSENSE
© 1983 PAWS, INC. All Rights Reserved.
IF A DOG CAN BE A WORLD WAR I FLYING ACE, I CAN SURELY FLY COMMERCIAL

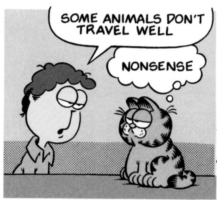

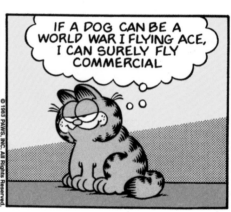

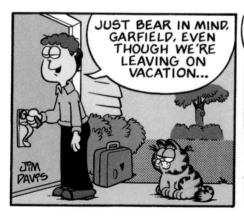

JUST BEAR IN MIND, GARFIELD, EVEN THOUGH WE'RE LEAVING ON VACATION...
JIM DAVIS
AND EVEN THOUGH WE'RE GOING TO HAVE FUN ...
4-9
© 1983 PAWS, INC. All Rights Reserved.
IT'S ALWAYS NICE TO GET BACK HOME

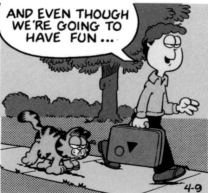

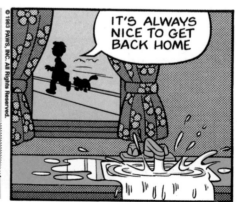

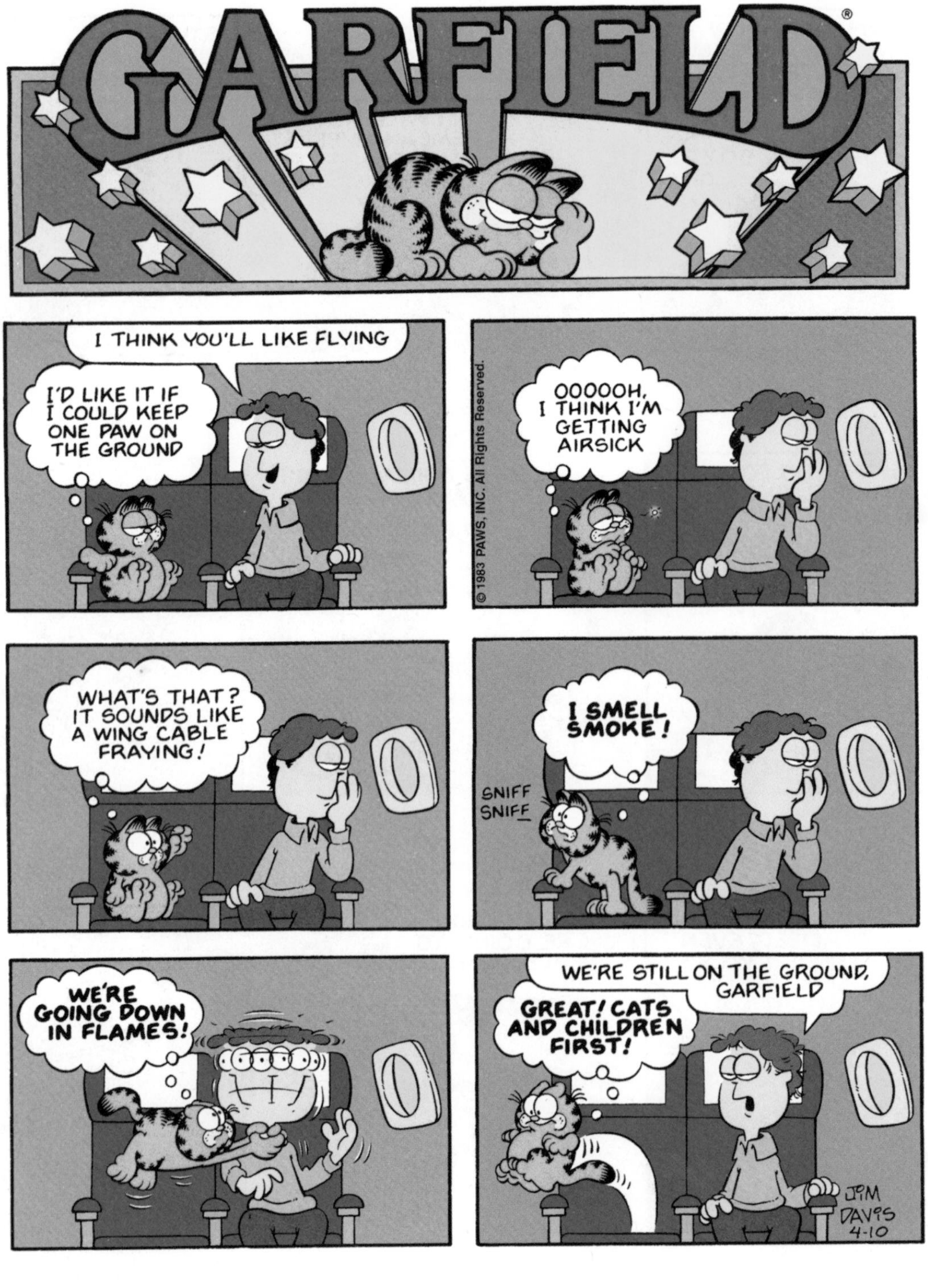
GARFIELD®
I THINK YOU'LL LIKE FLYING
I'D LIKE IT IF I COULD KEEP ONE PAW ON THE GROUND
OOOOOH, I THINK I'M GETTING AIRSICK
WHAT'S THAT? IT SOUNDS LIKE A WING CABLE FRAYING!
I SMELL SMOKE!
SNIFF SNIFF
WE'RE GOING DOWN IN FLAMES!
WE'RE STILL ON THE GROUND, GARFIELD
GREAT! CATS AND CHILDREN FIRST!
JIM DAVIS 4-10

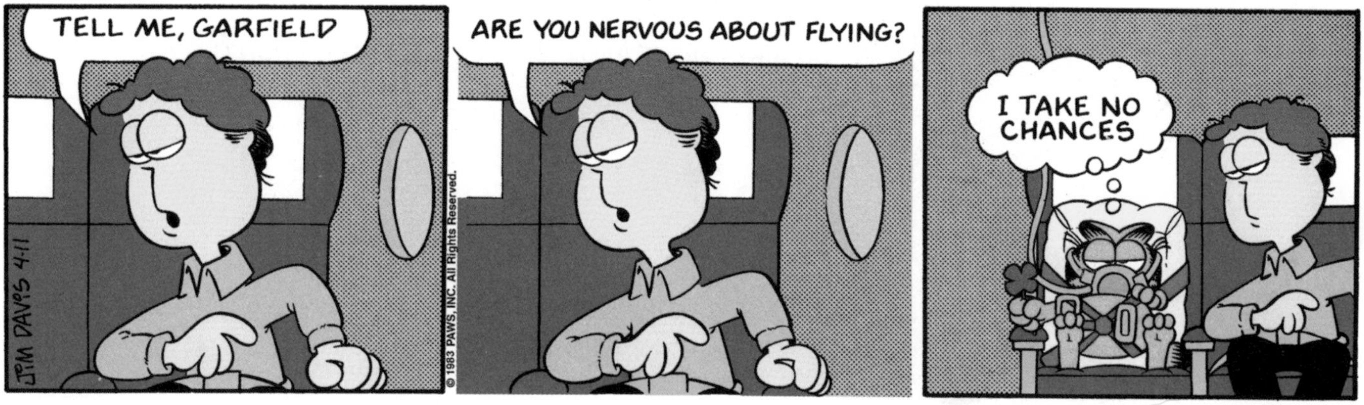
TELL ME, GARFIELD
JIM DAVIS 4-11
© 1983 PAWS, INC. All Rights Reserved.
ARE YOU NERVOUS ABOUT FLYING?
I TAKE NO CHANCES

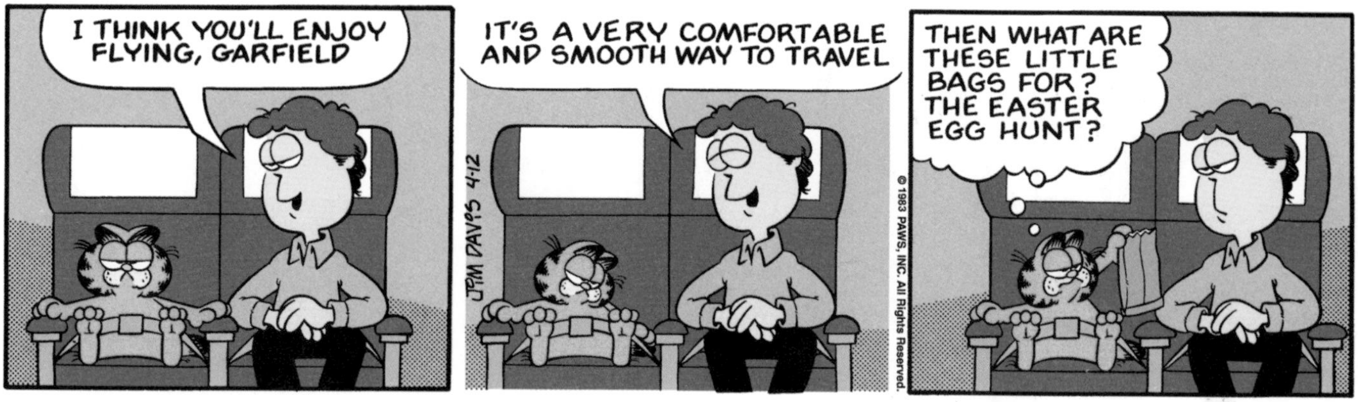
I THINK YOU'LL ENJOY FLYING, GARFIELD
IT'S A VERY COMFORTABLE AND SMOOTH WAY TO TRAVEL
JIM DAVIS 4-12
© 1983 PAWS, INC. All Rights Reserved.
THEN WHAT ARE THESE LITTLE BAGS FOR? THE EASTER EGG HUNT?

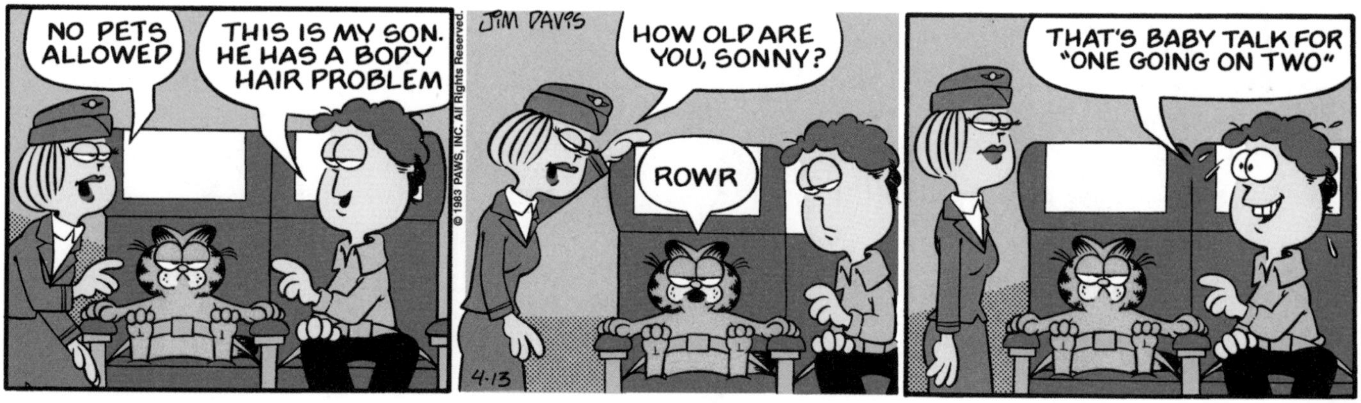
NO PETS ALLOWED
THIS IS MY SON. HE HAS A BODY HAIR PROBLEM
© 1983 PAWS, INC. All Rights Reserved.
JIM DAVIS
HOW OLD ARE YOU, SONNY?
ROWR
4-13
THAT'S BABY TALK FOR "ONE GOING ON TWO"

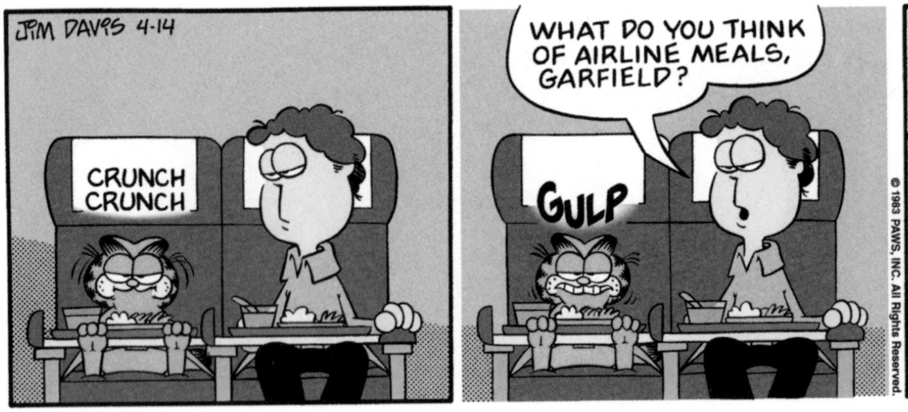
JIM DAVIS 4-14
CRUNCH CRUNCH
GULP
WHAT DO YOU THINK OF AIRLINE MEALS, GARFIELD?
THE ONLY THING WITH FOOD CONTENT WAS THE PLASTIC FORK I JUST ATE
© 1983 PAWS, INC. All Rights Reserved.

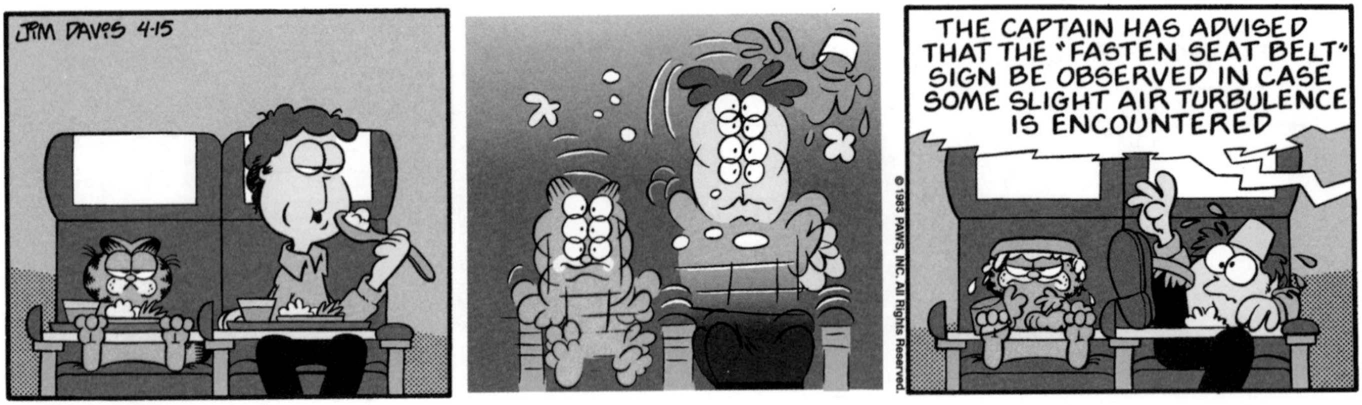
JIM DAVIS 4-15
THE CAPTAIN HAS ADVISED THAT THE "FASTEN SEAT BELT" SIGN BE OBSERVED IN CASE SOME SLIGHT AIR TURBULENCE IS ENCOUNTERED
© 1983 PAWS, INC. All Rights Reserved.

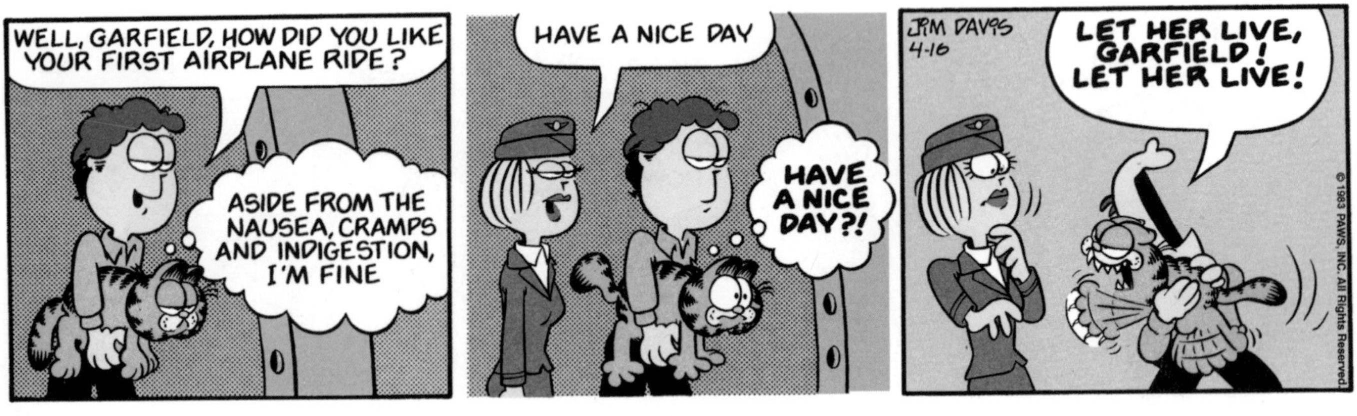
WELL, GARFIELD, HOW DID YOU LIKE YOUR FIRST AIRPLANE RIDE?
ASIDE FROM THE NAUSEA, CRAMPS AND INDIGESTION, I'M FINE
HAVE A NICE DAY
HAVE A NICE DAY?!
JIM DAVIS 4-16
LET HER LIVE, GARFIELD! LET HER LIVE!
© 1983 PAWS, INC. All Rights Reserved.

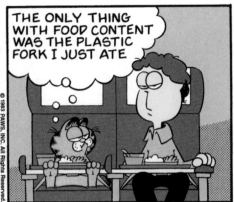

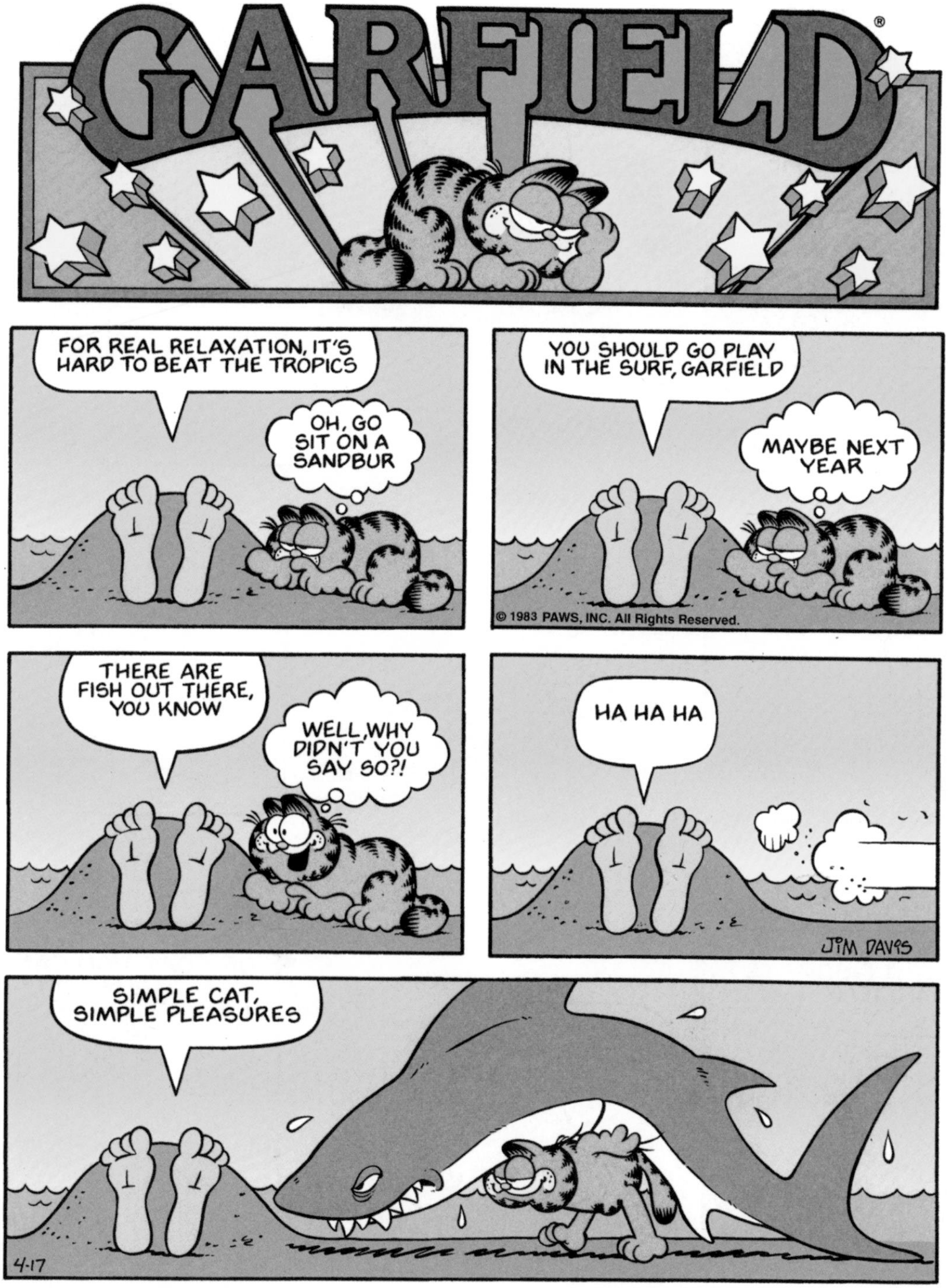
GARFIELD®
FOR REAL RELAXATION, IT'S HARD TO BEAT THE TROPICS
OH, GO SIT ON A SANDBUR
YOU SHOULD GO PLAY IN THE SURF, GARFIELD
MAYBE NEXT YEAR
© 1983 PAWS, INC. All Rights Reserved.
THERE ARE FISH OUT THERE, YOU KNOW
WELL, WHY DIDN'T YOU SAY SO?!
HA HA HA
JIM DAVIS
SIMPLE CAT, SIMPLE PLEASURES
4-17

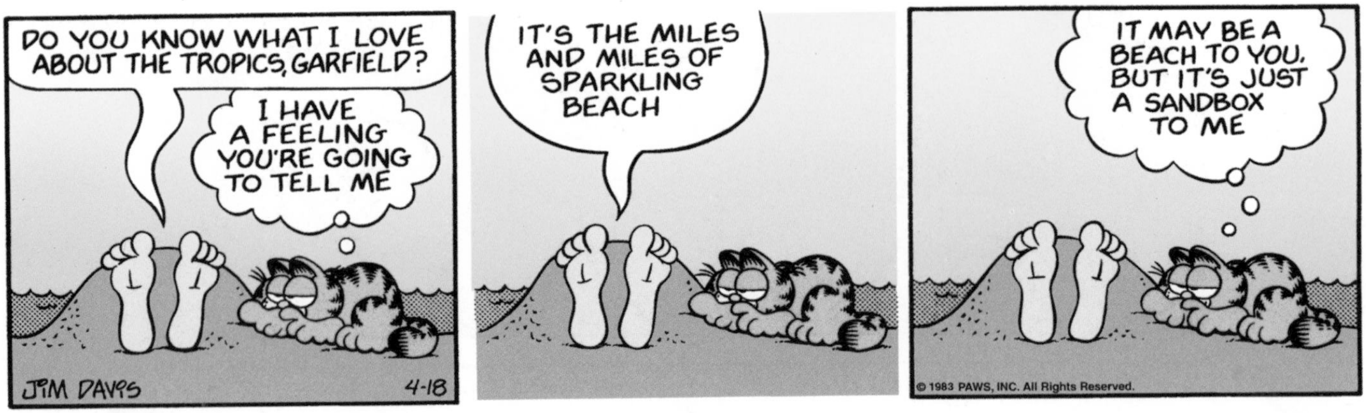
DO YOU KNOW WHAT I LOVE ABOUT THE TROPICS, GARFIELD?
I HAVE A FEELING YOU'RE GOING TO TELL ME
JIM DAVIS
4-18
IT'S THE MILES AND MILES OF SPARKLING BEACH
IT MAY BE A BEACH TO YOU, BUT IT'S JUST A SANDBOX TO ME
© 1983 PAWS, INC. All Rights Reserved.

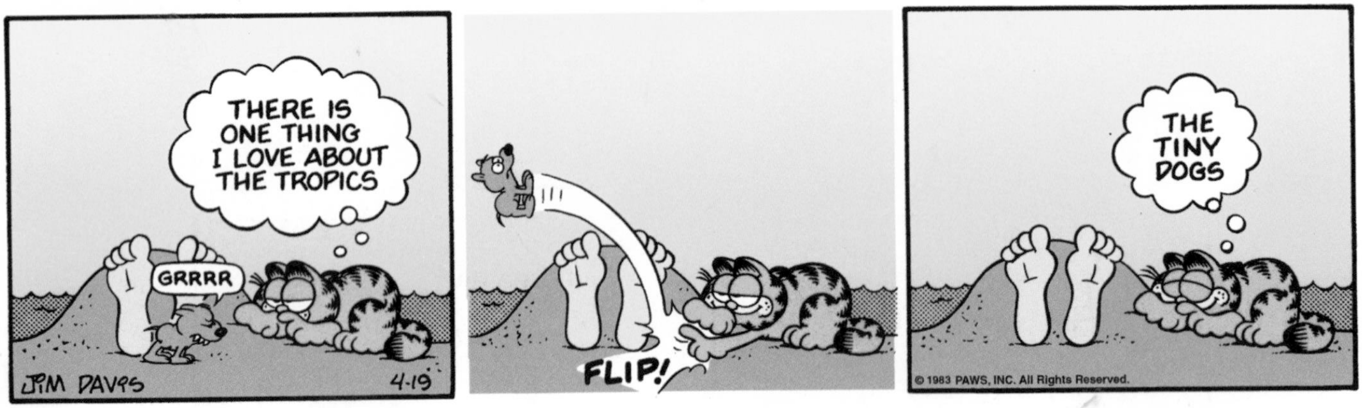
THERE IS ONE THING I LOVE ABOUT THE TROPICS
GRRRR
JIM DAVIS
4-19
FLIP!
THE TINY DOGS
© 1983 PAWS, INC. All Rights Reserved.

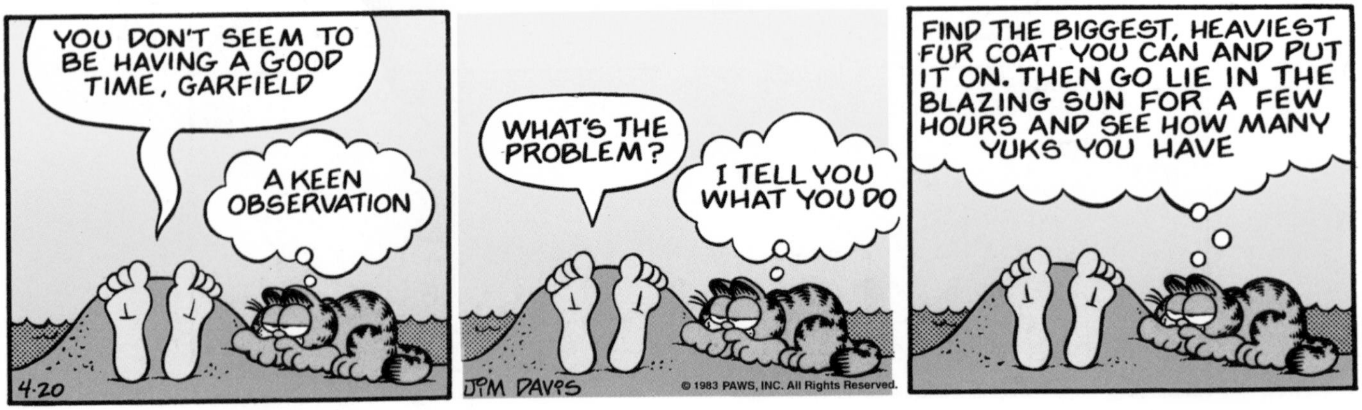
YOU DON'T SEEM TO BE HAVING A GOOD TIME, GARFIELD
A KEEN OBSERVATION
4-20
WHAT'S THE PROBLEM?
I TELL YOU WHAT YOU DO
JIM DAVIS
© 1983 PAWS, INC. All Rights Reserved.
FIND THE BIGGEST, HEAVIEST FUR COAT YOU CAN AND PUT IT ON. THEN GO LIE IN THE BLAZING SUN FOR A FEW HOURS AND SEE HOW MANY YUKS YOU HAVE

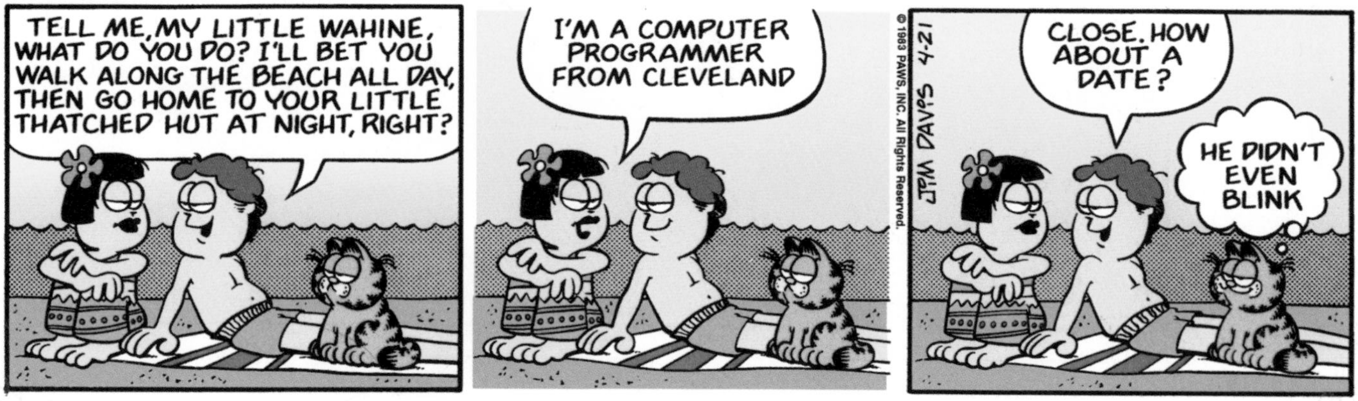
TELL ME, MY LITTLE WAHINE, WHAT DO YOU DO? I'LL BET YOU WALK ALONG THE BEACH ALL DAY, THEN GO HOME TO YOUR LITTLE THATCHED HUT AT NIGHT, RIGHT?
I'M A COMPUTER PROGRAMMER FROM CLEVELAND
© 1983 PAWS, INC. All Rights Reserved.
JIM DAVIS 4·21
CLOSE. HOW ABOUT A DATE?
HE DIDN'T EVEN BLINK

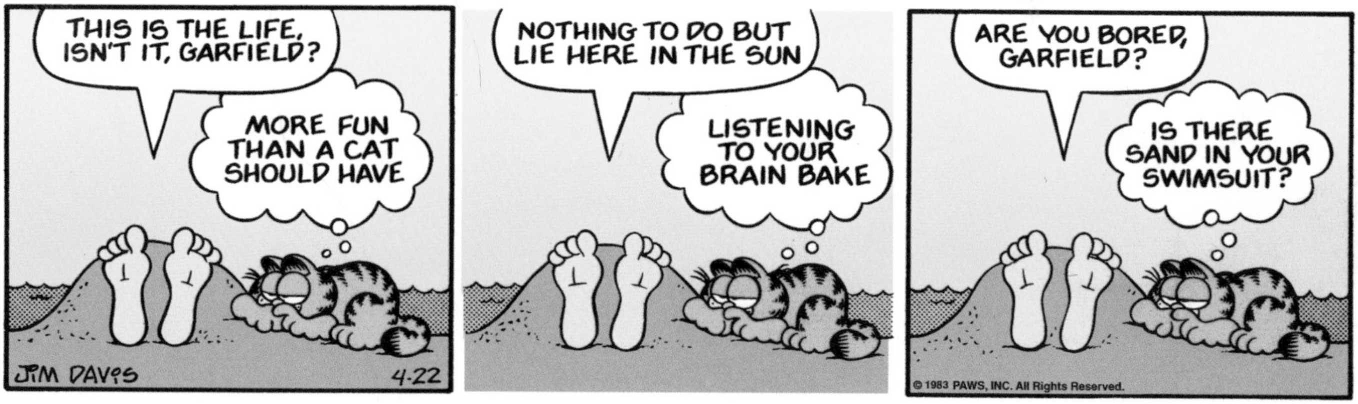
THIS IS THE LIFE, ISN'T IT, GARFIELD?
MORE FUN THAN A CAT SHOULD HAVE
JIM DAVIS
4·22
NOTHING TO DO BUT LIE HERE IN THE SUN
LISTENING TO YOUR BRAIN BAKE
ARE YOU BORED, GARFIELD?
IS THERE SAND IN YOUR SWIMSUIT?
© 1983 PAWS, INC. All Rights Reserved.

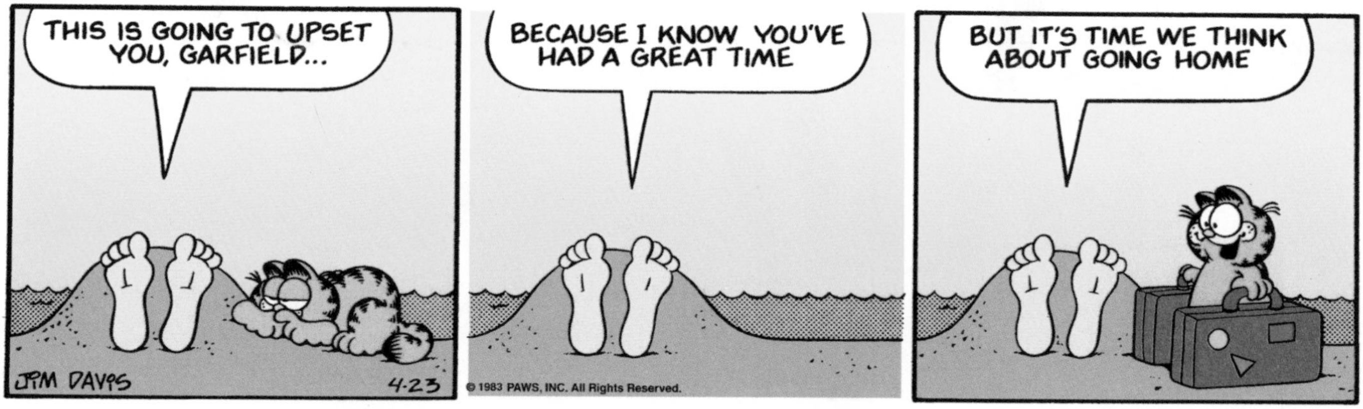
THIS IS GOING TO UPSET YOU, GARFIELD...
JIM DAVIS
4·23
BECAUSE I KNOW YOU'VE HAD A GREAT TIME
© 1983 PAWS, INC. All Rights Reserved.
BUT IT'S TIME WE THINK ABOUT GOING HOME

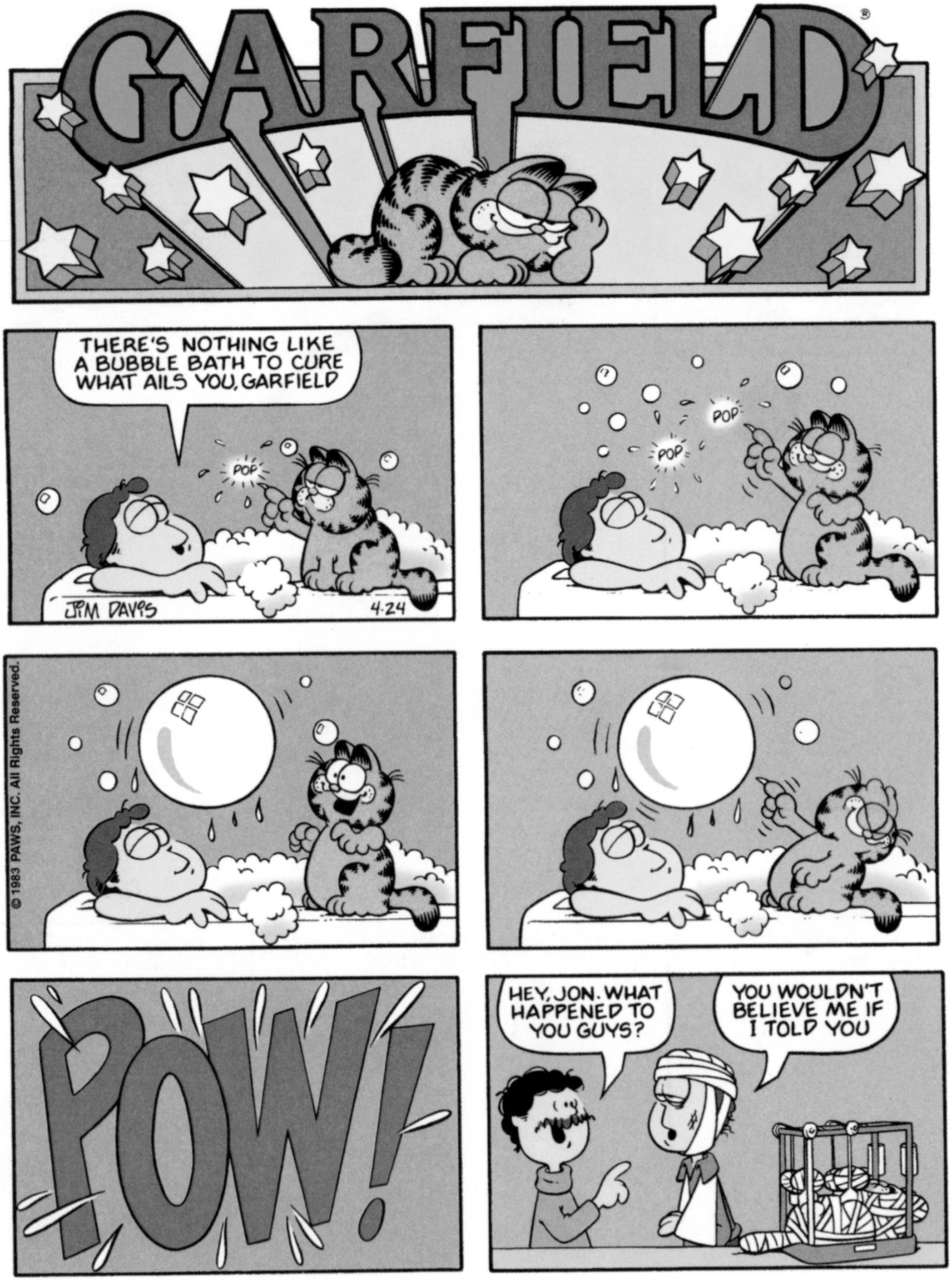
GARFIELD
THERE'S NOTHING LIKE A BUBBLE BATH TO CURE WHAT AILS YOU, GARFIELD
POP
JIM DAVIS
4·24
POP
POP
© 1983 PAWS, INC. All Rights Reserved.
POW!
HEY, JON. WHAT HAPPENED TO YOU GUYS?
YOU WOULDN'T BELIEVE ME IF I TOLD YOU

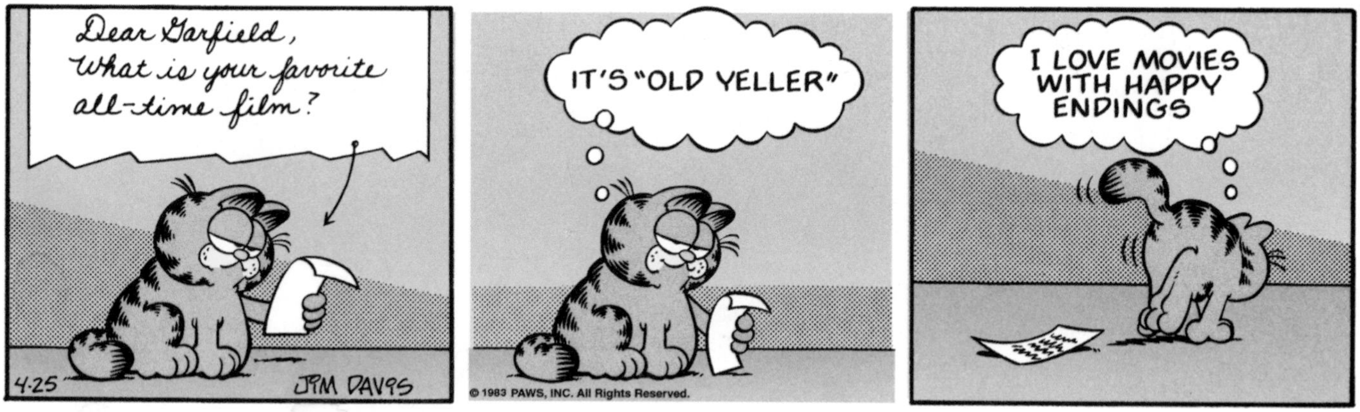
Dear Garfield,
What is your favorite all-time film?
4-25
JIM DAVIS
IT'S "OLD YELLER"
© 1983 PAWS, INC. All Rights Reserved.
I LOVE MOVIES WITH HAPPY ENDINGS

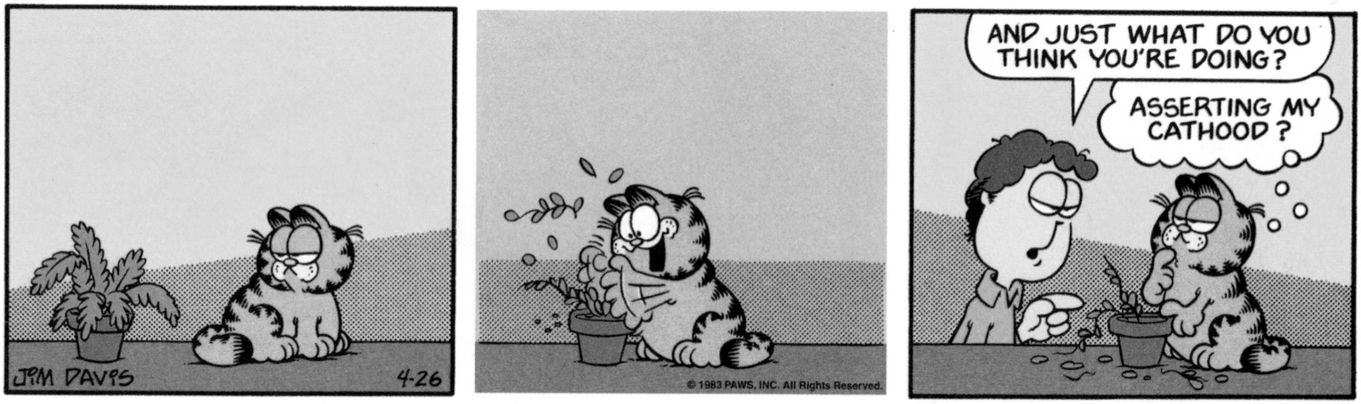
JIM DAVIS
4-26
© 1983 PAWS, INC. All Rights Reserved.
AND JUST WHAT DO YOU THINK YOU'RE DOING?
ASSERTING MY CATHOOD?

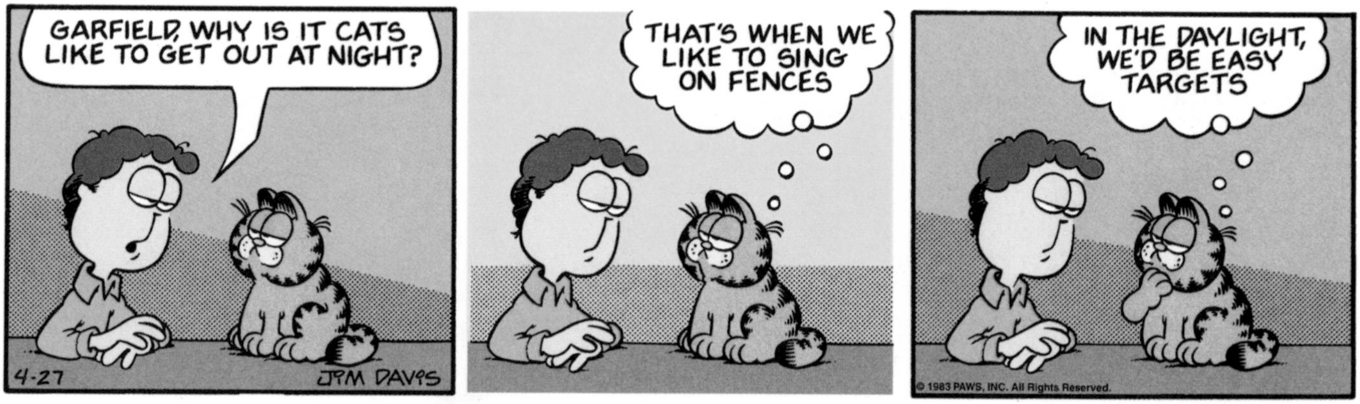
GARFIELD, WHY IS IT CATS LIKE TO GET OUT AT NIGHT?
4-27
JIM DAVIS
THAT'S WHEN WE LIKE TO SING ON FENCES
IN THE DAYLIGHT, WE'D BE EASY TARGETS
© 1983 PAWS, INC. All Rights Reserved.

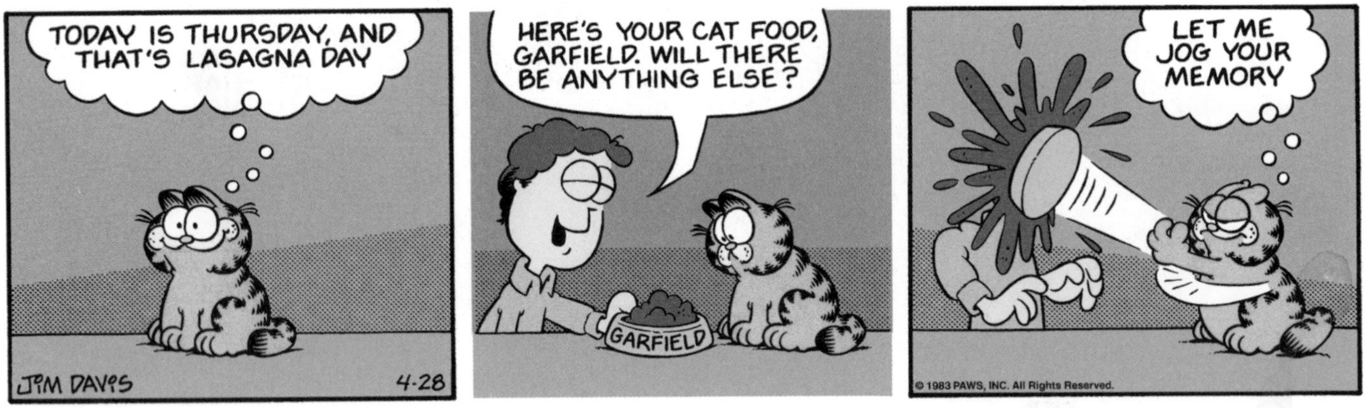
TODAY IS THURSDAY, AND THAT'S LASAGNA DAY
JIM DAVIS
4-28
HERE'S YOUR CAT FOOD, GARFIELD. WILL THERE BE ANYTHING ELSE?
GARFIELD
LET ME JOG YOUR MEMORY
© 1983 PAWS, INC. All Rights Reserved.

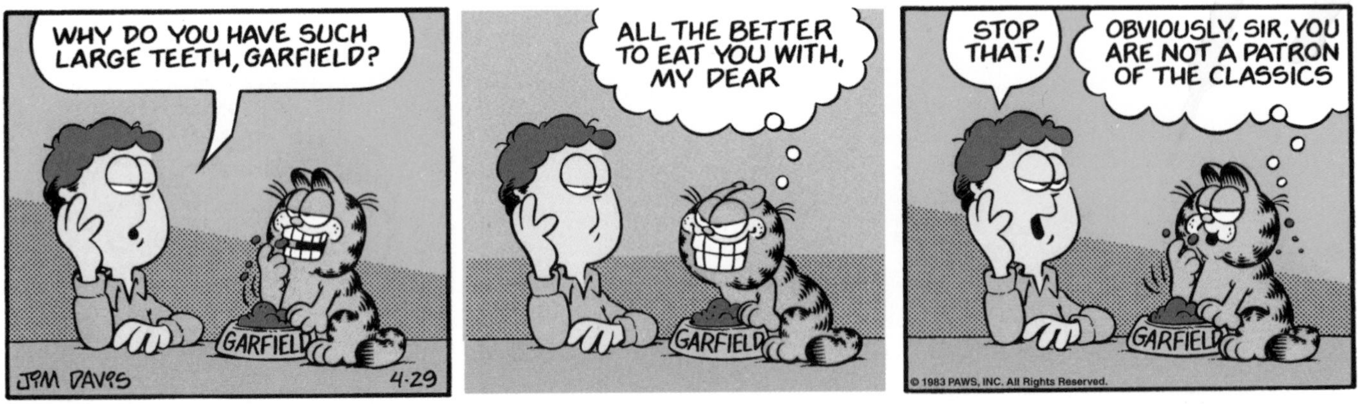
WHY DO YOU HAVE SUCH LARGE TEETH, GARFIELD?
GARFIELD
JIM DAVIS
4-29
ALL THE BETTER TO EAT YOU WITH, MY DEAR
GARFIELD
STOP THAT!
OBVIOUSLY, SIR, YOU ARE NOT A PATRON OF THE CLASSICS
GARFIELD
© 1983 PAWS, INC. All Rights Reserved.

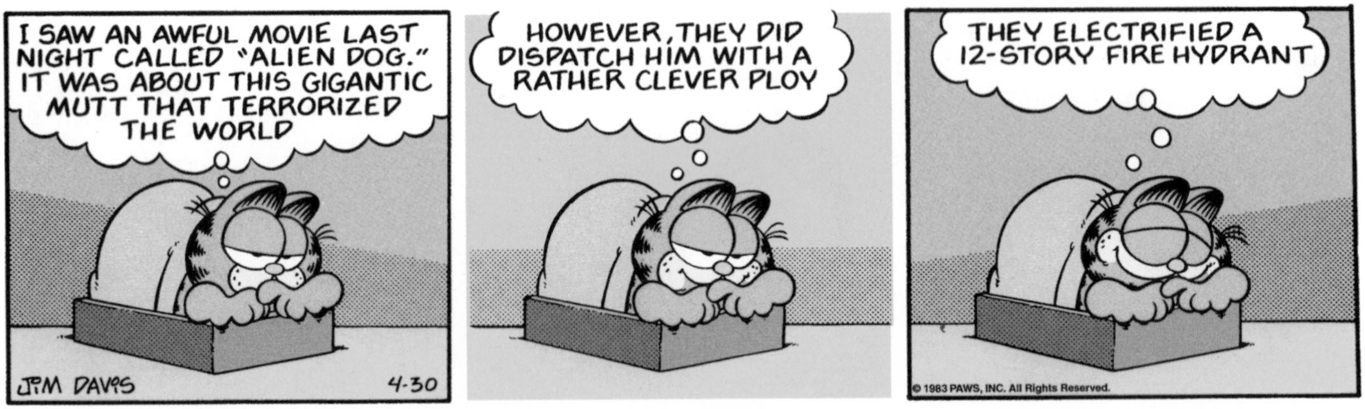
I SAW AN AWFUL MOVIE LAST NIGHT CALLED "ALIEN DOG." IT WAS ABOUT THIS GIGANTIC MUTT THAT TERRORIZED THE WORLD
JIM DAVIS
4-30
HOWEVER, THEY DID DISPATCH HIM WITH A RATHER CLEVER PLOY
THEY ELECTRIFIED A 12-STORY FIRE HYDRANT
© 1983 PAWS, INC. All Rights Reserved.

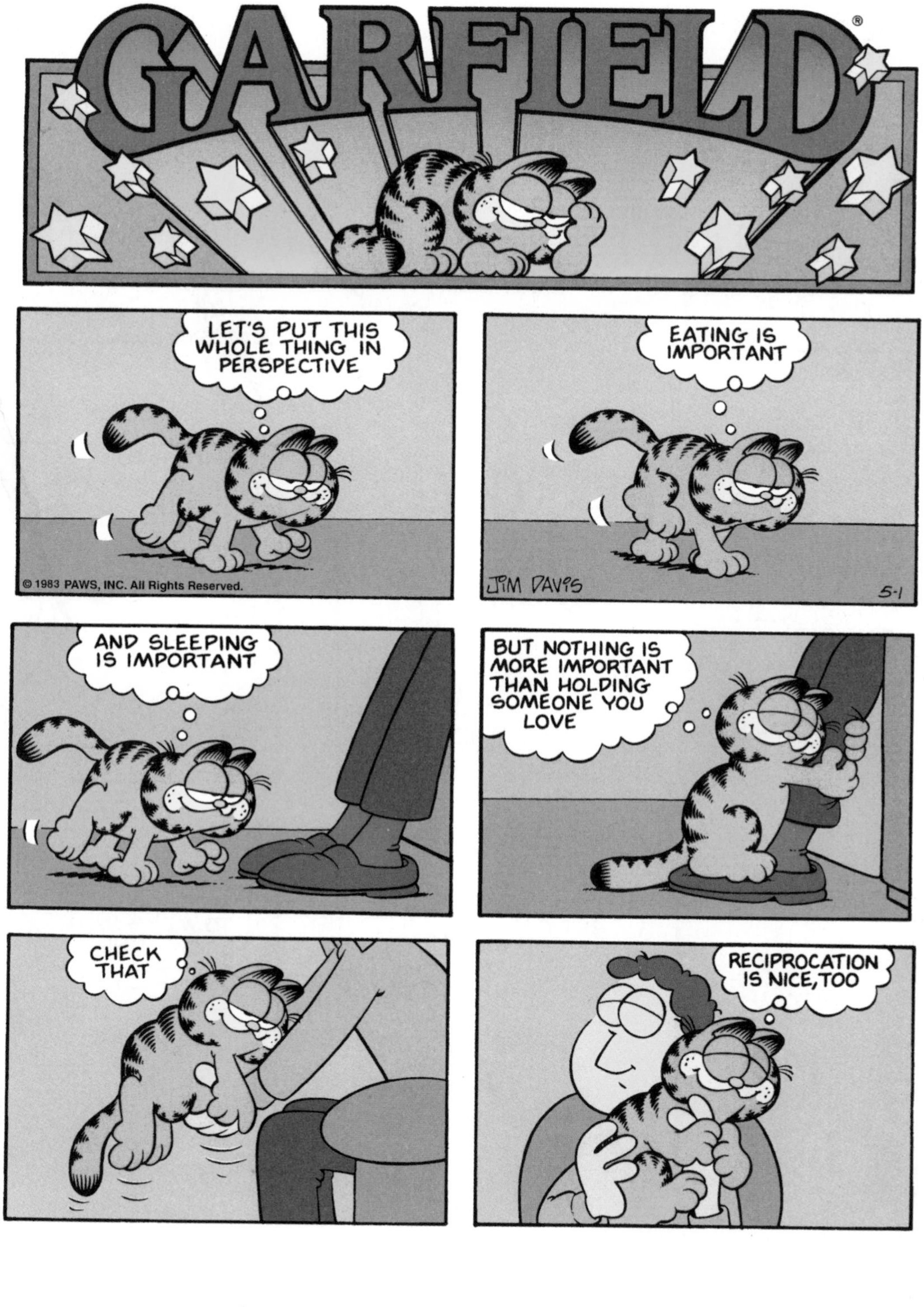
GARFIELD
LET'S PUT THIS WHOLE THING IN PERSPECTIVE
© 1983 PAWS, INC. All Rights Reserved.
EATING IS IMPORTANT
JIM DAVIS
5-1
AND SLEEPING IS IMPORTANT
BUT NOTHING IS MORE IMPORTANT THAN HOLDING SOMEONE YOU LOVE
CHECK THAT
RECIPROCATION IS NICE, TOO

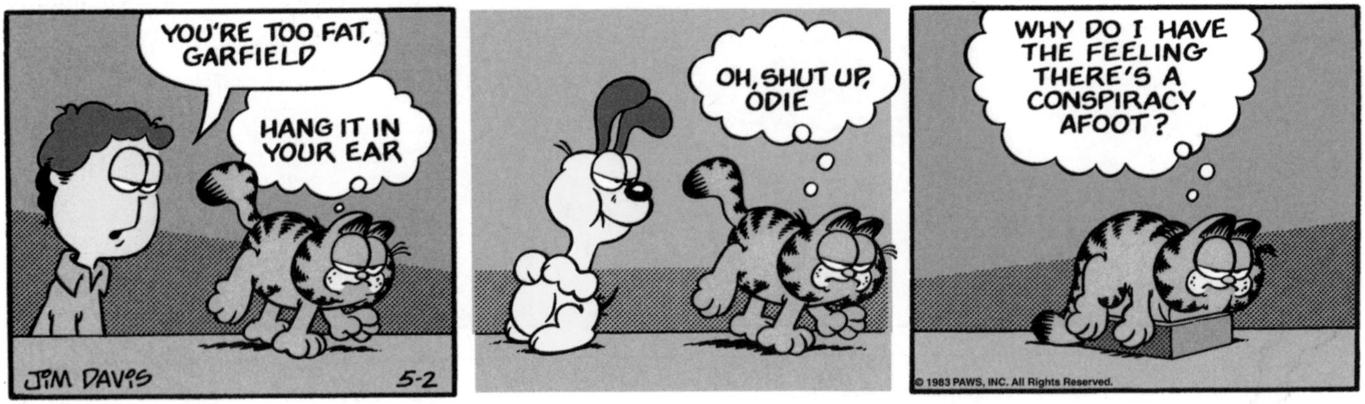
YOU'RE TOO FAT, GARFIELD
HANG IT IN YOUR EAR
JIM DAVIS
5-2
OH, SHUT UP, ODIE
WHY DO I HAVE THE FEELING THERE'S A CONSPIRACY AFOOT?
© 1983 PAWS, INC. All Rights Reserved.

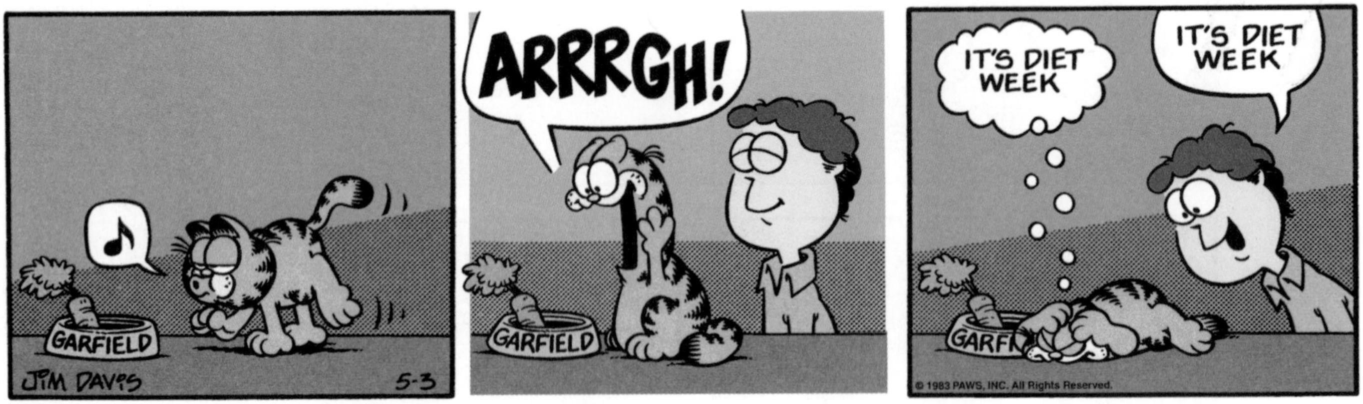
♪
GARFIELD
JIM DAVIS
5-3
ARRRGH!
GARFIELD
IT'S DIET WEEK
IT'S DIET WEEK
© 1983 PAWS, INC. All Rights Reserved.

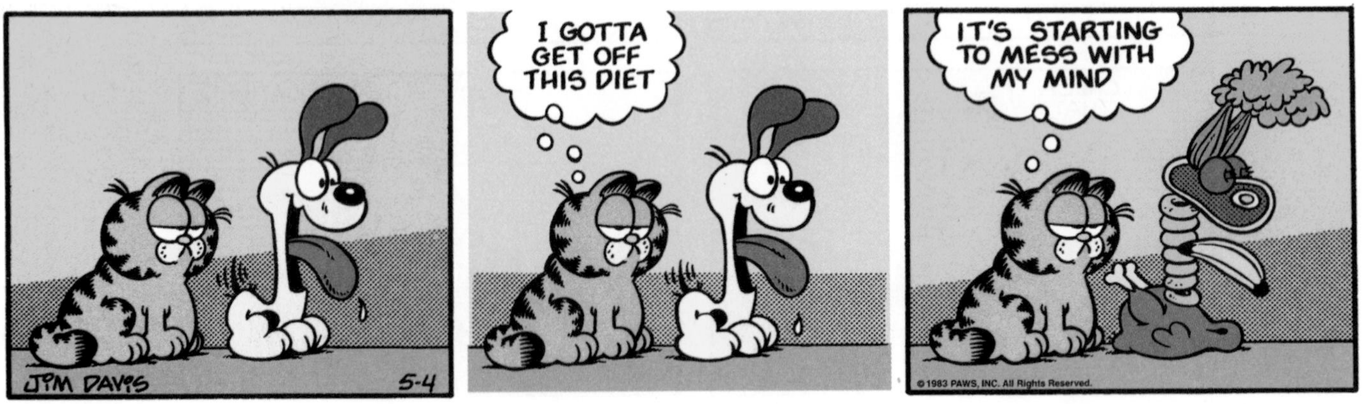
JIM DAVIS
5-4
I GOTTA GET OFF THIS DIET
IT'S STARTING TO MESS WITH MY MIND
© 1983 PAWS, INC. All Rights Reserved.

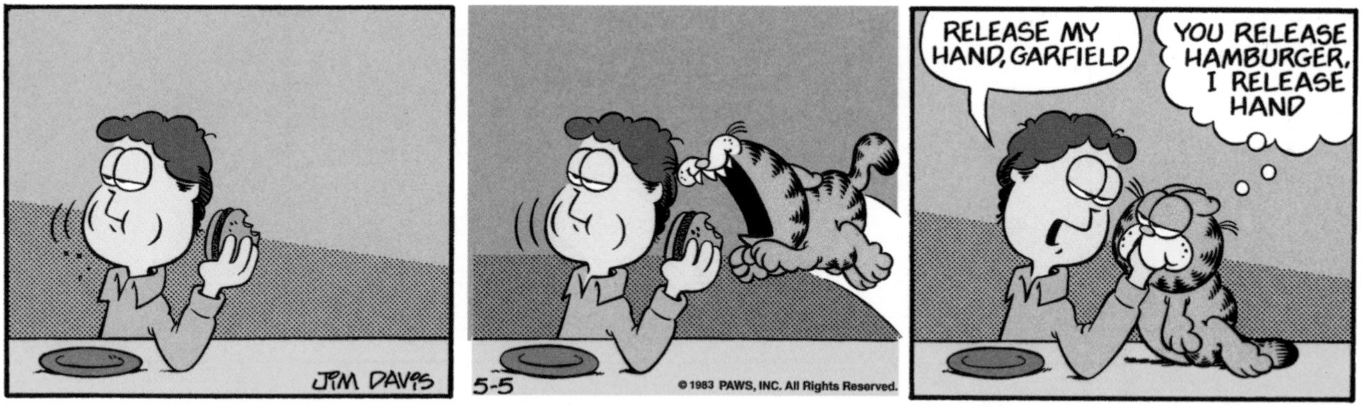
JIM DAVIS
5-5
© 1983 PAWS, INC. All Rights Reserved.
RELEASE MY HAND, GARFIELD
YOU RELEASE HAMBURGER, I RELEASE HAND

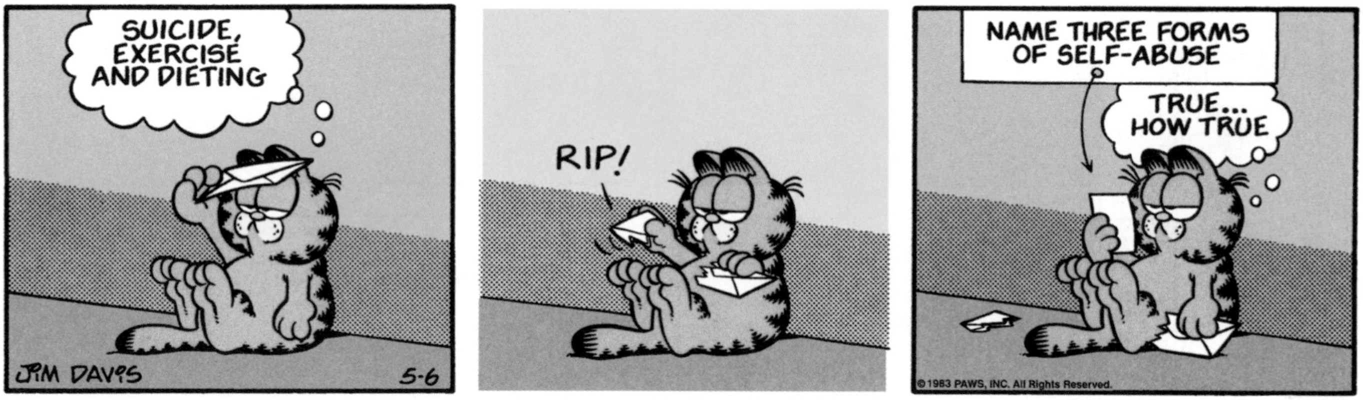
SUICIDE, EXERCISE AND DIETING
JIM DAVIS
5-6
RIP!
NAME THREE FORMS OF SELF-ABUSE
TRUE... HOW TRUE
©1983 PAWS, INC. All Rights Reserved.

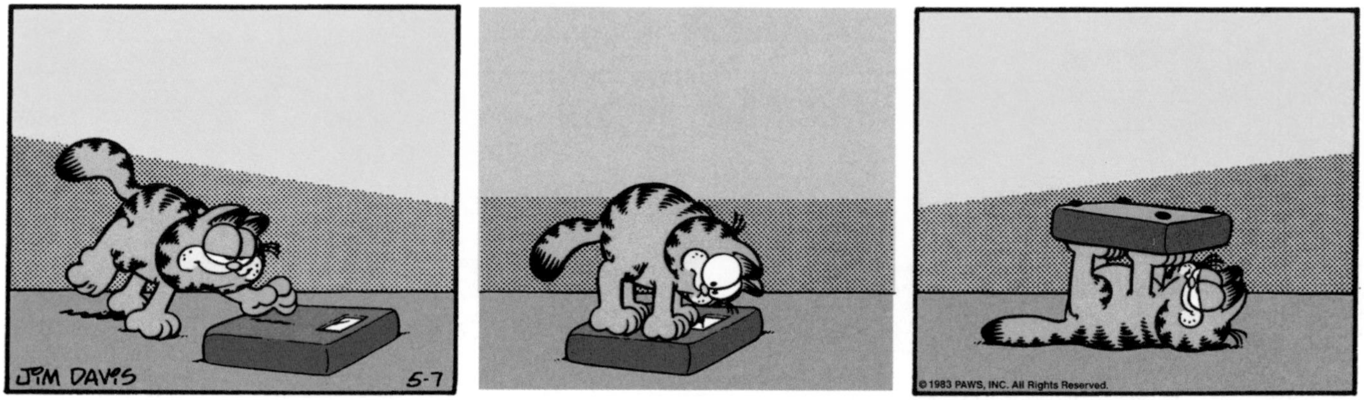
JIM DAVIS
5-7
©1983 PAWS, INC. All Rights Reserved.

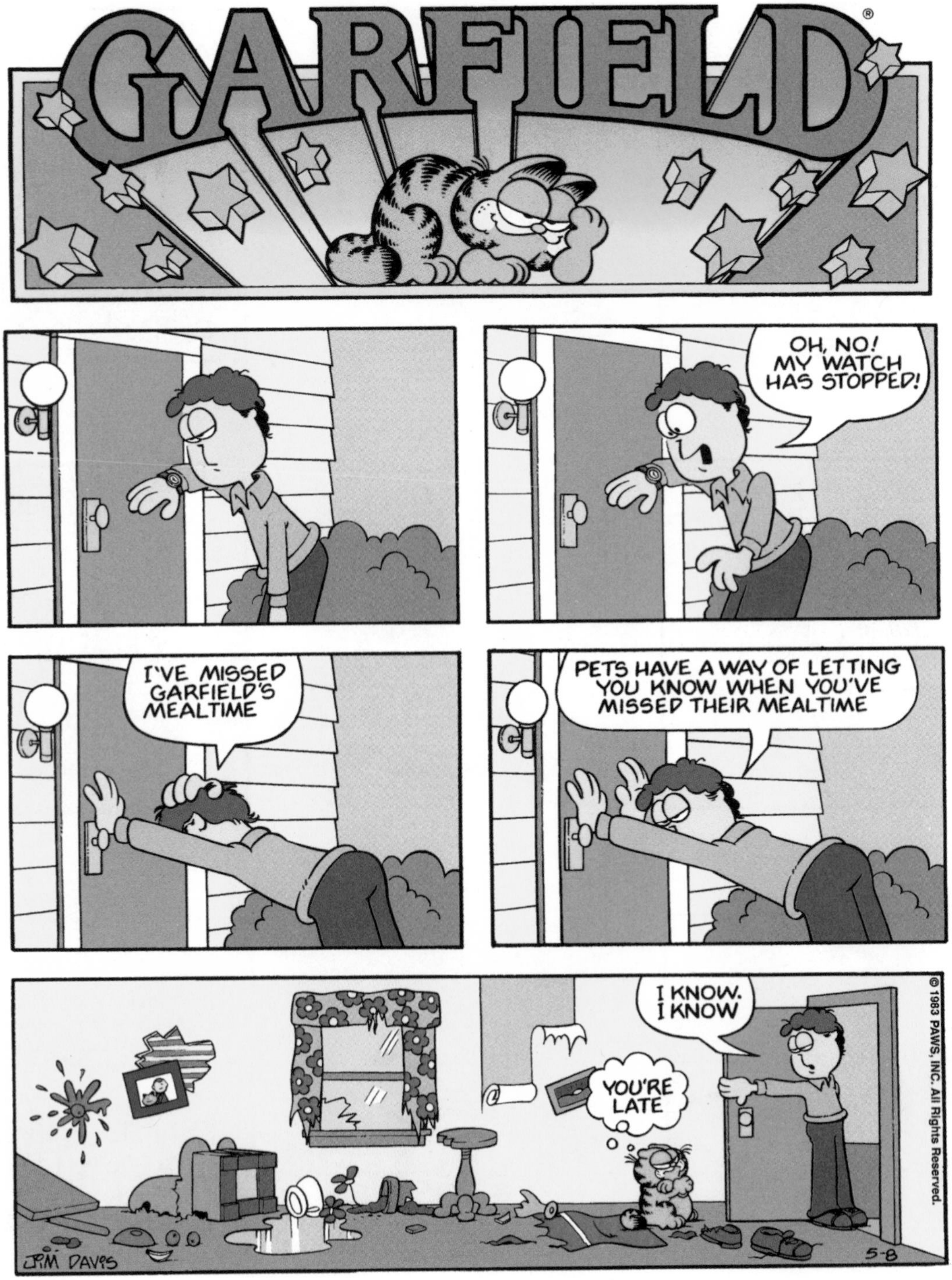
GARFIELD
OH, NO! MY WATCH HAS STOPPED!
I'VE MISSED GARFIELD'S MEALTIME
PETS HAVE A WAY OF LETTING YOU KNOW WHEN YOU'VE MISSED THEIR MEALTIME
I KNOW. I KNOW
YOU'RE LATE
JIM DAVIS
5-8
© 1983 PAWS, INC. All Rights Reserved.

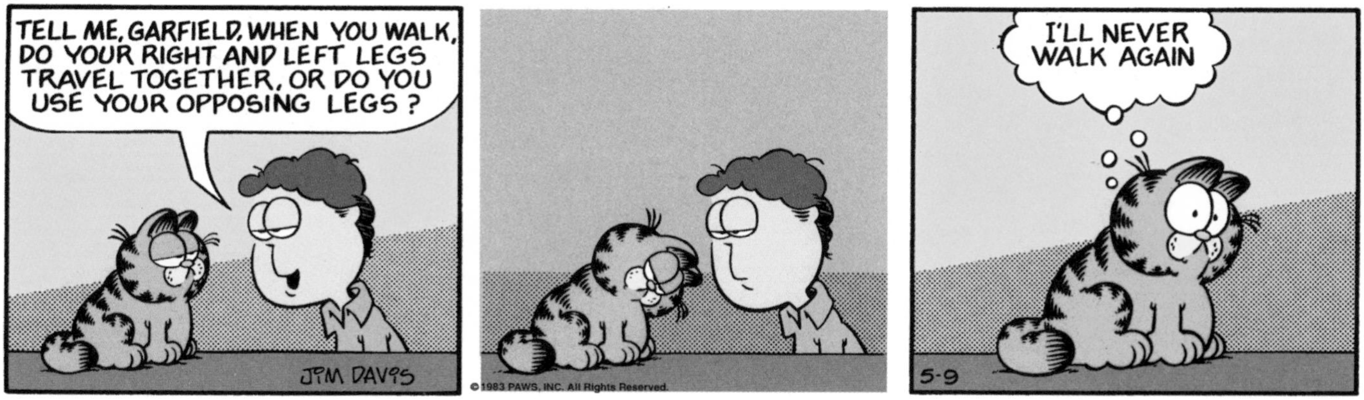
TELL ME, GARFIELD, WHEN YOU WALK, DO YOUR RIGHT AND LEFT LEGS TRAVEL TOGETHER, OR DO YOU USE YOUR OPPOSING LEGS?
I'LL NEVER WALK AGAIN
JIM DAVIS
©1983 PAWS, INC. All Rights Reserved.
5-9

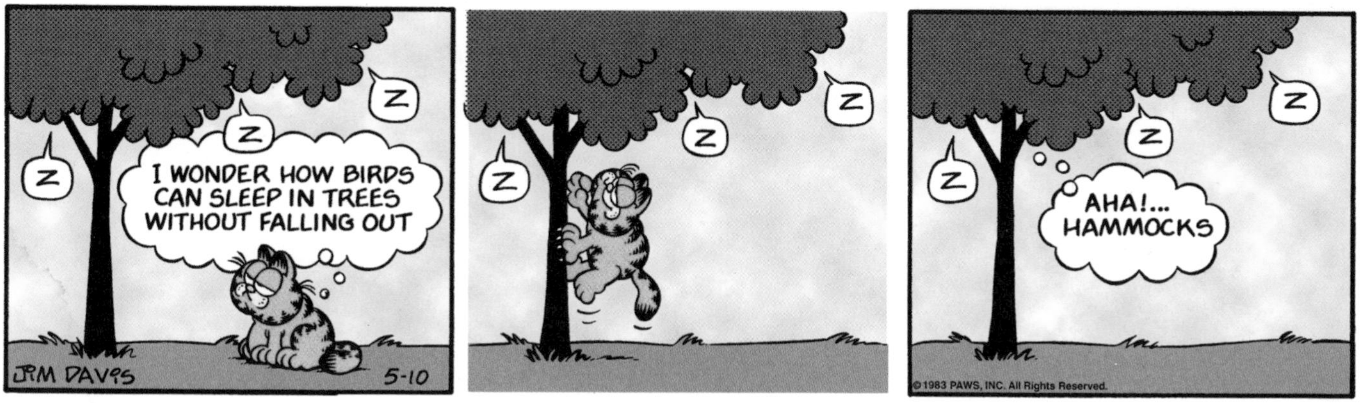
Z
Z
Z
I WONDER HOW BIRDS CAN SLEEP IN TREES WITHOUT FALLING OUT
JIM DAVIS
5-10
Z
Z
Z
Z
Z
Z
AHA!... HAMMOCKS
©1983 PAWS, INC. All Rights Reserved.

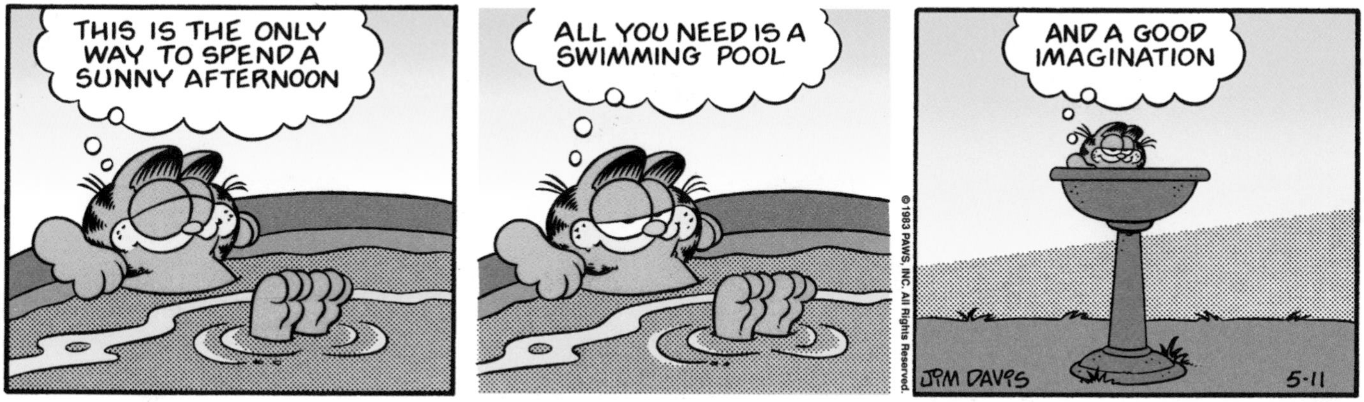
THIS IS THE ONLY WAY TO SPEND A SUNNY AFTERNOON
ALL YOU NEED IS A SWIMMING POOL
©1983 PAWS, INC. All Rights Reserved.
AND A GOOD IMAGINATION
JIM DAVIS
5-11

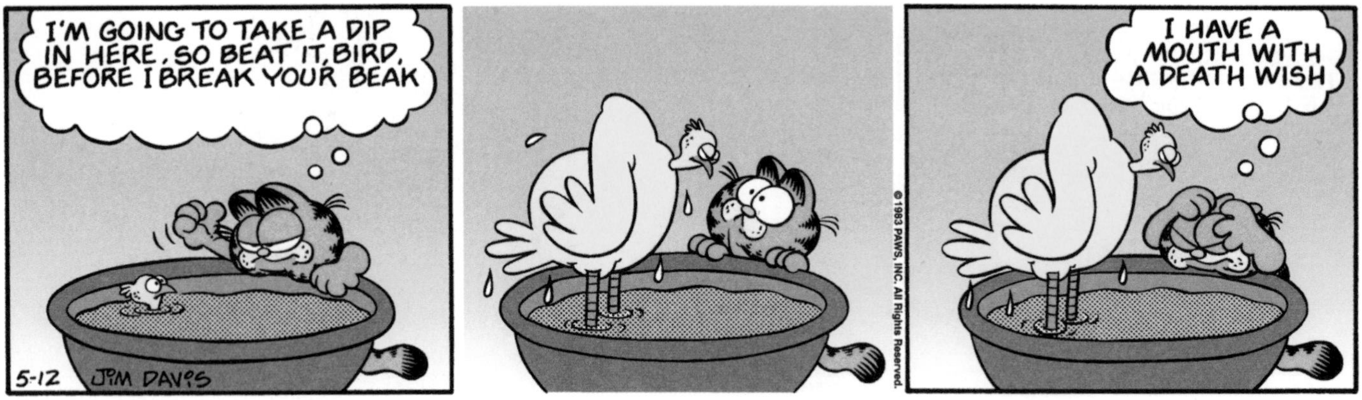
I'M GOING TO TAKE A DIP IN HERE, SO BEAT IT, BIRD, BEFORE I BREAK YOUR BEAK
5-12 JIM DAVIS
© 1983 PAWS, INC. All Rights Reserved.
I HAVE A MOUTH WITH A DEATH WISH

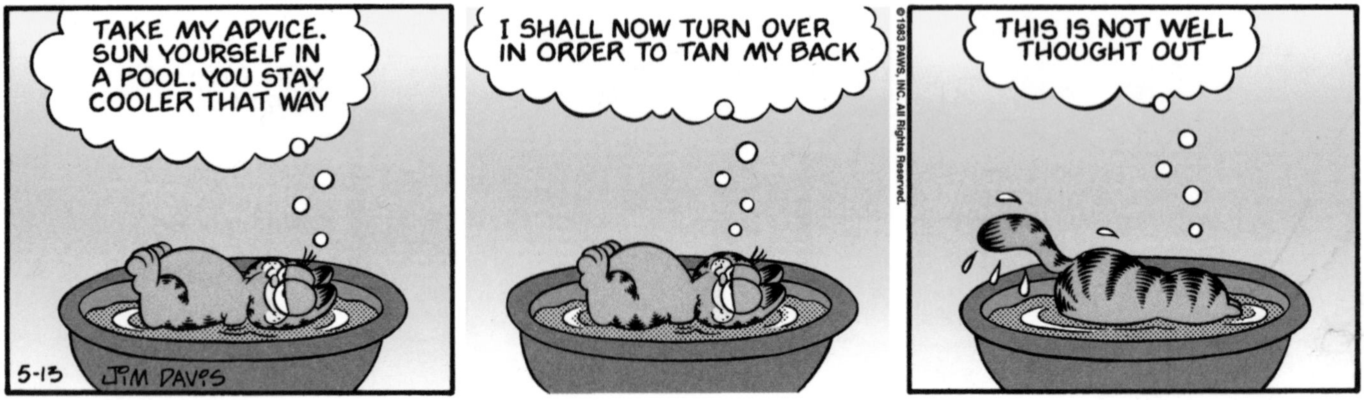
TAKE MY ADVICE. SUN YOURSELF IN A POOL. YOU STAY COOLER THAT WAY
5-13 JIM DAVIS
I SHALL NOW TURN OVER IN ORDER TO TAN MY BACK
© 1983 PAWS, INC. All Rights Reserved.
THIS IS NOT WELL THOUGHT OUT

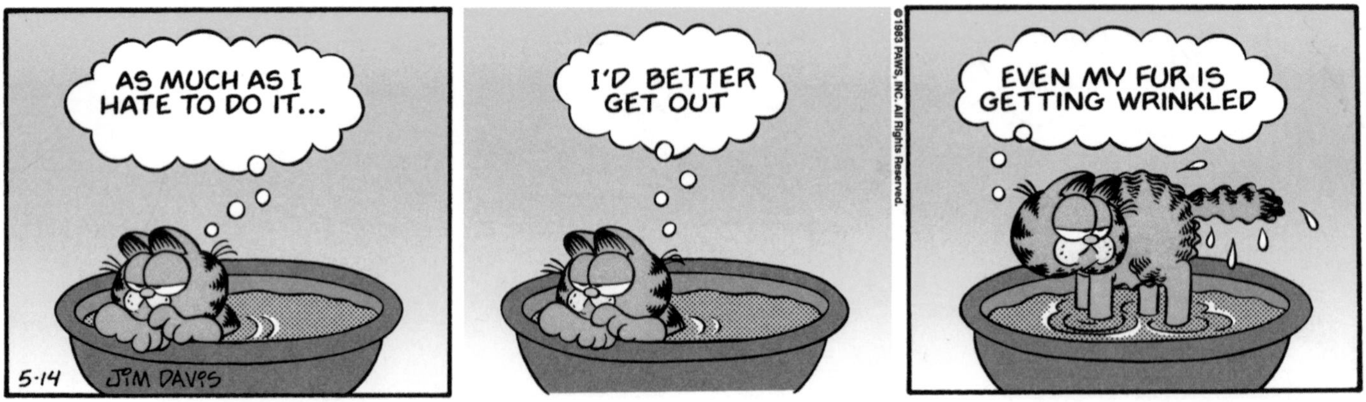
AS MUCH AS I HATE TO DO IT...
5-14 JIM DAVIS
I'D BETTER GET OUT
© 1983 PAWS, INC. All Rights Reserved.
EVEN MY FUR IS GETTING WRINKLED

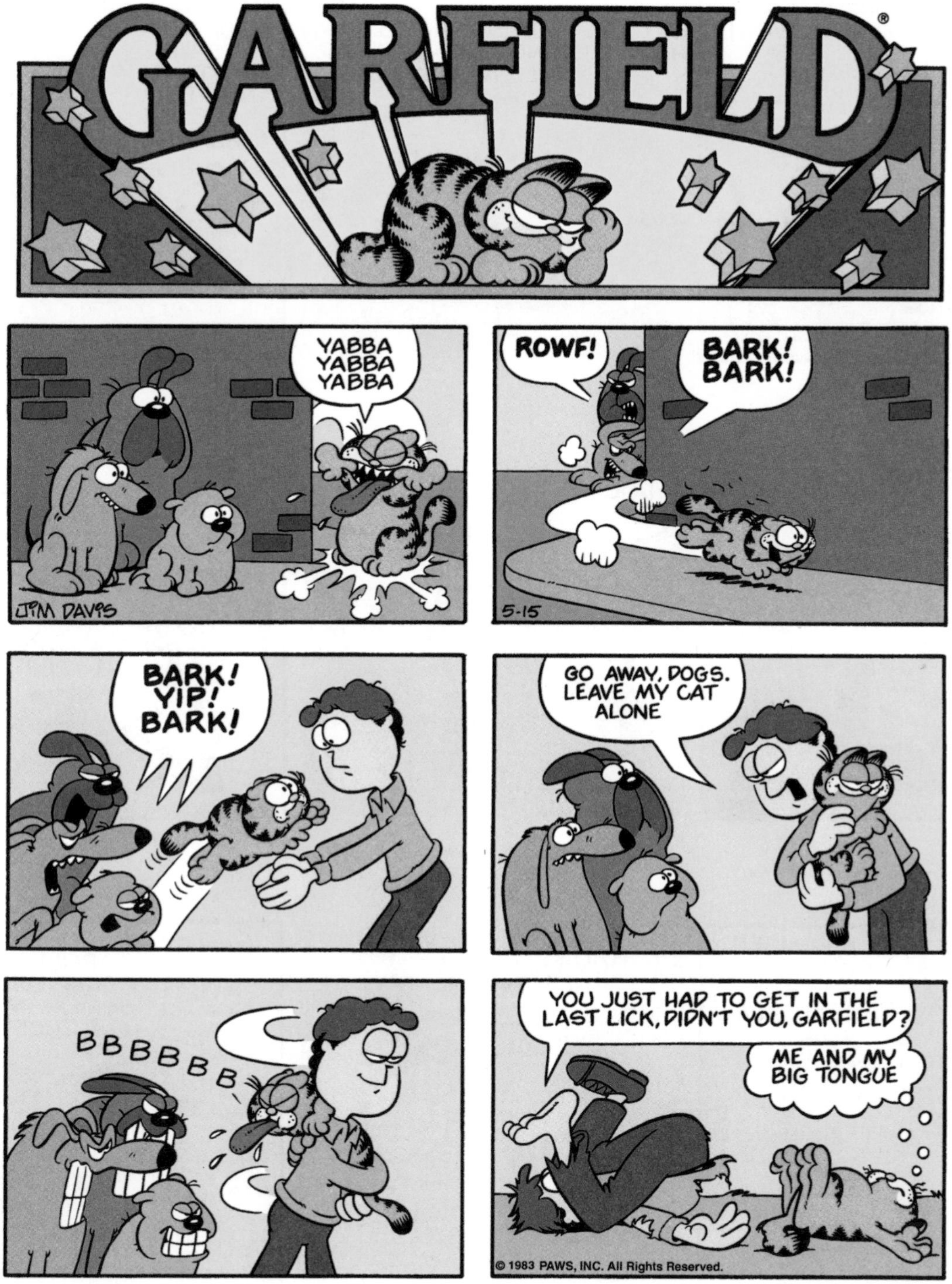
GARFIELD®
YABBA YABBA YABBA
JIM DAVIS
ROWF!
BARK! BARK!
5-15
BARK! YIP! BARK!
GO AWAY, DOGS. LEAVE MY CAT ALONE
BBBBBBB
YOU JUST HAD TO GET IN THE LAST LICK, DIDN'T YOU, GARFIELD?
ME AND MY BIG TONGUE
© 1983 PAWS, INC. All Rights Reserved.

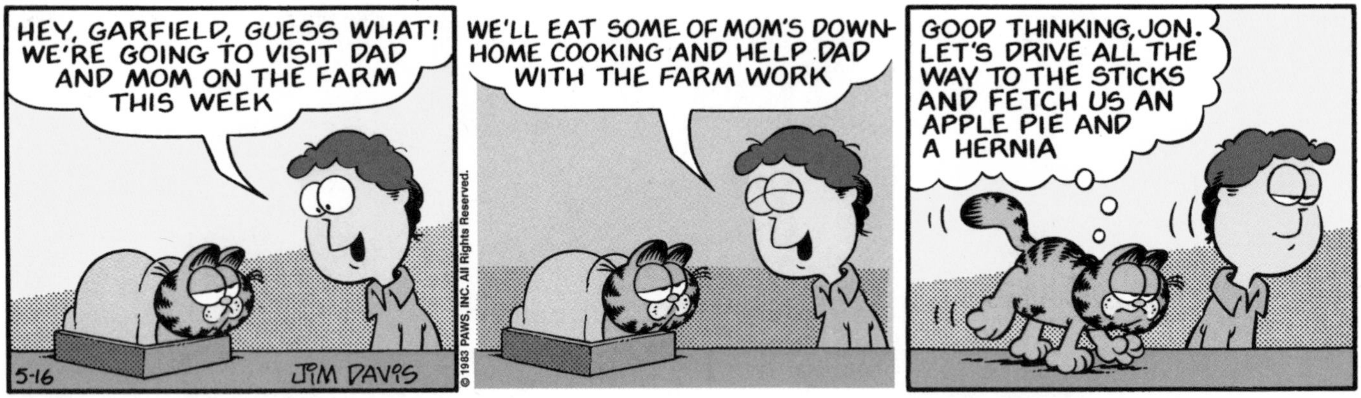
HEY, GARFIELD, GUESS WHAT! WE'RE GOING TO VISIT DAD AND MOM ON THE FARM THIS WEEK
5-16
JIM DAVIS
© 1983 PAWS, INC. All Rights Reserved.
WE'LL EAT SOME OF MOM'S DOWN-HOME COOKING AND HELP DAD WITH THE FARM WORK
GOOD THINKING, JON. LET'S DRIVE ALL THE WAY TO THE STICKS AND FETCH US AN APPLE PIE AND A HERNIA

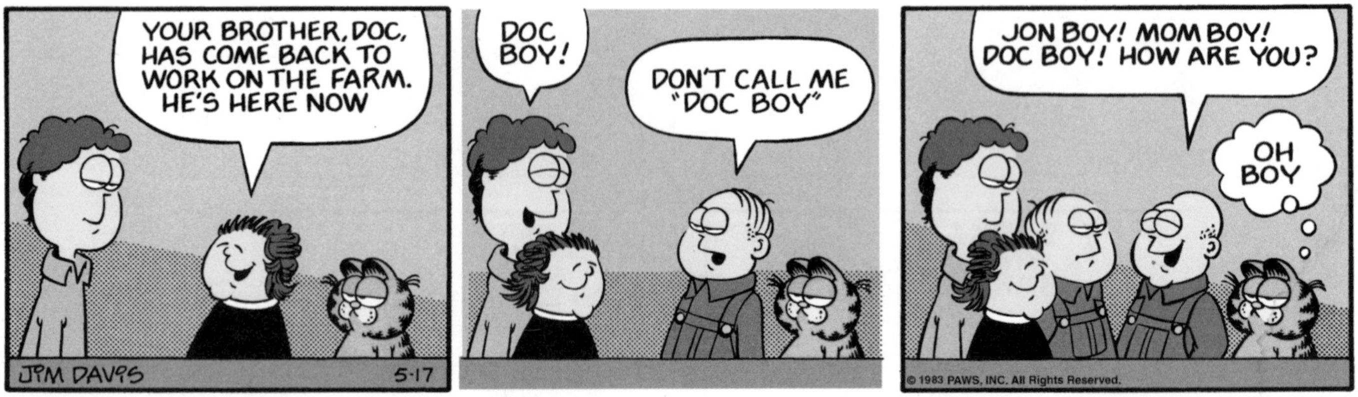
YOUR BROTHER, DOC, HAS COME BACK TO WORK ON THE FARM. HE'S HERE NOW
JIM DAVIS
5-17
DOC BOY!
DON'T CALL ME "DOC BOY"
JON BOY! MOM BOY! DOC BOY! HOW ARE YOU?
OH BOY
© 1983 PAWS, INC. All Rights Reserved.

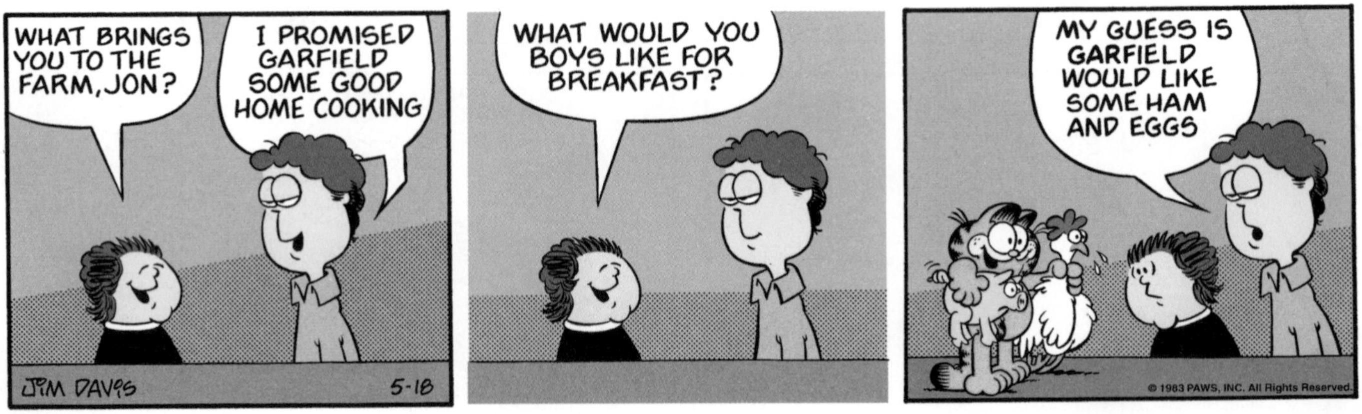
WHAT BRINGS YOU TO THE FARM, JON?
I PROMISED GARFIELD SOME GOOD HOME COOKING
JIM DAVIS
5-18
WHAT WOULD YOU BOYS LIKE FOR BREAKFAST?
MY GUESS IS GARFIELD WOULD LIKE SOME HAM AND EGGS
© 1983 PAWS, INC. All Rights Reserved.

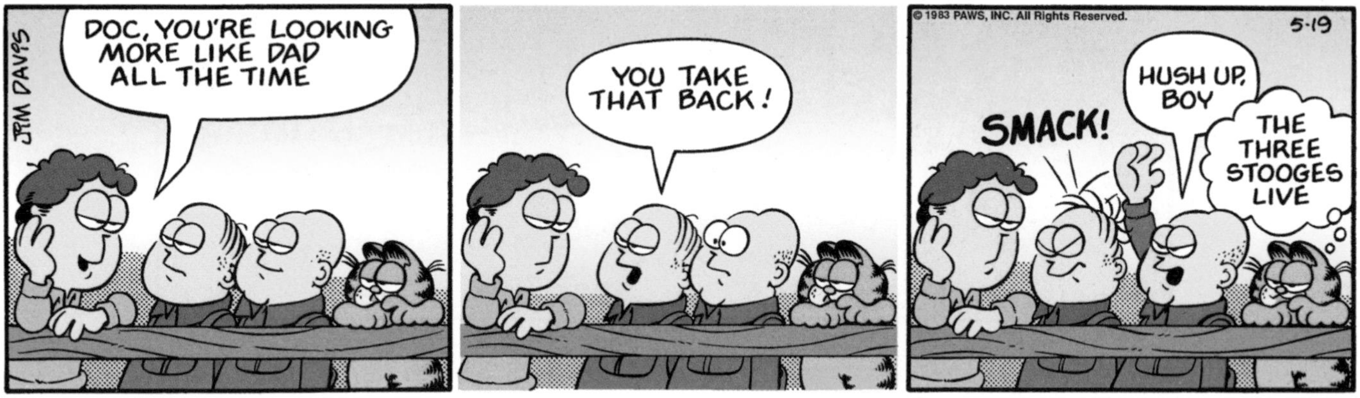
JIM DAVIS
DOC, YOU'RE LOOKING MORE LIKE DAD ALL THE TIME
YOU TAKE THAT BACK!
© 1983 PAWS, INC. All Rights Reserved.
5-19
SMACK!
HUSH UP, BOY
THE THREE STOOGES LIVE

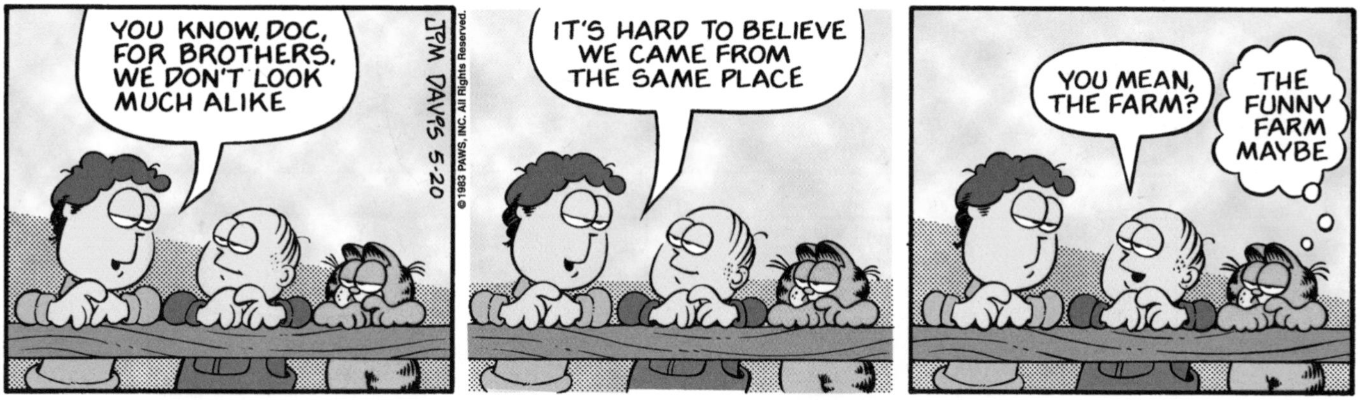
YOU KNOW, DOC, FOR BROTHERS, WE DON'T LOOK MUCH ALIKE
JIM DAVIS 5-20
© 1983 PAWS, INC. All Rights Reserved.
IT'S HARD TO BELIEVE WE CAME FROM THE SAME PLACE
YOU MEAN, THE FARM?
THE FUNNY FARM MAYBE

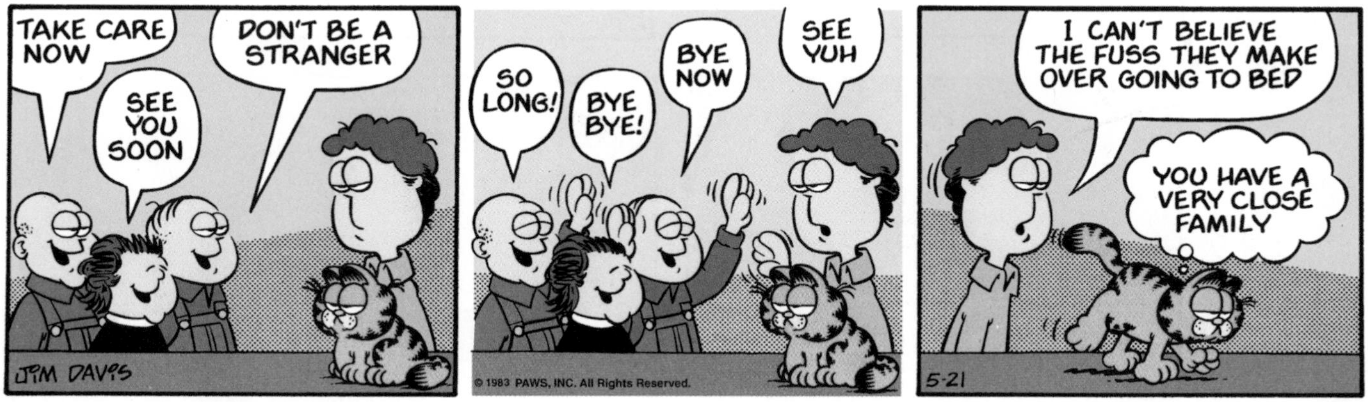
TAKE CARE NOW
SEE YOU SOON
DON'T BE A STRANGER
JIM DAVIS
SO LONG!
BYE BYE!
BYE NOW
SEE YUH
© 1983 PAWS, INC. All Rights Reserved.
I CAN'T BELIEVE THE FUSS THEY MAKE OVER GOING TO BED
YOU HAVE A VERY CLOSE FAMILY
5-21

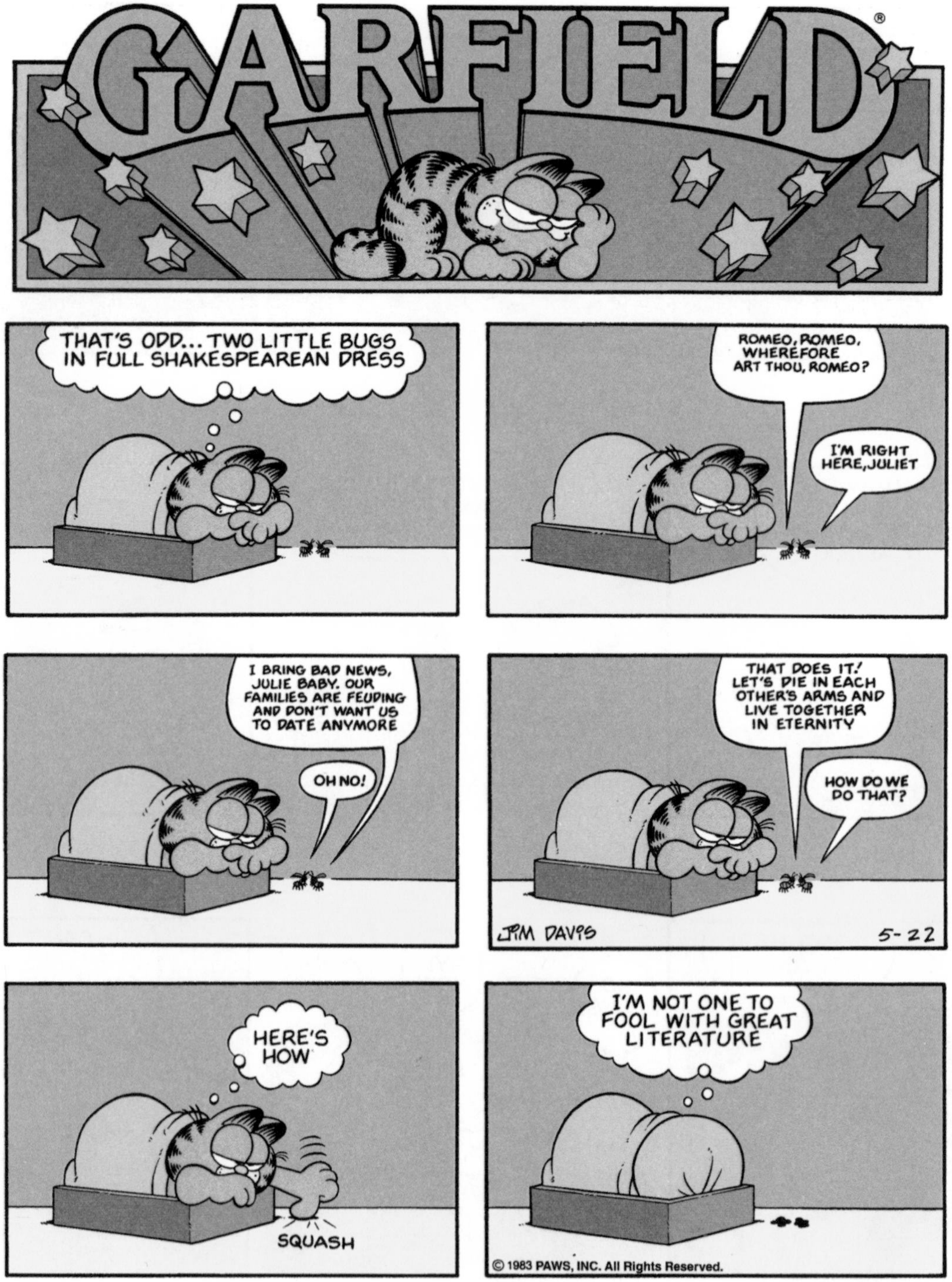
GARFIELD®
THAT'S ODD... TWO LITTLE BUGS IN FULL SHAKESPEAREAN DRESS
ROMEO, ROMEO, WHEREFORE ART THOU, ROMEO?
I'M RIGHT HERE, JULIET
I BRING BAD NEWS, JULIE BABY. OUR FAMILIES ARE FEUDING AND DON'T WANT US TO DATE ANYMORE
OH NO!
THAT DOES IT! LET'S DIE IN EACH OTHER'S ARMS AND LIVE TOGETHER IN ETERNITY
HOW DO WE DO THAT?
JIM DAVIS
5-22
HERE'S HOW
SQUASH
I'M NOT ONE TO FOOL WITH GREAT LITERATURE

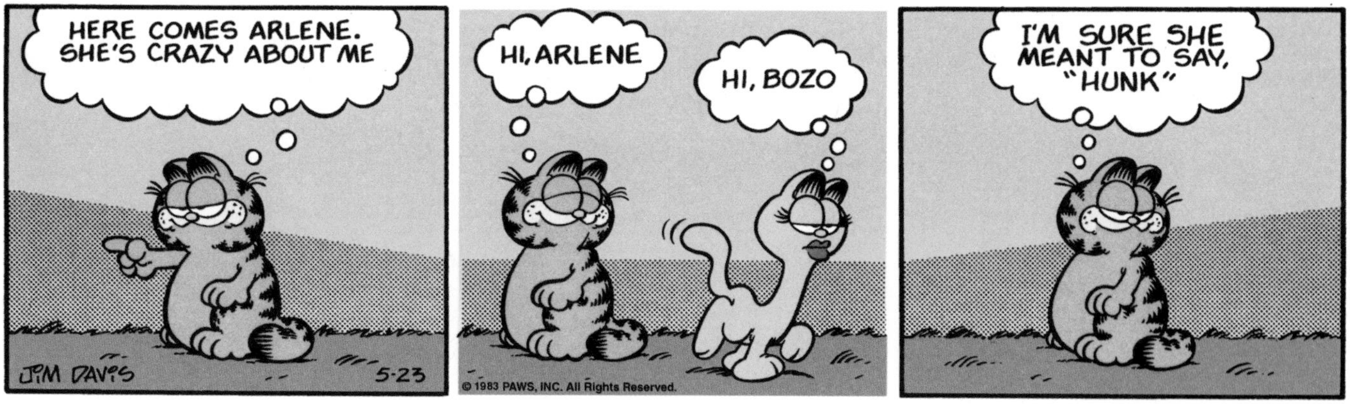
HERE COMES ARLENE. SHE'S CRAZY ABOUT ME
JIM DAVIS
5-23
HI, ARLENE
HI, BOZO
© 1983 PAWS, INC. All Rights Reserved.
I'M SURE SHE MEANT TO SAY, "HUNK"

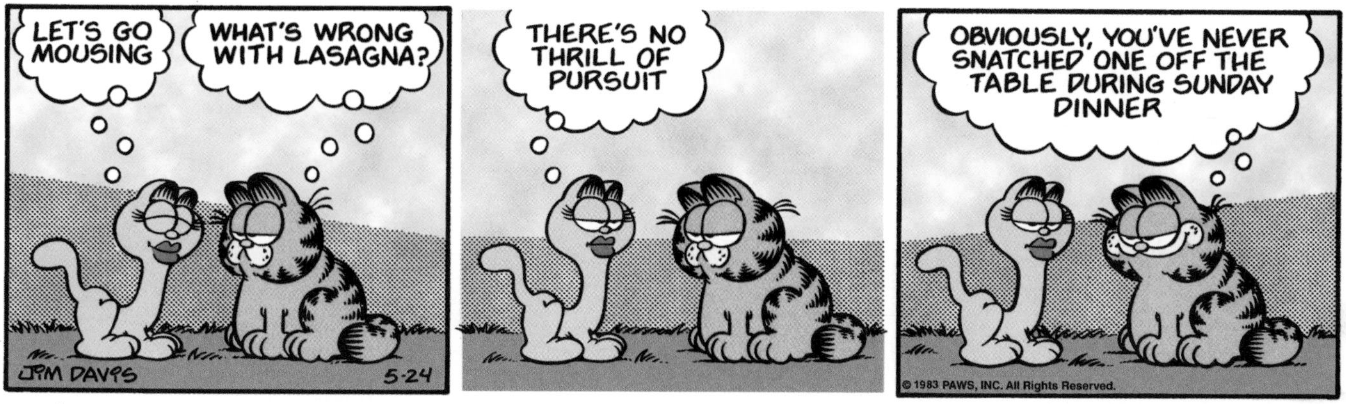
LET'S GO MOUSING
WHAT'S WRONG WITH LASAGNA?
JIM DAVIS
5-24
THERE'S NO THRILL OF PURSUIT
OBVIOUSLY, YOU'VE NEVER SNATCHED ONE OFF THE TABLE DURING SUNDAY DINNER
© 1983 PAWS, INC. All Rights Reserved.

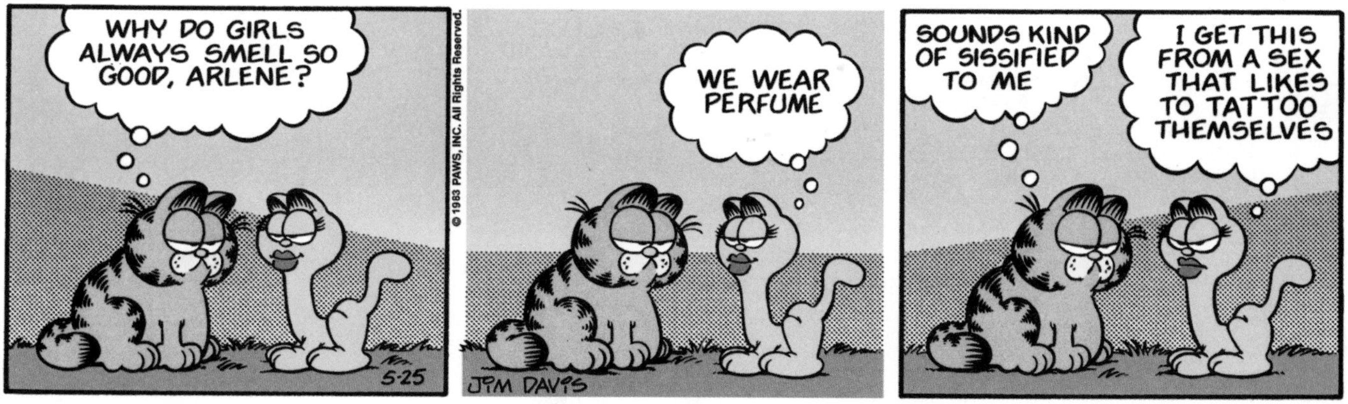
WHY DO GIRLS ALWAYS SMELL SO GOOD, ARLENE?
5-25
© 1983 PAWS, INC. All Rights Reserved.
WE WEAR PERFUME
JIM DAVIS
SOUNDS KIND OF SISSIFIED TO ME
I GET THIS FROM A SEX THAT LIKES TO TATTOO THEMSELVES

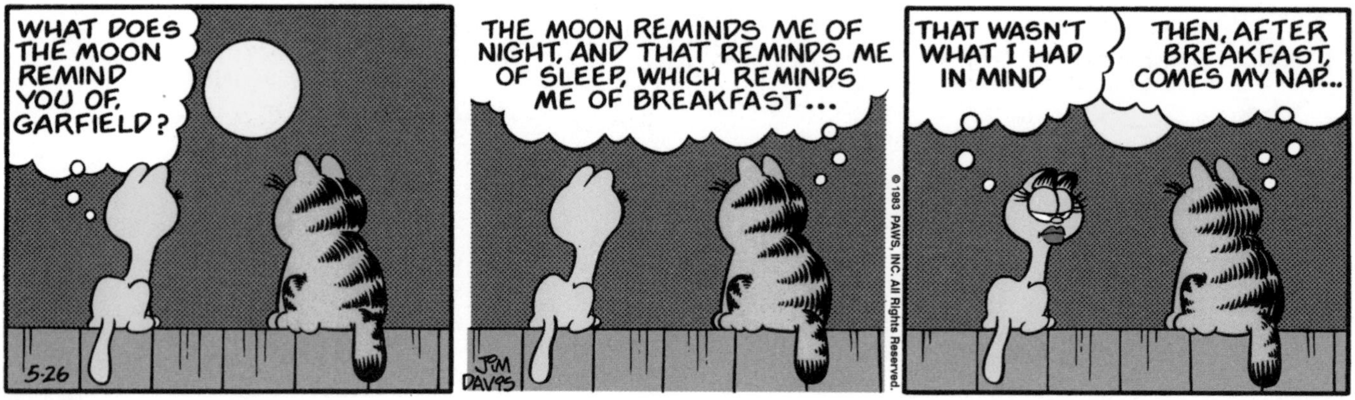
WHAT DOES THE MOON REMIND YOU OF, GARFIELD?
5-26
THE MOON REMINDS ME OF NIGHT, AND THAT REMINDS ME OF SLEEP, WHICH REMINDS ME OF BREAKFAST...
JIM DAVIS
© 1983 PAWS, INC. All Rights Reserved.
THAT WASN'T WHAT I HAD IN MIND
THEN, AFTER BREAKFAST, COMES MY NAP...

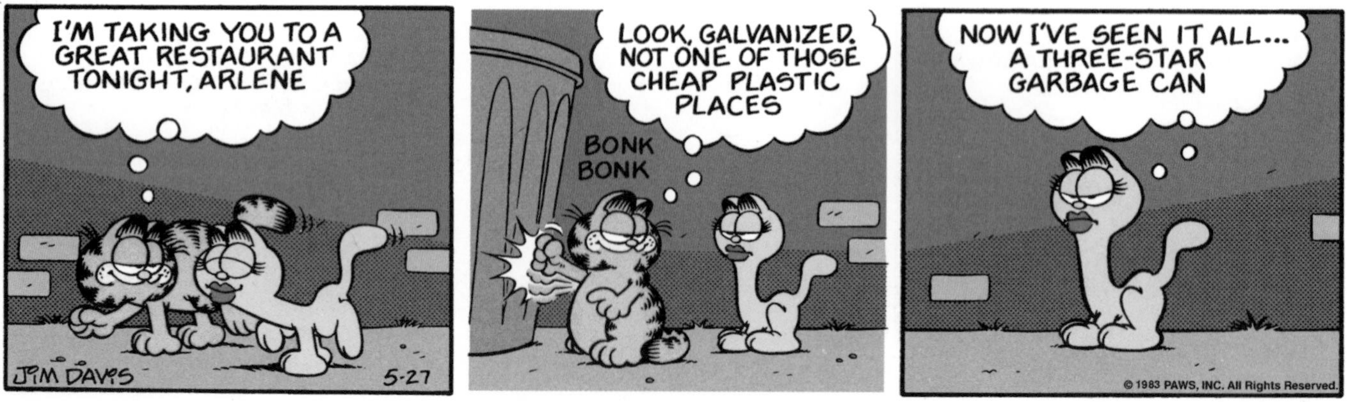
I'M TAKING YOU TO A GREAT RESTAURANT TONIGHT, ARLENE
JIM DAVIS
5-27
LOOK, GALVANIZED. NOT ONE OF THOSE CHEAP PLASTIC PLACES
BONK BONK
NOW I'VE SEEN IT ALL... A THREE-STAR GARBAGE CAN
© 1983 PAWS, INC. All Rights Reserved.

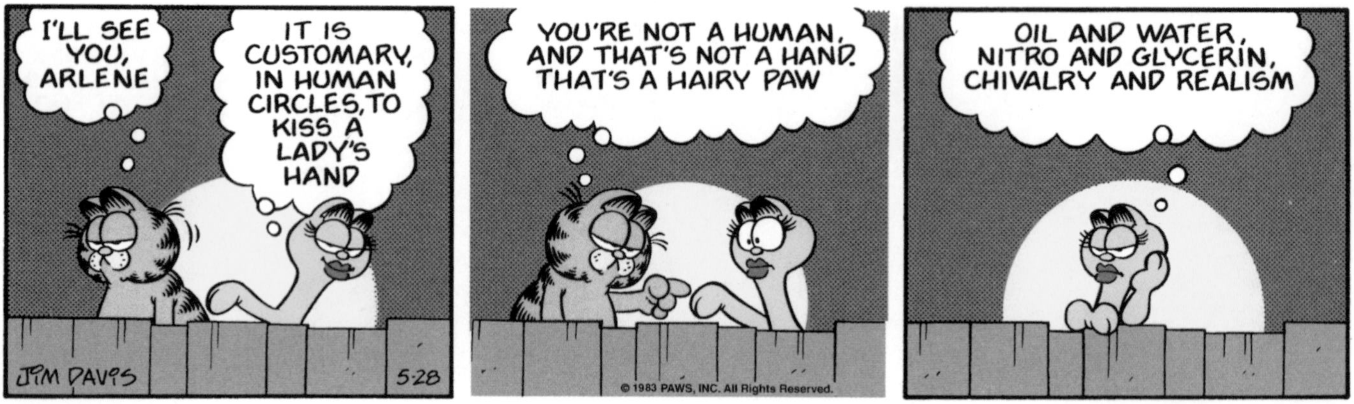
I'LL SEE YOU, ARLENE
IT IS CUSTOMARY, IN HUMAN CIRCLES, TO KISS A LADY'S HAND
JIM DAVIS
5-28
YOU'RE NOT A HUMAN, AND THAT'S NOT A HAND. THAT'S A HAIRY PAW
© 1983 PAWS, INC. All Rights Reserved.
OIL AND WATER, NITRO AND GLYCERIN, CHIVALRY AND REALISM

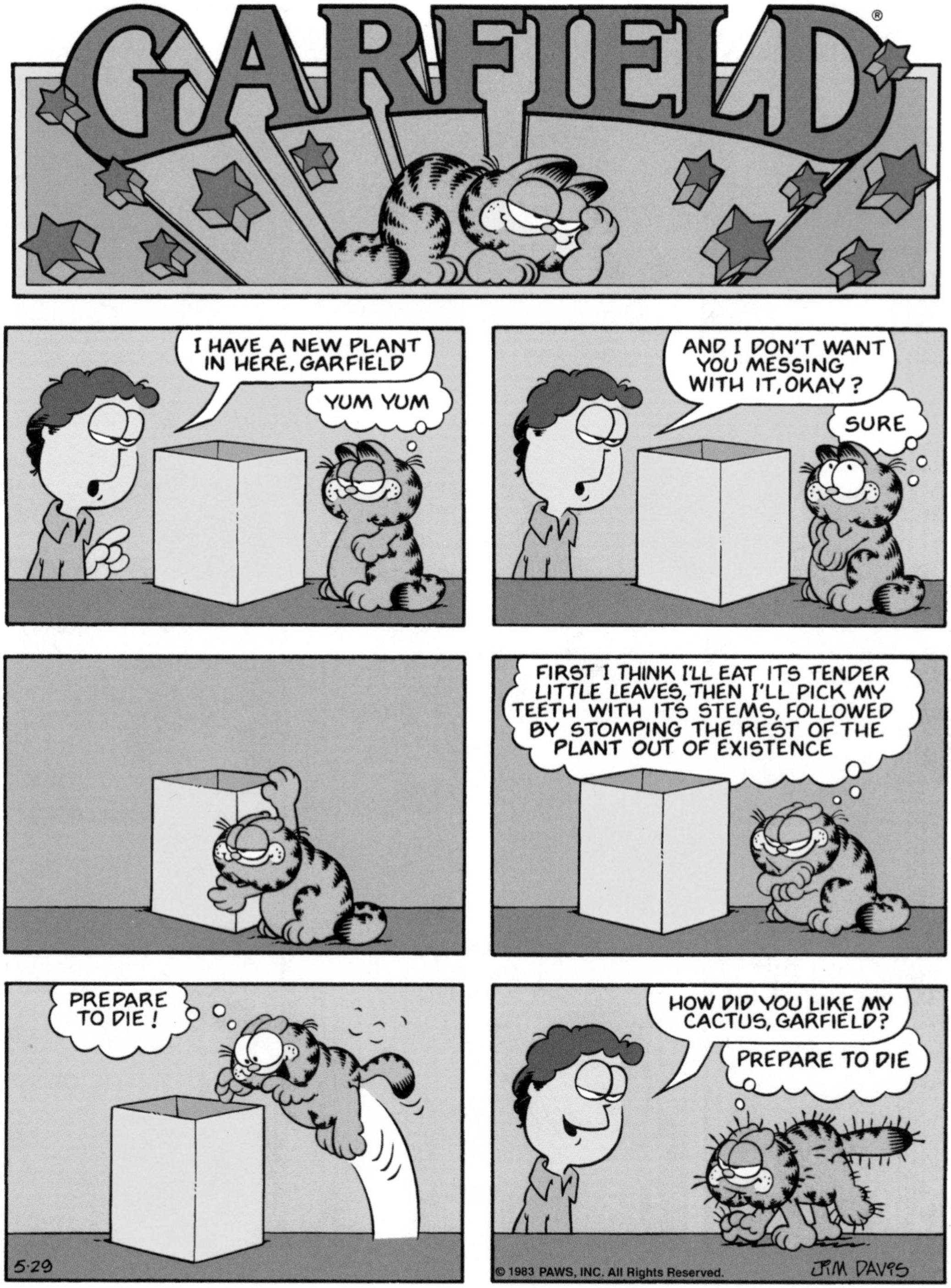
GARFIELD
I HAVE A NEW PLANT IN HERE, GARFIELD
YUM YUM
AND I DON'T WANT YOU MESSING WITH IT, OKAY?
SURE
FIRST I THINK I'LL EAT ITS TENDER LITTLE LEAVES, THEN I'LL PICK MY TEETH WITH ITS STEMS, FOLLOWED BY STOMPING THE REST OF THE PLANT OUT OF EXISTENCE
PREPARE TO DIE!
HOW DID YOU LIKE MY CACTUS, GARFIELD?
PREPARE TO DIE
5·29
© 1983 PAWS, INC. All Rights Reserved.
JIM DAVIS

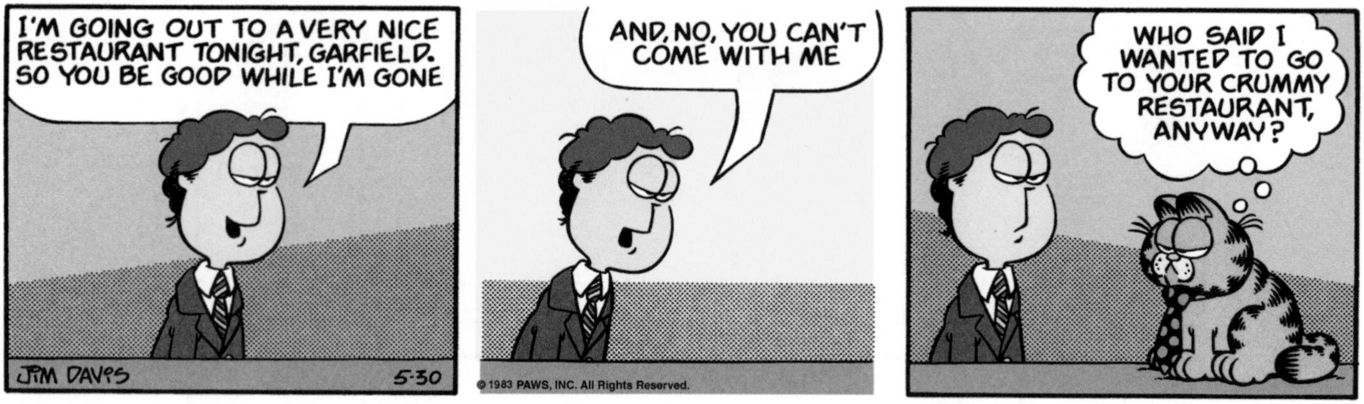
I'M GOING OUT TO A VERY NICE RESTAURANT TONIGHT, GARFIELD. SO YOU BE GOOD WHILE I'M GONE
JIM DAVIS
5-30
AND, NO, YOU CAN'T COME WITH ME
© 1983 PAWS, INC. All Rights Reserved.
WHO SAID I WANTED TO GO TO YOUR CRUMMY RESTAURANT, ANYWAY?

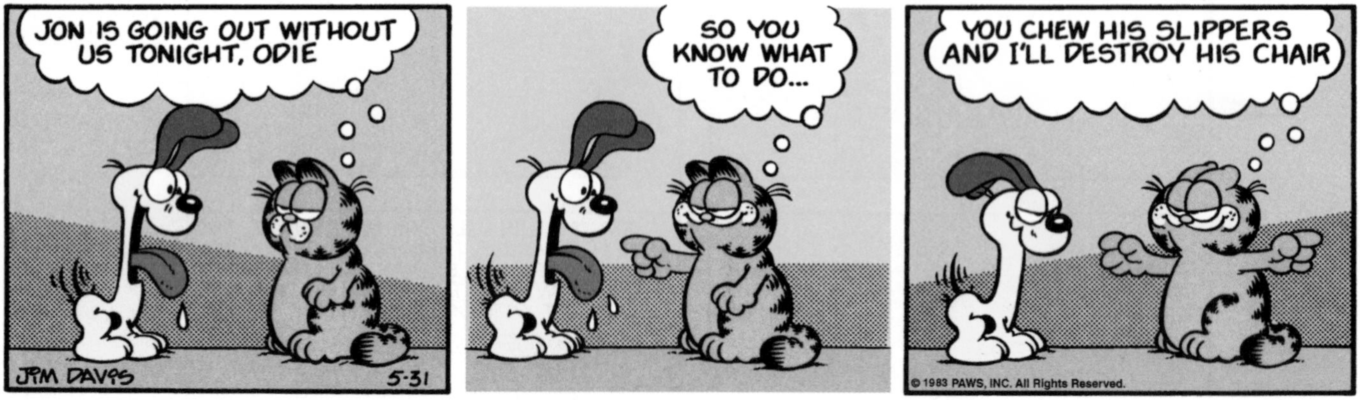
JON IS GOING OUT WITHOUT US TONIGHT, ODIE
JIM DAVIS
5-31
SO YOU KNOW WHAT TO DO...
YOU CHEW HIS SLIPPERS AND I'LL DESTROY HIS CHAIR
© 1983 PAWS, INC. All Rights Reserved.

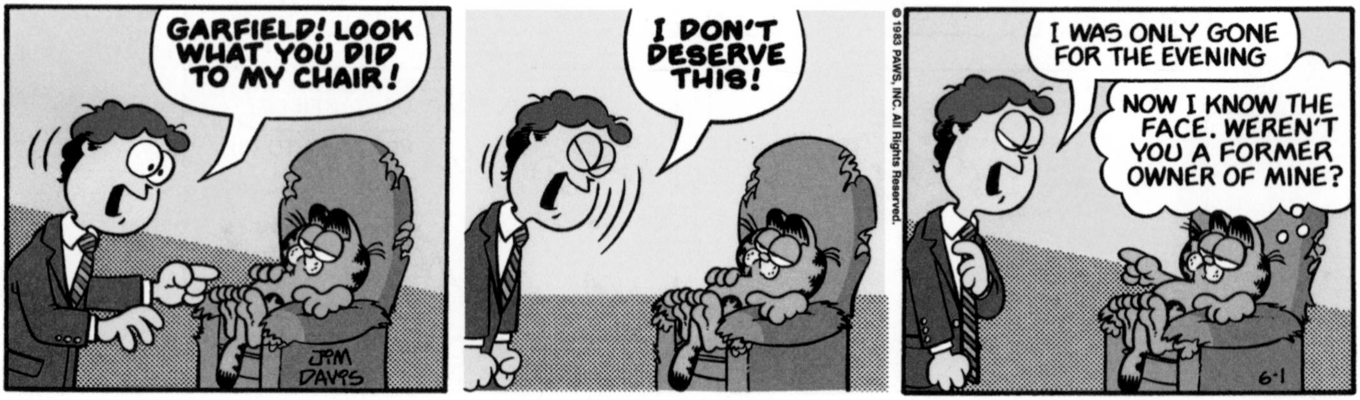
GARFIELD! LOOK WHAT YOU DID TO MY CHAIR!
JIM DAVIS
I DON'T DESERVE THIS!
© 1983 PAWS, INC. All Rights Reserved.
I WAS ONLY GONE FOR THE EVENING
NOW I KNOW THE FACE. WEREN'T YOU A FORMER OWNER OF MINE?
6-1

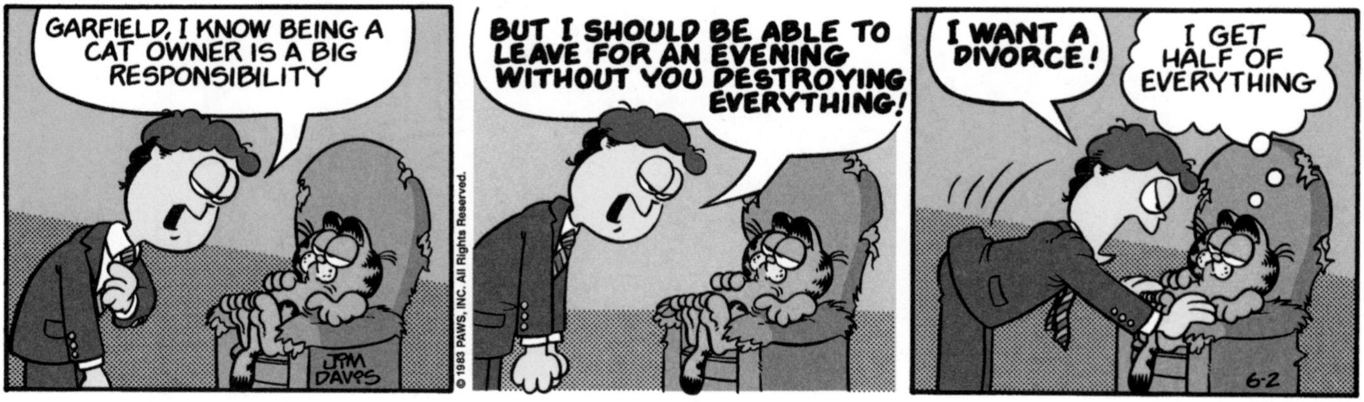
GARFIELD, I KNOW BEING A CAT OWNER IS A BIG RESPONSIBILITY
JPM DAVPS
© 1983 PAWS, INC. All Rights Reserved.
BUT I SHOULD BE ABLE TO LEAVE FOR AN EVENING WITHOUT YOU DESTROYING EVERYTHING!
I WANT A DIVORCE!
I GET HALF OF EVERYTHING
6-2

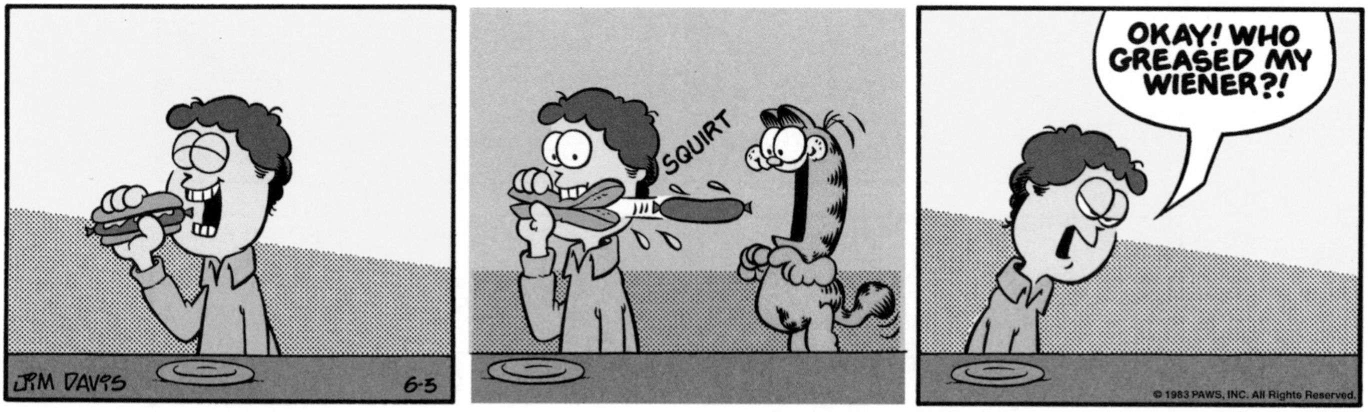
JPM DAVPS
6-3
SQUIRT
OKAY! WHO GREASED MY WIENER?!
© 1983 PAWS, INC. All Rights Reserved.

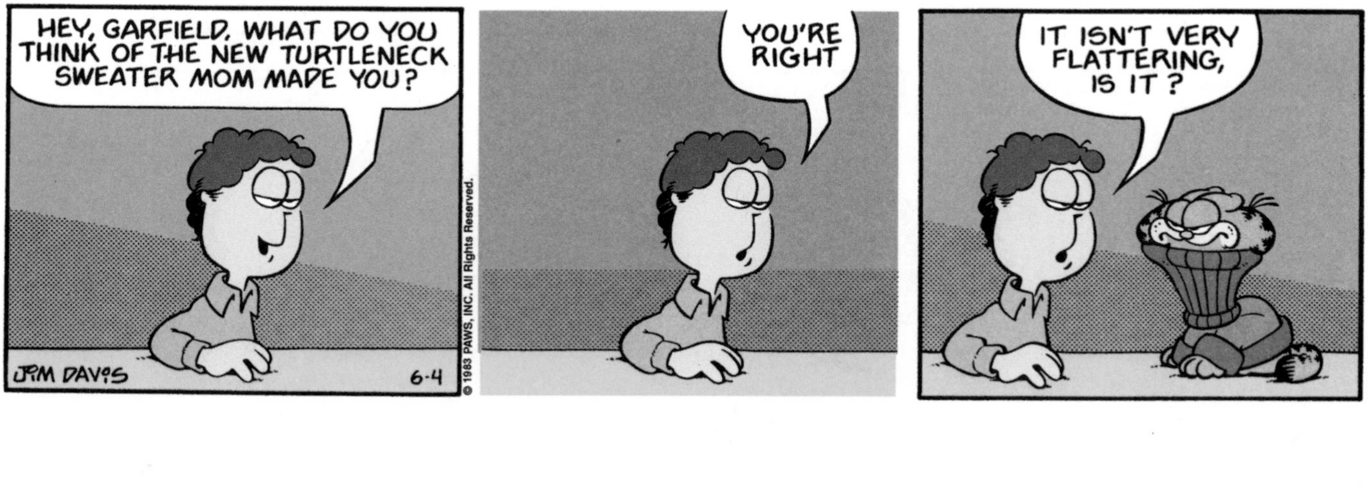
HEY, GARFIELD, WHAT DO YOU THINK OF THE NEW TURTLENECK SWEATER MOM MADE YOU?
JPM DAVPS
6-4
© 1983 PAWS, INC. All Rights Reserved.
YOU'RE RIGHT
IT ISN'T VERY FLATTERING, IS IT?

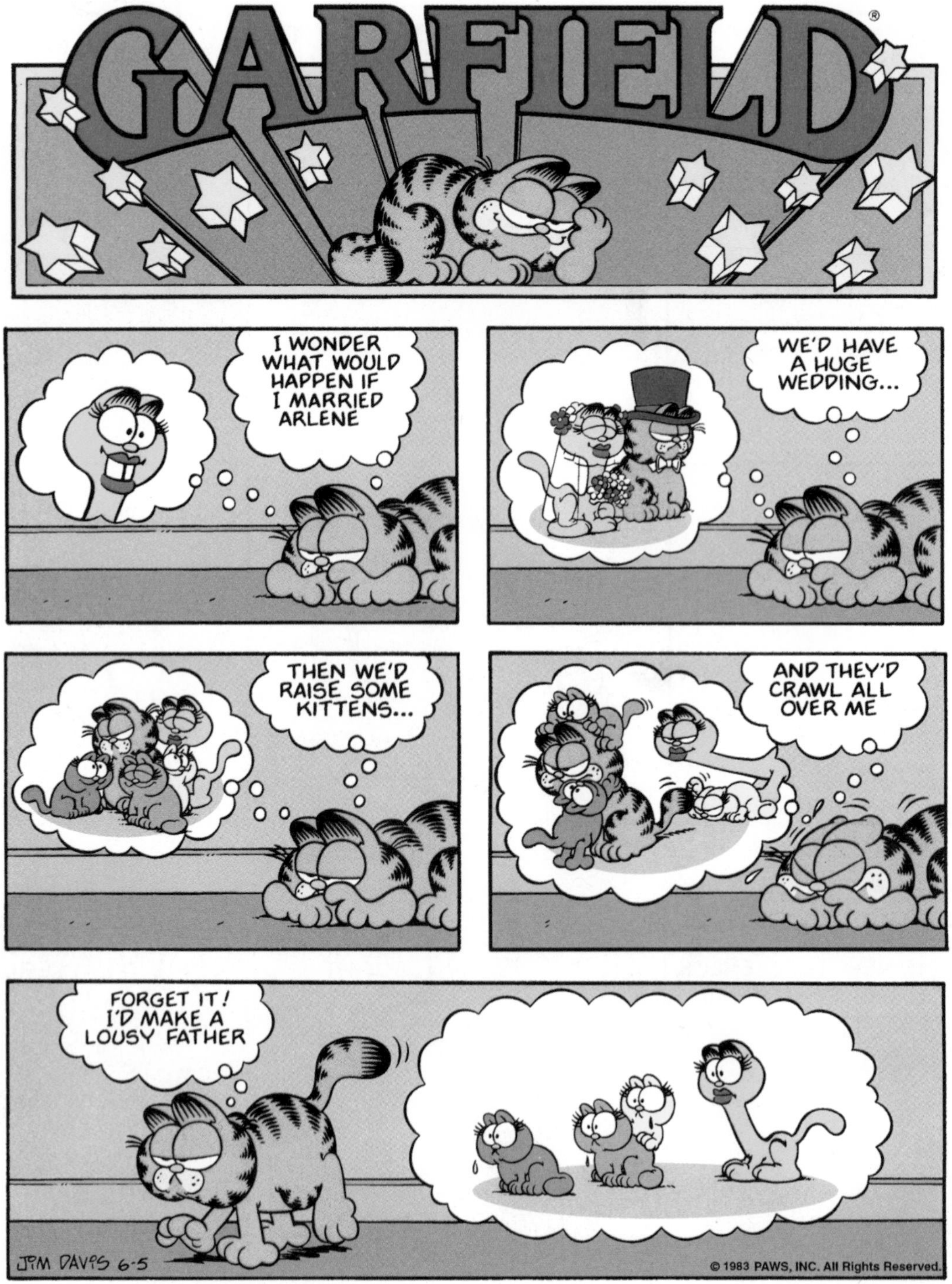
GARFIELD®
I WONDER WHAT WOULD HAPPEN IF I MARRIED ARLENE
WE'D HAVE A HUGE WEDDING...
THEN WE'D RAISE SOME KITTENS...
AND THEY'D CRAWL ALL OVER ME
FORGET IT! I'D MAKE A LOUSY FATHER
JIM DAVIS 6-5
© 1983 PAWS, INC. All Rights Reserved.

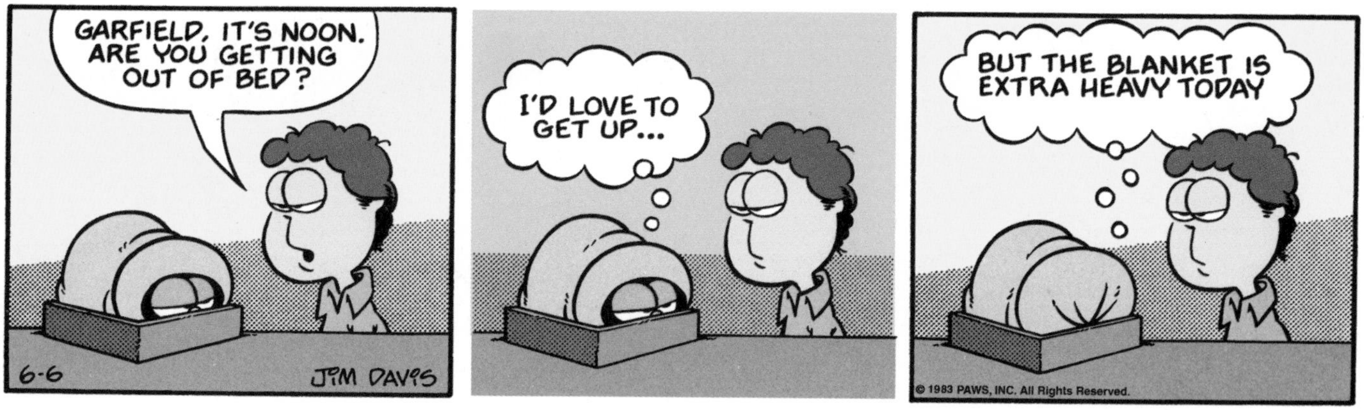
GARFIELD, IT'S NOON. ARE YOU GETTING OUT OF BED?
6-6
JIM DAVIS
I'D LOVE TO GET UP...
BUT THE BLANKET IS EXTRA HEAVY TODAY
© 1983 PAWS, INC. All Rights Reserved.

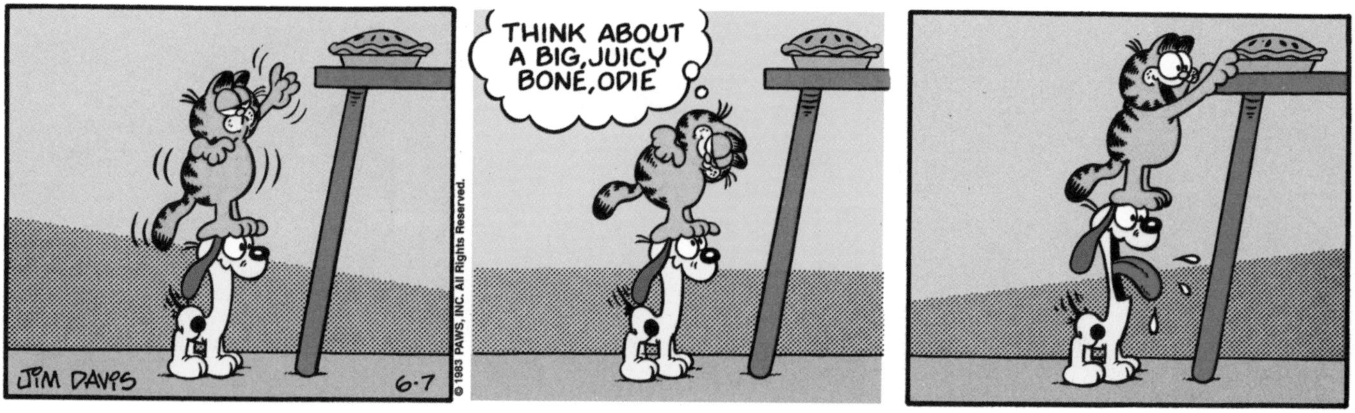
JIM DAVIS
6-7
© 1983 PAWS, INC. All Rights Reserved.
THINK ABOUT A BIG, JUICY BONE, ODIE

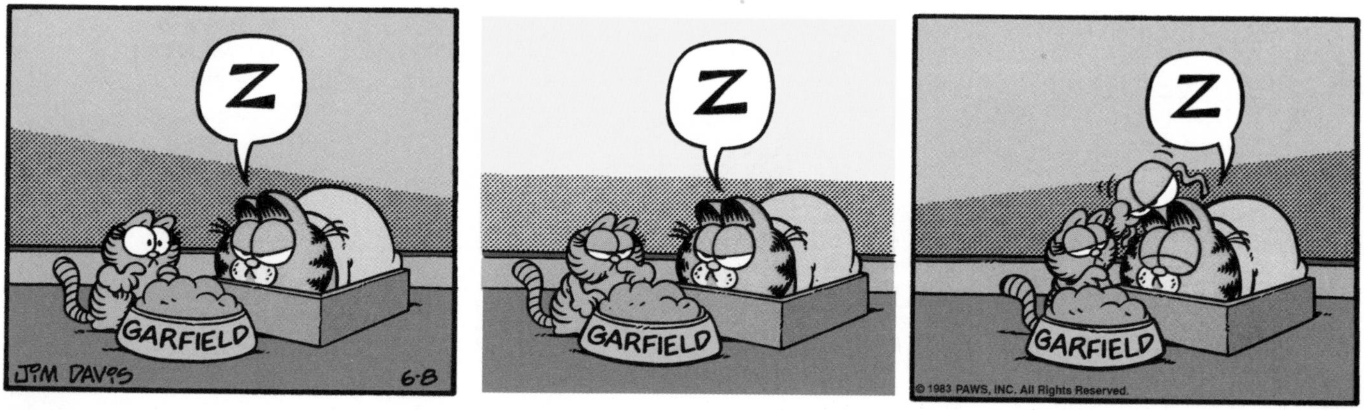
Z
GARFIELD
JIM DAVIS
6-8
Z
GARFIELD
Z
GARFIELD
© 1983 PAWS, INC. All Rights Reserved.

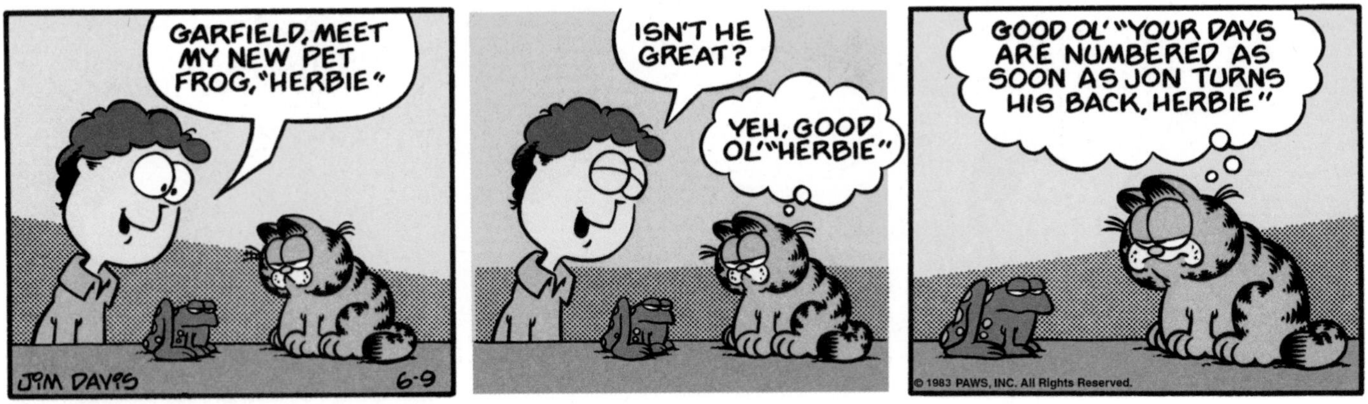
GARFIELD, MEET MY NEW PET FROG, "HERBIE"
JIM DAVIS
6-9
ISN'T HE GREAT?
YEH, GOOD OL' "HERBIE"
GOOD OL' "YOUR DAYS ARE NUMBERED AS SOON AS JON TURNS HIS BACK, HERBIE"
© 1983 PAWS, INC. All Rights Reserved.

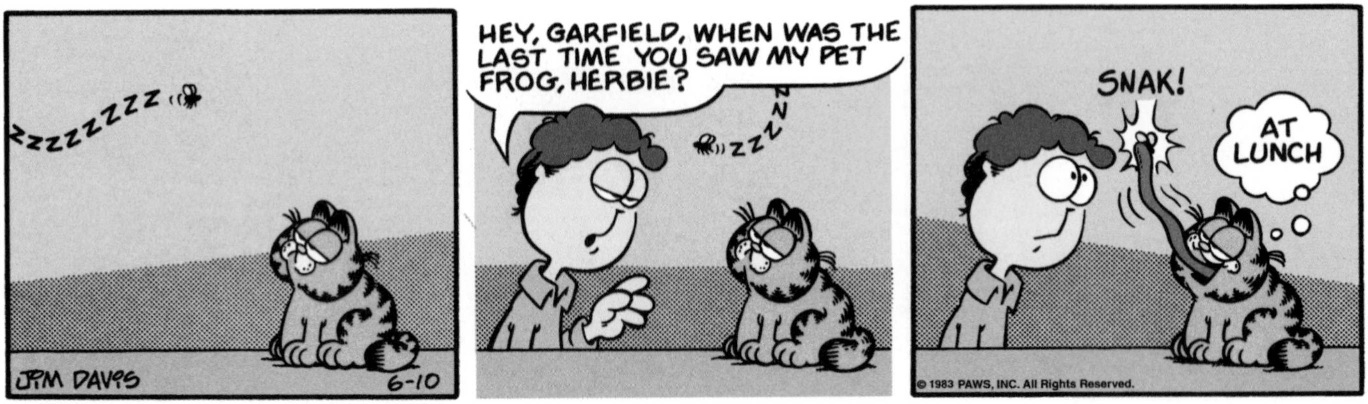
ZZZZZZZZZ
JIM DAVIS
6-10
HEY, GARFIELD, WHEN WAS THE LAST TIME YOU SAW MY PET FROG, HERBIE?
ZZZZ
SNAK!
AT LUNCH
© 1983 PAWS, INC. All Rights Reserved.

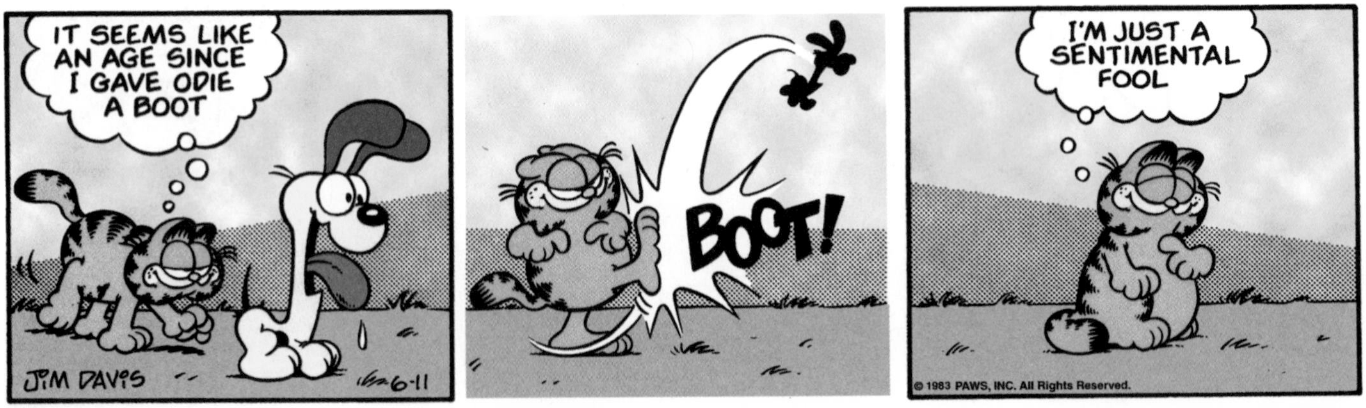
IT SEEMS LIKE AN AGE SINCE I GAVE ODIE A BOOT
JIM DAVIS
6-11
BOOT!
I'M JUST A SENTIMENTAL FOOL
© 1983 PAWS, INC. All Rights Reserved.

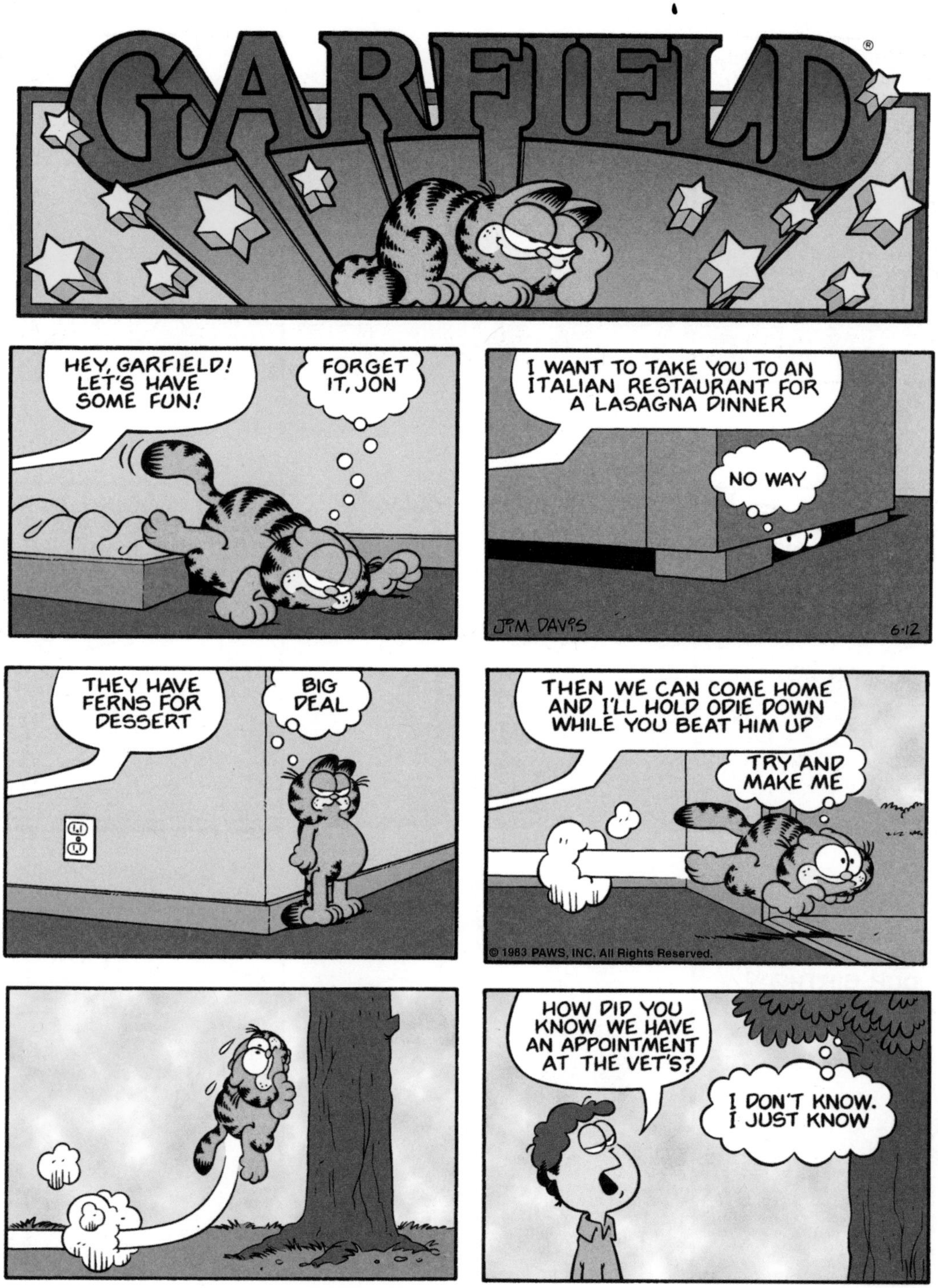
GARFIELD®
HEY, GARFIELD! LET'S HAVE SOME FUN!
FORGET IT, JON
I WANT TO TAKE YOU TO AN ITALIAN RESTAURANT FOR A LASAGNA DINNER
NO WAY
JIM DAVIS 6-12
THEY HAVE FERNS FOR DESSERT
BIG DEAL
THEN WE CAN COME HOME AND I'LL HOLD ODIE DOWN WHILE YOU BEAT HIM UP
TRY AND MAKE ME
© 1983 PAWS, INC. All Rights Reserved.
HOW DID YOU KNOW WE HAVE AN APPOINTMENT AT THE VET'S?
I DON'T KNOW. I JUST KNOW

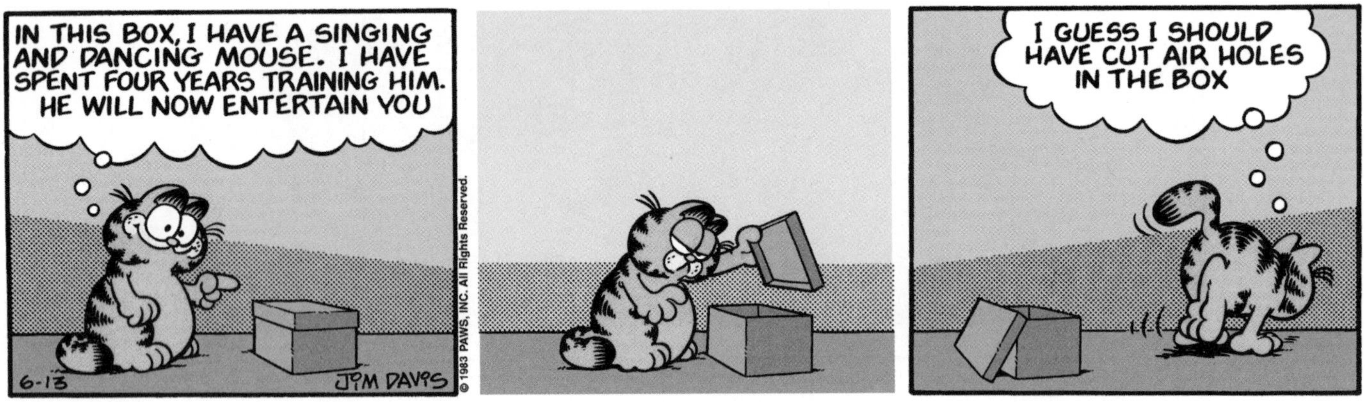
IN THIS BOX, I HAVE A SINGING AND DANCING MOUSE. I HAVE SPENT FOUR YEARS TRAINING HIM. HE WILL NOW ENTERTAIN YOU
6-13
JIM DAVIS
© 1983 PAWS, INC. All Rights Reserved.
I GUESS I SHOULD HAVE CUT AIR HOLES IN THE BOX

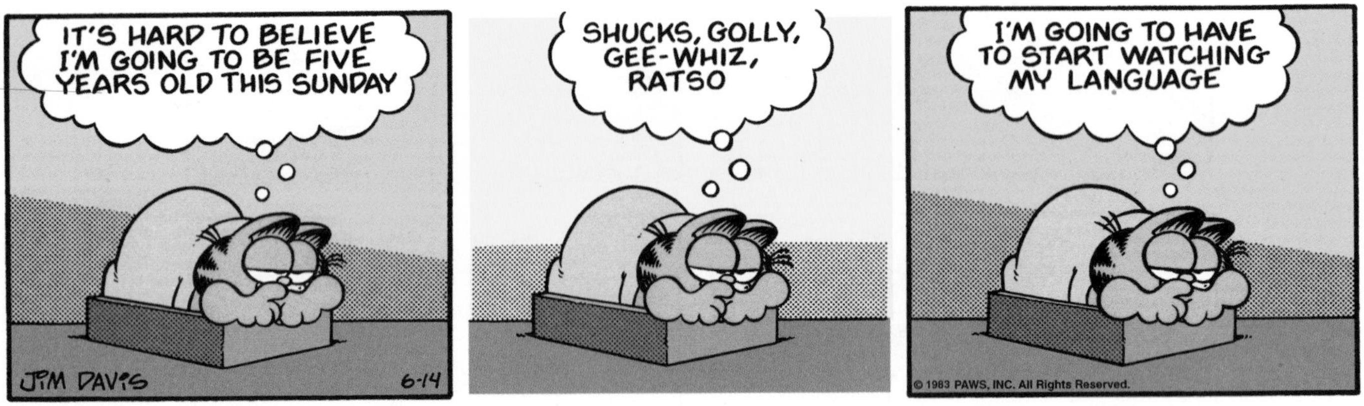
IT'S HARD TO BELIEVE I'M GOING TO BE FIVE YEARS OLD THIS SUNDAY
JIM DAVIS
6-14
SHUCKS, GOLLY, GEE-WHIZ, RATSO
I'M GOING TO HAVE TO START WATCHING MY LANGUAGE
© 1983 PAWS, INC. All Rights Reserved.

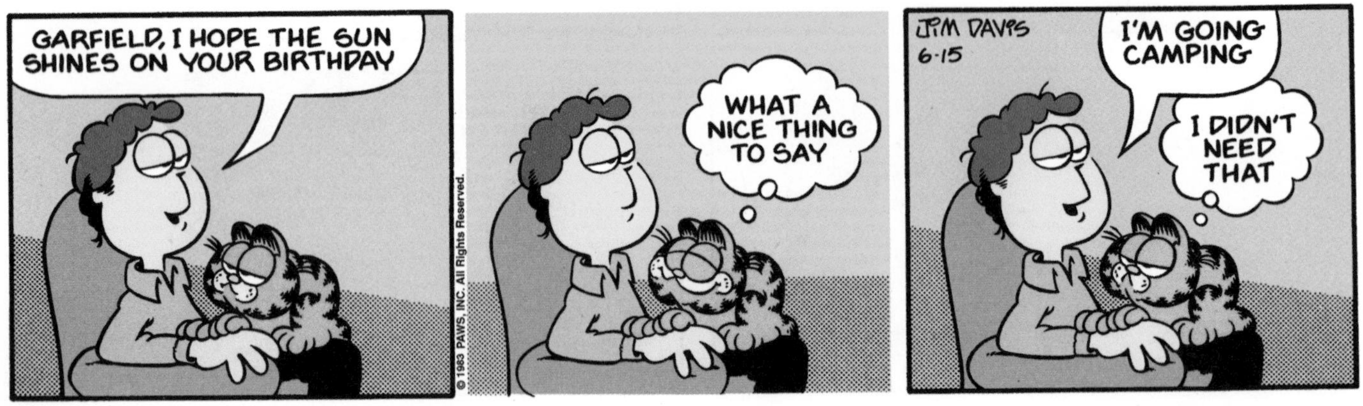
GARFIELD, I HOPE THE SUN SHINES ON YOUR BIRTHDAY
© 1983 PAWS, INC. All Rights Reserved.
WHAT A NICE THING TO SAY
JIM DAVIS
6-15
I'M GOING CAMPING
I DIDN'T NEED THAT

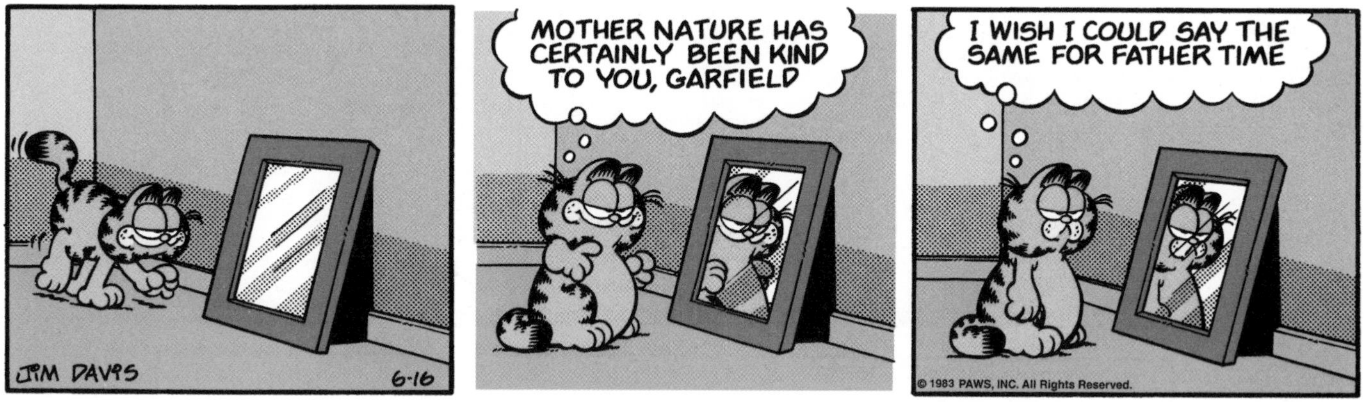
JIM DAVIS 6-16
MOTHER NATURE HAS CERTAINLY BEEN KIND TO YOU, GARFIELD
I WISH I COULD SAY THE SAME FOR FATHER TIME
© 1983 PAWS, INC. All Rights Reserved.

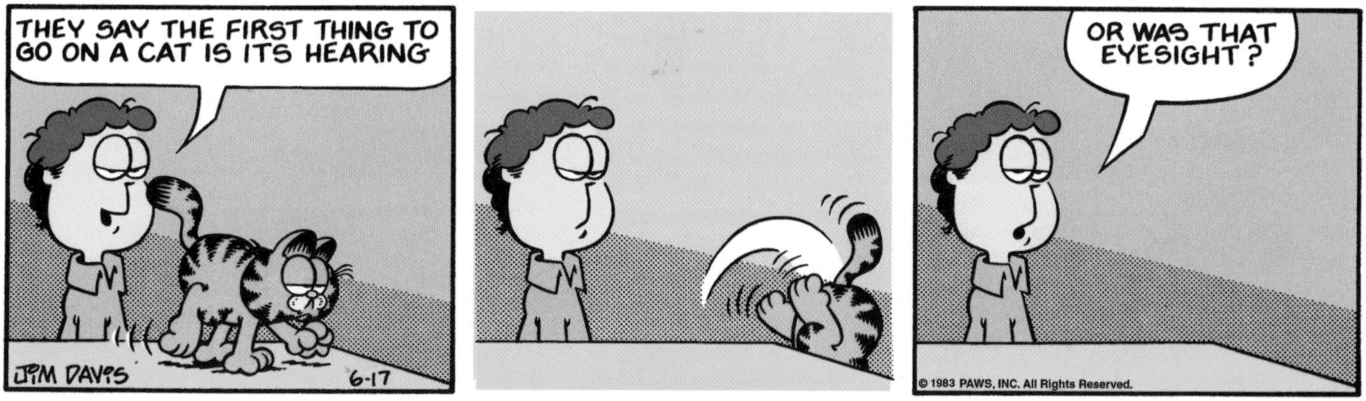
THEY SAY THE FIRST THING TO GO ON A CAT IS ITS HEARING
JIM DAVIS 6-17
OR WAS THAT EYESIGHT ?
© 1983 PAWS, INC. All Rights Reserved.

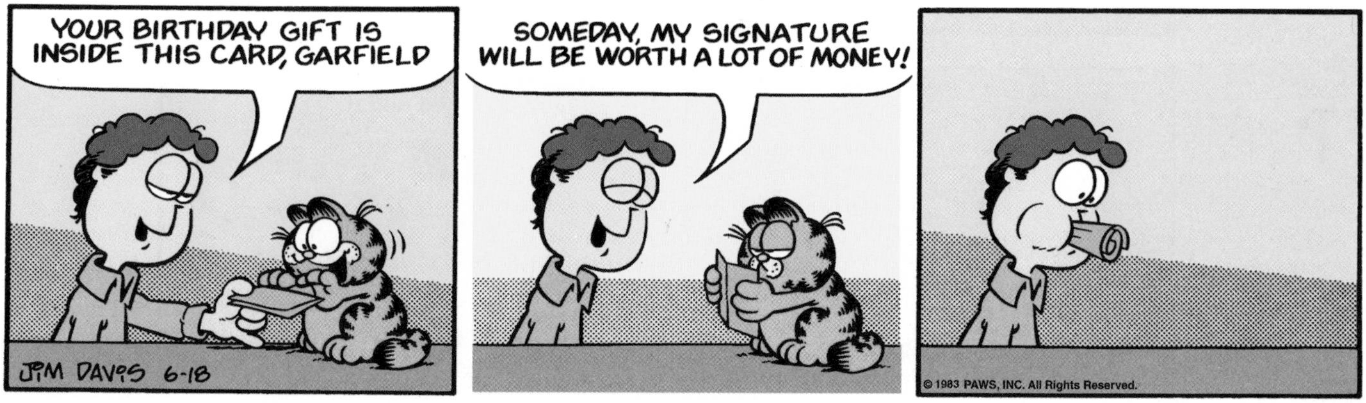
YOUR BIRTHDAY GIFT IS INSIDE THIS CARD, GARFIELD
JIM DAVIS 6-18
SOMEDAY, MY SIGNATURE WILL BE WORTH A LOT OF MONEY!
© 1983 PAWS, INC. All Rights Reserved.

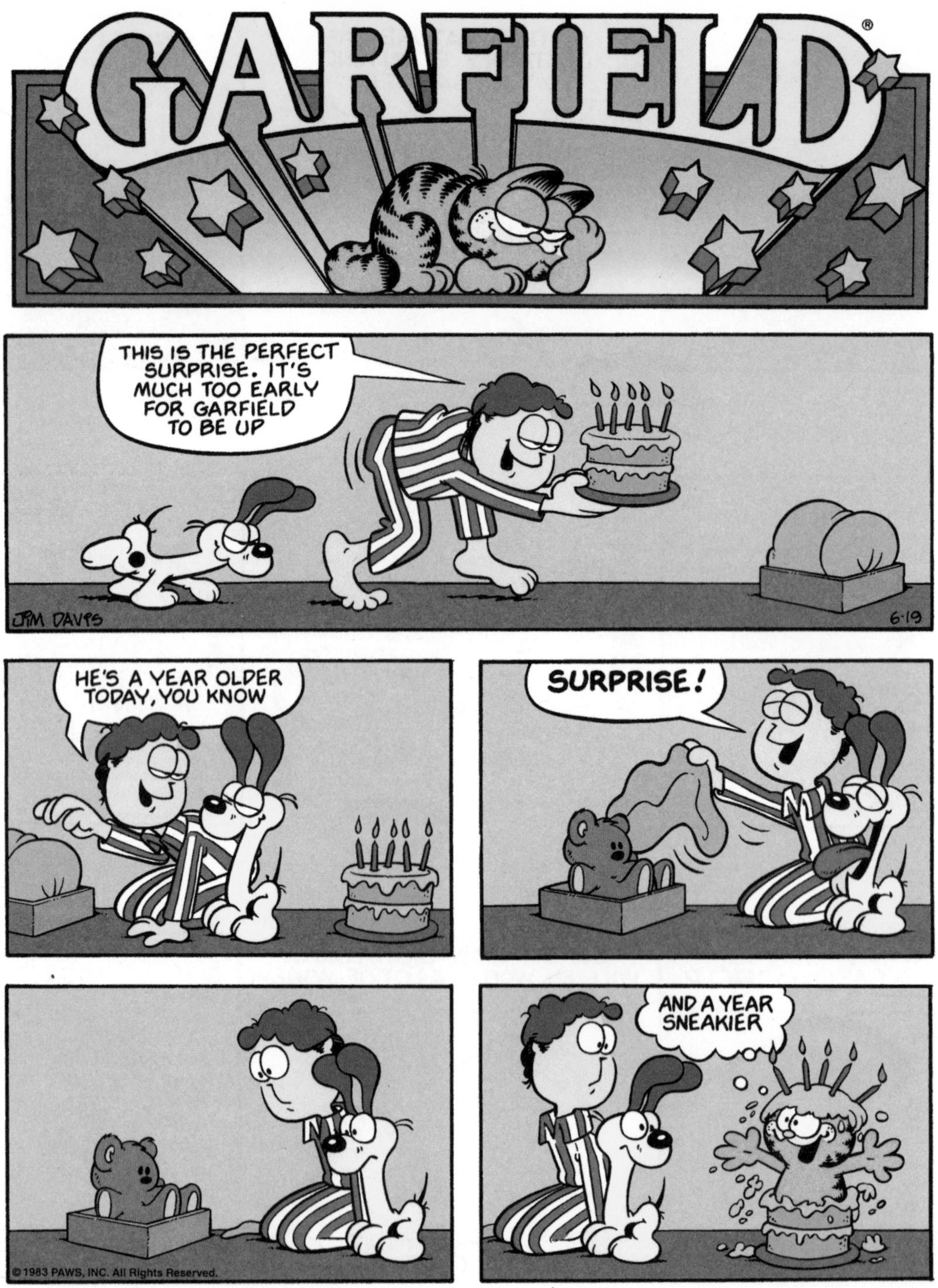
GARFIELD®
THIS IS THE PERFECT SURPRISE. IT'S MUCH TOO EARLY FOR GARFIELD TO BE UP
JIM DAVIS
6-19
HE'S A YEAR OLDER TODAY, YOU KNOW
SURPRISE!
AND A YEAR SNEAKIER
© 1983 PAWS, INC. All Rights Reserved.

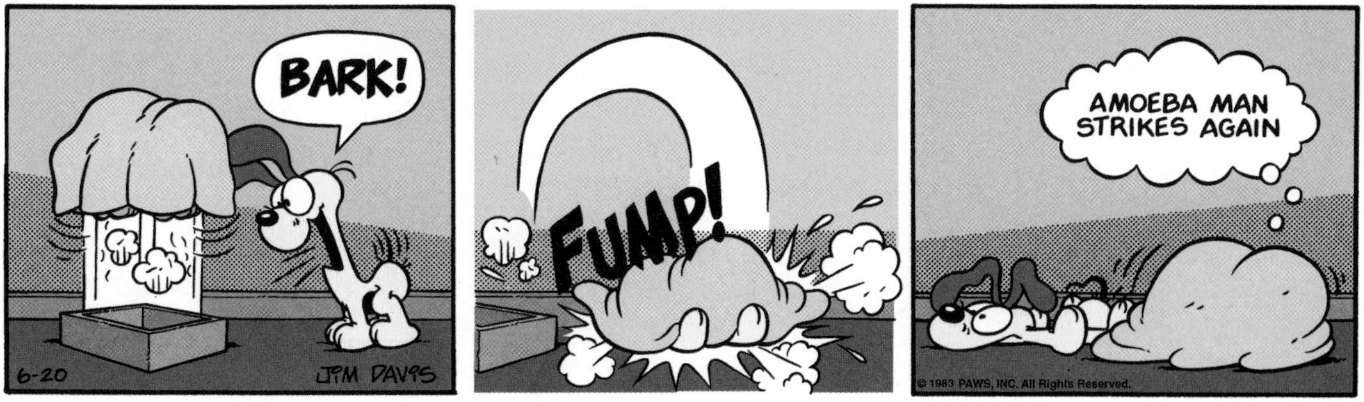
BARK!
6-20
JIM DAVIS
FUMP!
AMOEBA MAN STRIKES AGAIN
© 1983 PAWS, INC. All Rights Reserved.

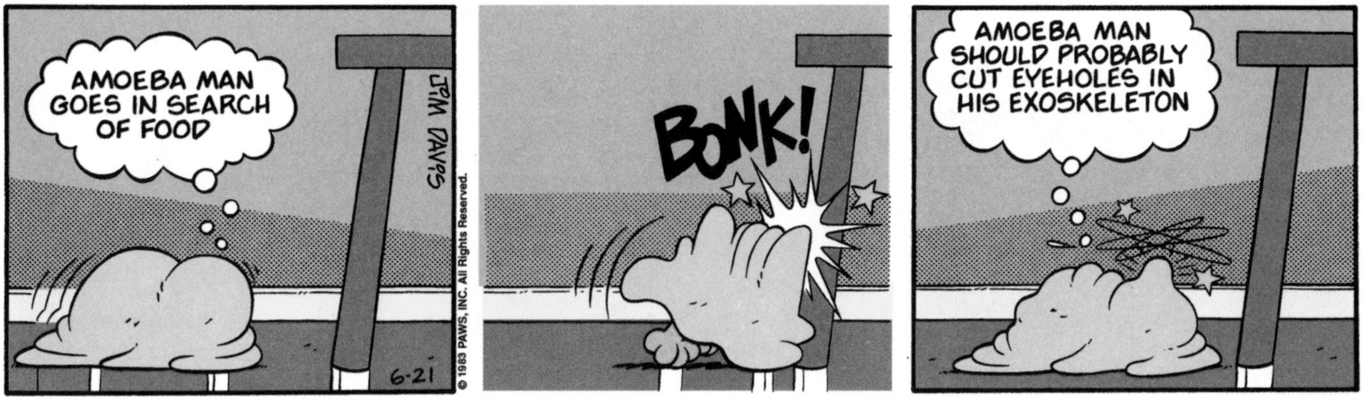
AMOEBA MAN GOES IN SEARCH OF FOOD
JIM DAVIS
6-21
© 1983 PAWS, INC. All Rights Reserved.
BONK!
AMOEBA MAN SHOULD PROBABLY CUT EYEHOLES IN HIS EXOSKELETON

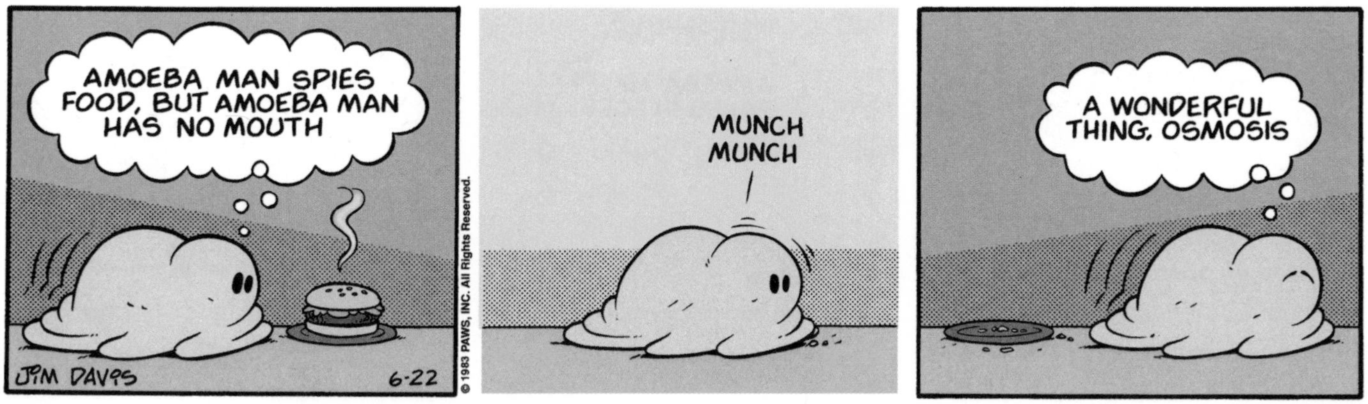
AMOEBA MAN SPIES FOOD, BUT AMOEBA MAN HAS NO MOUTH
JIM DAVIS
6-22
© 1983 PAWS, INC. All Rights Reserved.
MUNCH MUNCH
A WONDERFUL THING, OSMOSIS

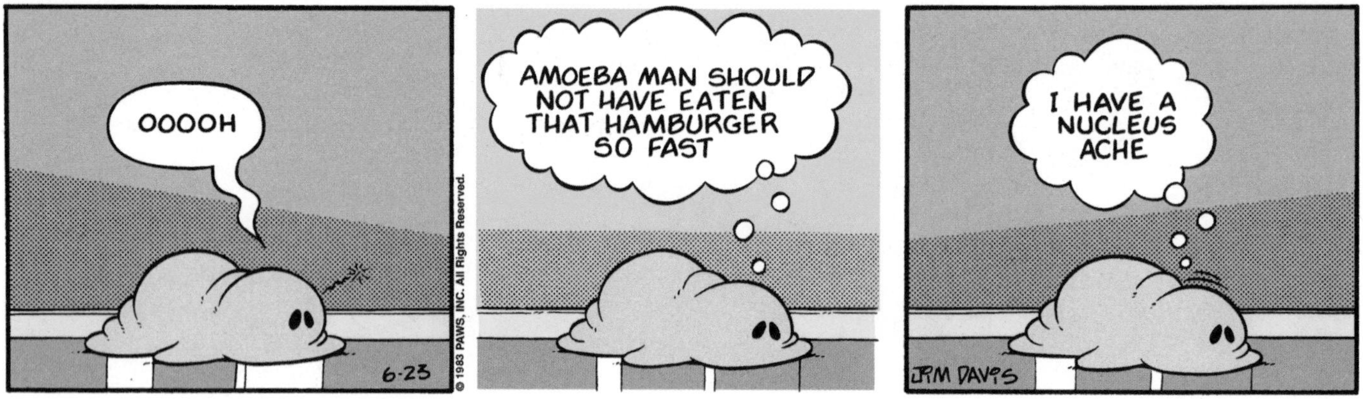
OOOOH
AMOEBA MAN SHOULD NOT HAVE EATEN THAT HAMBURGER SO FAST
I HAVE A NUCLEUS ACHE
6-23
JIM DAVIS
© 1983 PAWS, INC. All Rights Reserved.

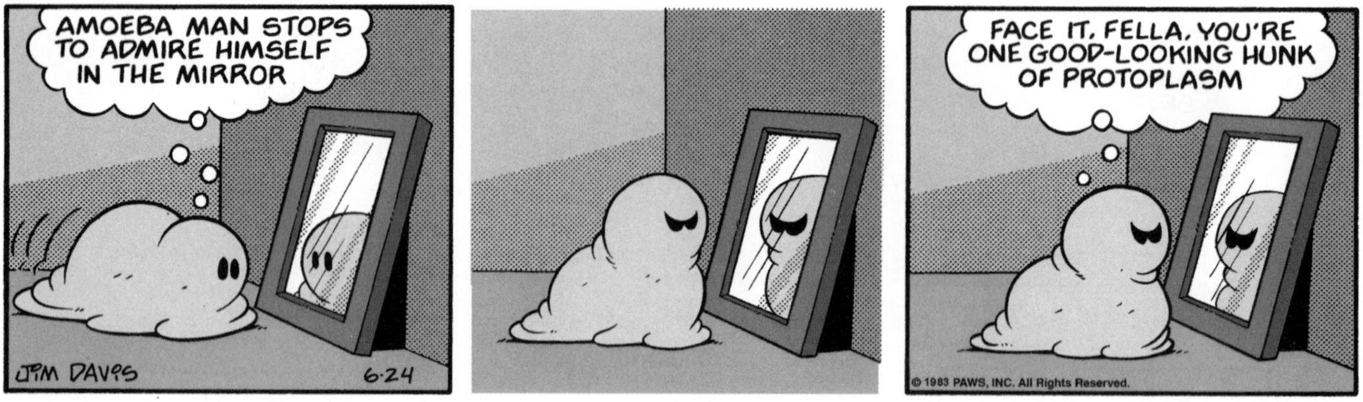
AMOEBA MAN STOPS TO ADMIRE HIMSELF IN THE MIRROR
FACE IT, FELLA, YOU'RE ONE GOOD-LOOKING HUNK OF PROTOPLASM
JIM DAVIS
6-24
© 1983 PAWS, INC. All Rights Reserved.

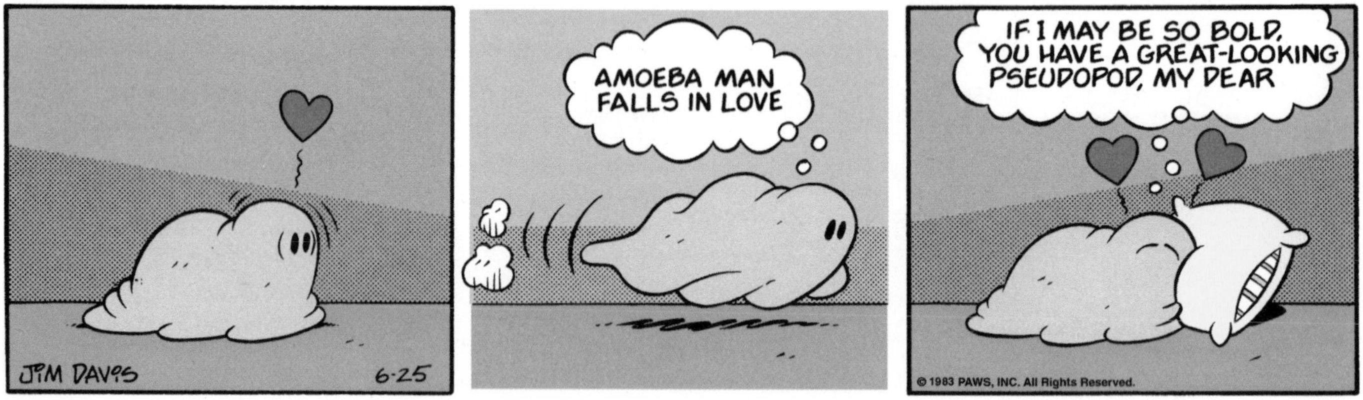
AMOEBA MAN FALLS IN LOVE
IF I MAY BE SO BOLD, YOU HAVE A GREAT-LOOKING PSEUDOPOD, MY DEAR
JIM DAVIS
6-25
© 1983 PAWS, INC. All Rights Reserved.

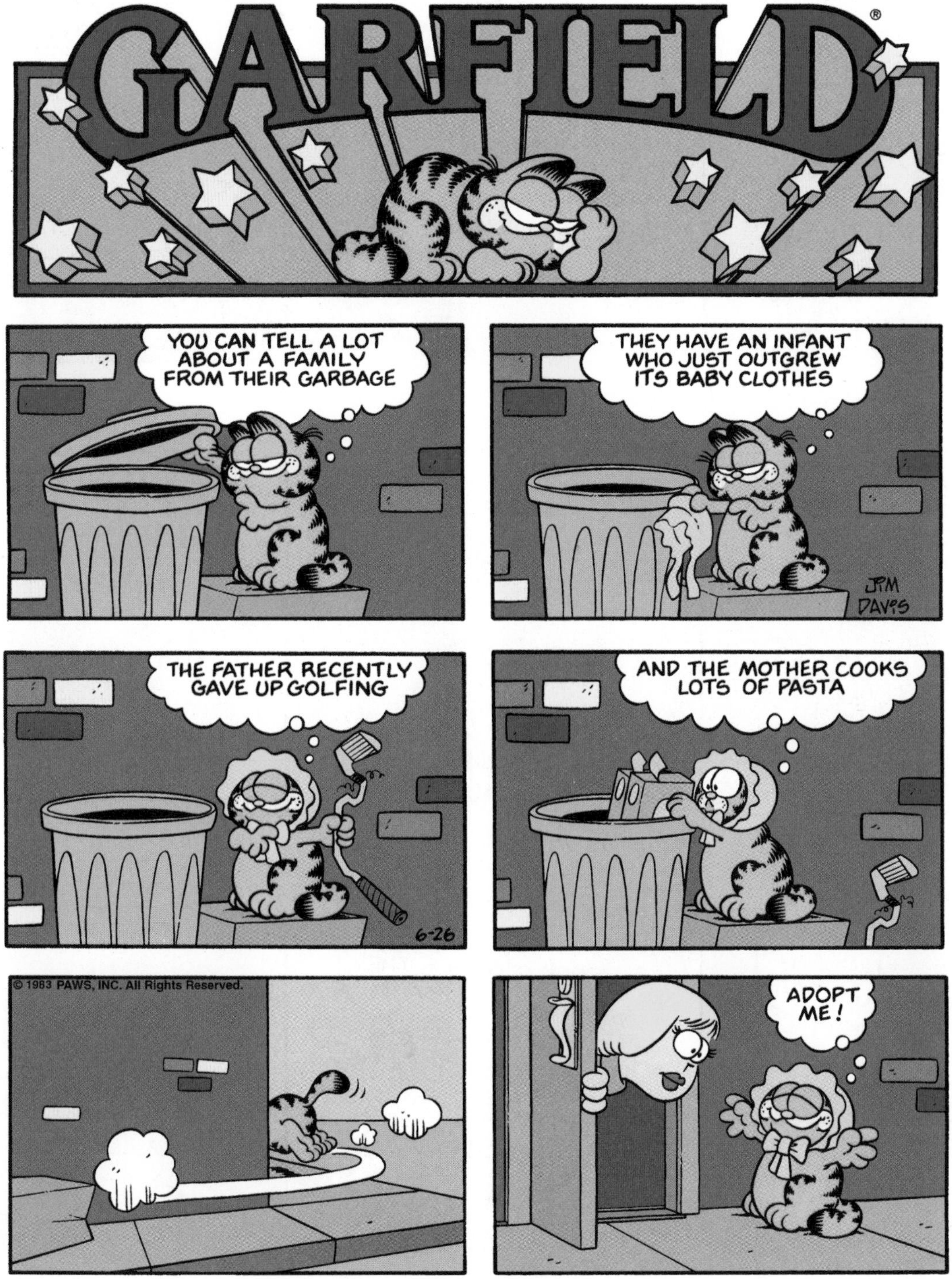
GARFIELD
YOU CAN TELL A LOT ABOUT A FAMILY FROM THEIR GARBAGE
THEY HAVE AN INFANT WHO JUST OUTGREW ITS BABY CLOTHES
JIM DAVIS
THE FATHER RECENTLY GAVE UP GOLFING
6-26
AND THE MOTHER COOKS LOTS OF PASTA
© 1983 PAWS, INC. All Rights Reserved.
ADOPT ME!

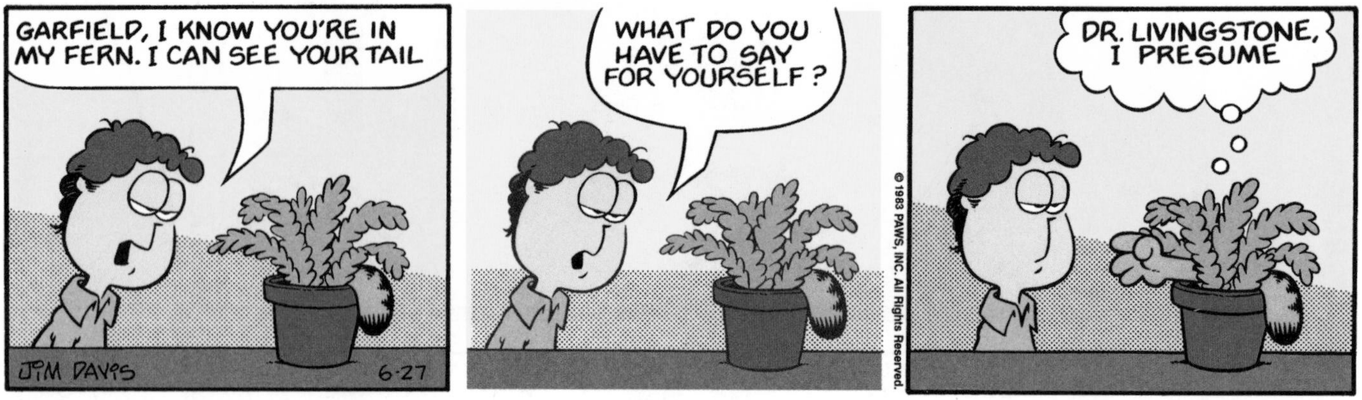
GARFIELD, I KNOW YOU'RE IN MY FERN. I CAN SEE YOUR TAIL
WHAT DO YOU HAVE TO SAY FOR YOURSELF ?
DR. LIVINGSTONE, I PRESUME
JIM DAVIS
6-27
© 1983 PAWS, INC. All Rights Reserved.

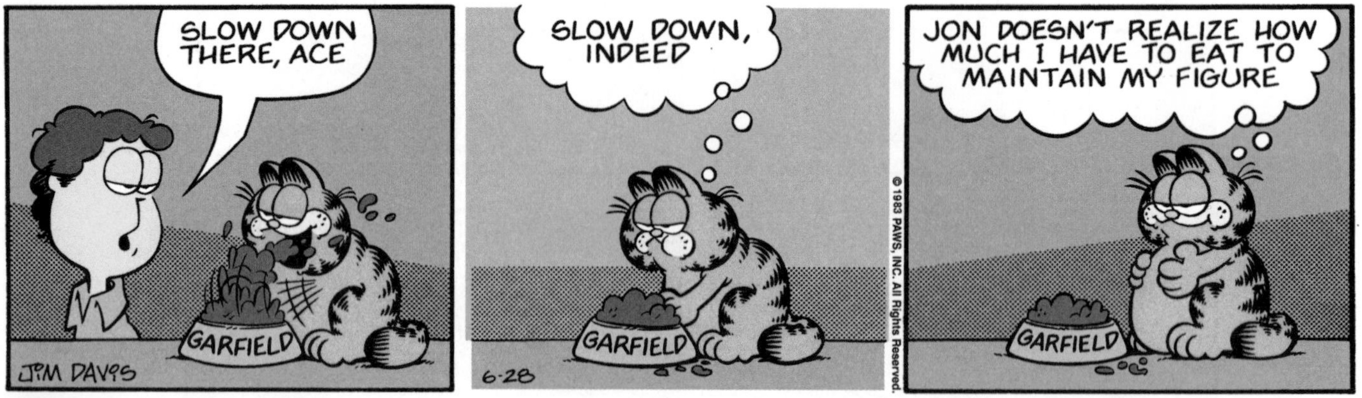
SLOW DOWN THERE, ACE
SLOW DOWN, INDEED
JON DOESN'T REALIZE HOW MUCH I HAVE TO EAT TO MAINTAIN MY FIGURE
GARFIELD
JIM DAVIS
6-28
© 1983 PAWS, INC. All Rights Reserved.

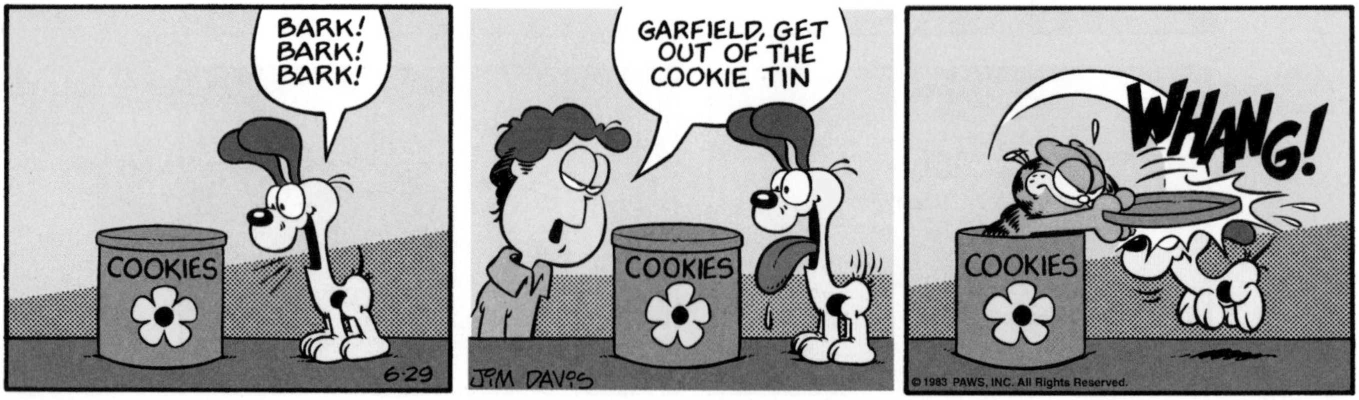
BARK! BARK! BARK!
COOKIES
GARFIELD, GET OUT OF THE COOKIE TIN
WHANG!
6-29
JIM DAVIS
© 1983 PAWS, INC. All Rights Reserved.

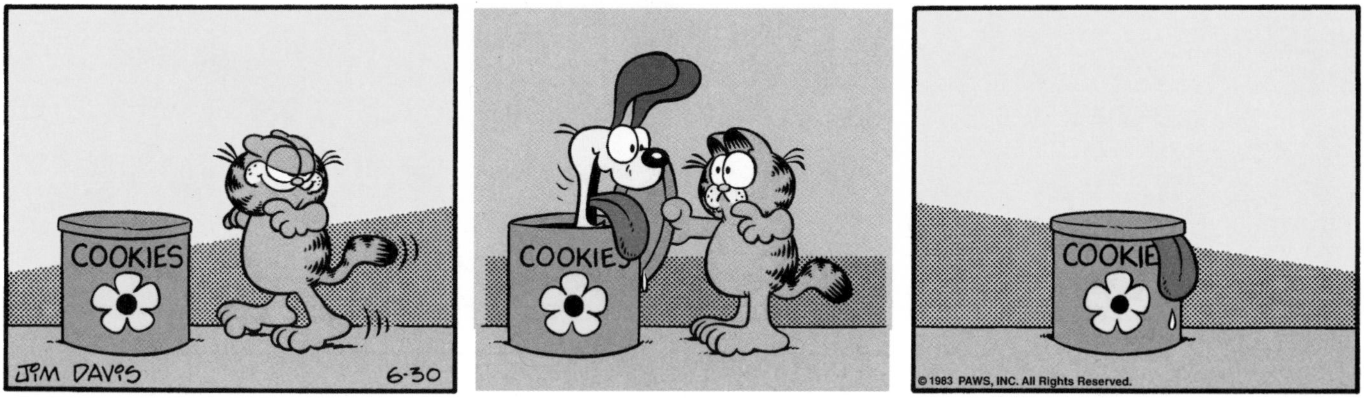
COOKIES
JIM DAVIS
6-30
COOKIES
COOKIE
© 1983 PAWS, INC. All Rights Reserved.

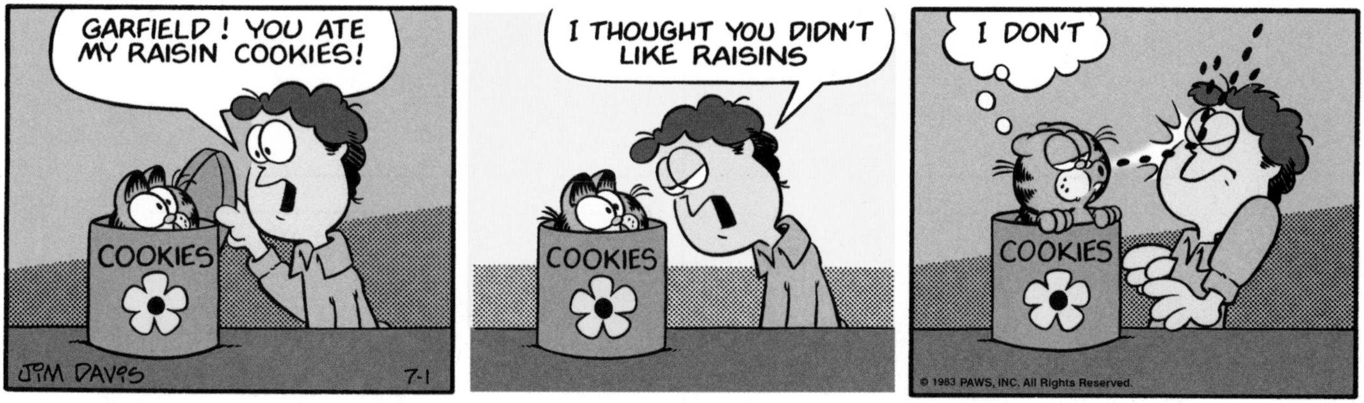
GARFIELD! YOU ATE MY RAISIN COOKIES!
COOKIES
JIM DAVIS
7-1
I THOUGHT YOU DIDN'T LIKE RAISINS
COOKIES
I DON'T
COOKIES
© 1983 PAWS, INC. All Rights Reserved.

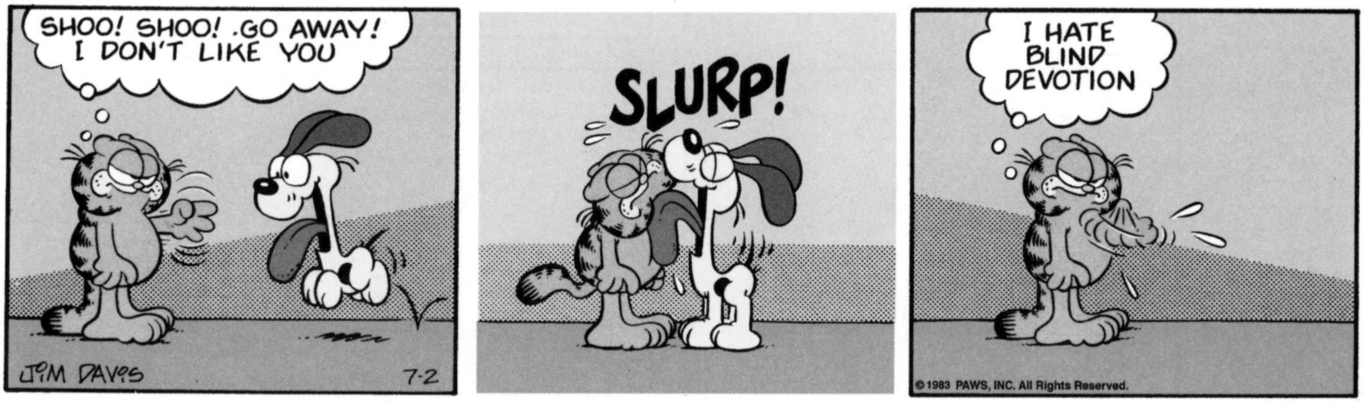
SHOO! SHOO! .GO AWAY! I DON'T LIKE YOU
JIM DAVIS
7-2
SLURP!
I HATE BLIND DEVOTION
© 1983 PAWS, INC. All Rights Reserved.

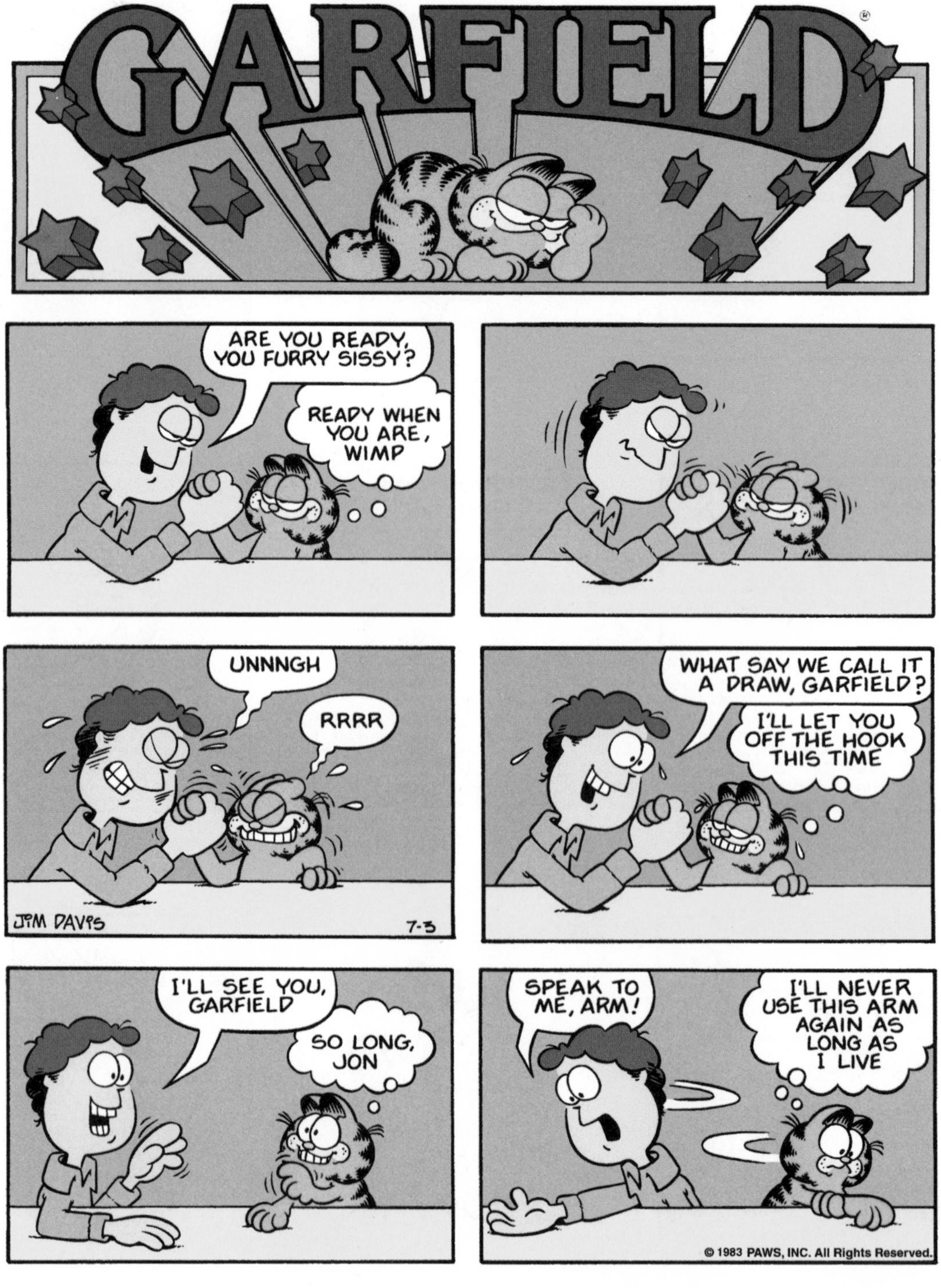
GARFIELD
ARE YOU READY, YOU FURRY SISSY?
READY WHEN YOU ARE, WIMP
UNNNGH
RRRR
JIM DAVIS
7-3
WHAT SAY WE CALL IT A DRAW, GARFIELD?
I'LL LET YOU OFF THE HOOK THIS TIME
I'LL SEE YOU, GARFIELD
SO LONG, JON
SPEAK TO ME, ARM!
I'LL NEVER USE THIS ARM AGAIN AS LONG AS I LIVE
© 1983 PAWS, INC. All Rights Reserved.

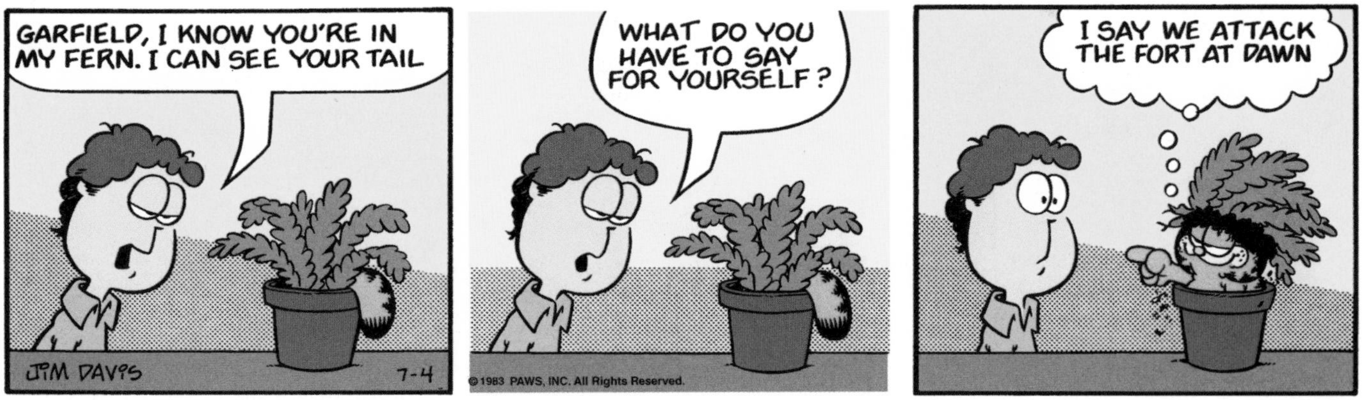
GARFIELD, I KNOW YOU'RE IN MY FERN. I CAN SEE YOUR TAIL
WHAT DO YOU HAVE TO SAY FOR YOURSELF?
I SAY WE ATTACK THE FORT AT DAWN
JIM DAVIS 7-4
© 1983 PAWS, INC. All Rights Reserved.

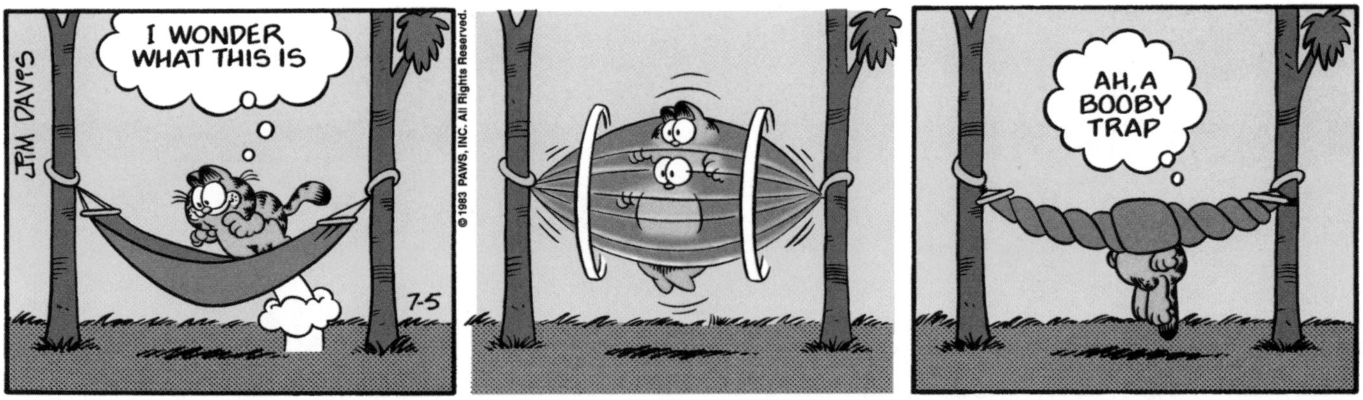
I WONDER WHAT THIS IS
AH, A BOOBY TRAP
JIM DAVIS 7-5
© 1983 PAWS, INC. All Rights Reserved.

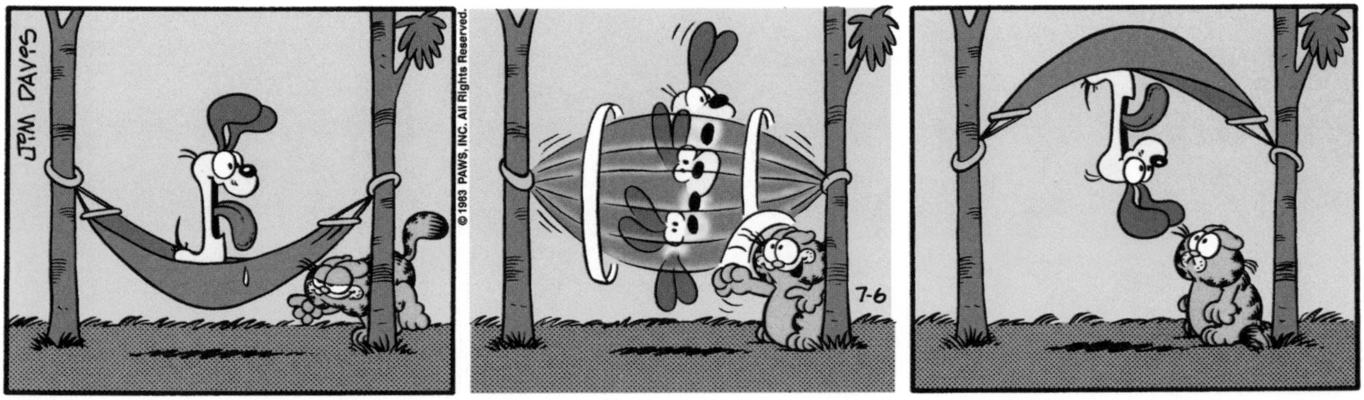
JIM DAVIS 7-6
© 1983 PAWS, INC. All Rights Reserved.

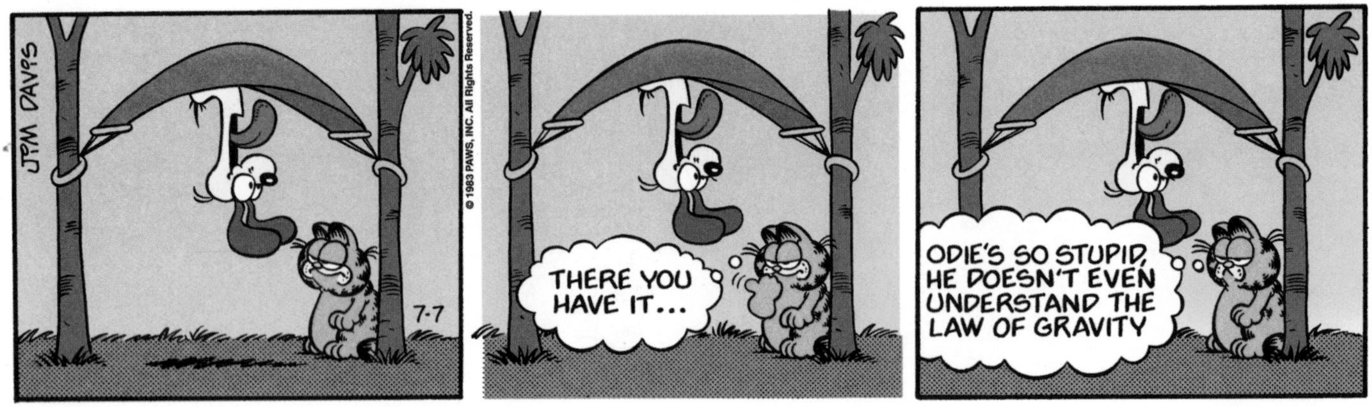
JIM DAVIS
7-7
© 1983 PAWS, INC. All Rights Reserved.
THERE YOU HAVE IT...
ODIE'S SO STUPID, HE DOESN'T EVEN UNDERSTAND THE LAW OF GRAVITY

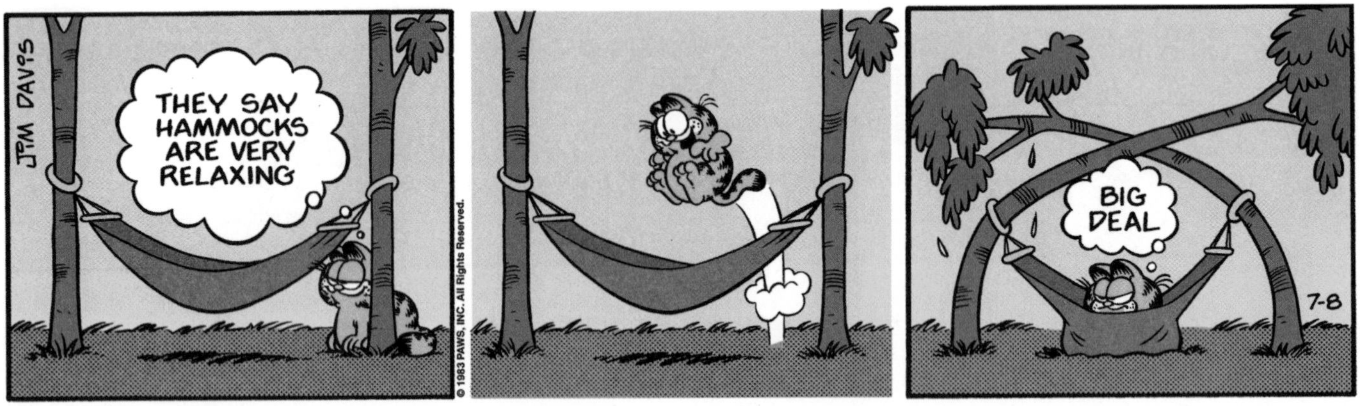
JIM DAVIS
THEY SAY HAMMOCKS ARE VERY RELAXING
© 1983 PAWS, INC. All Rights Reserved.
BIG DEAL
7-8

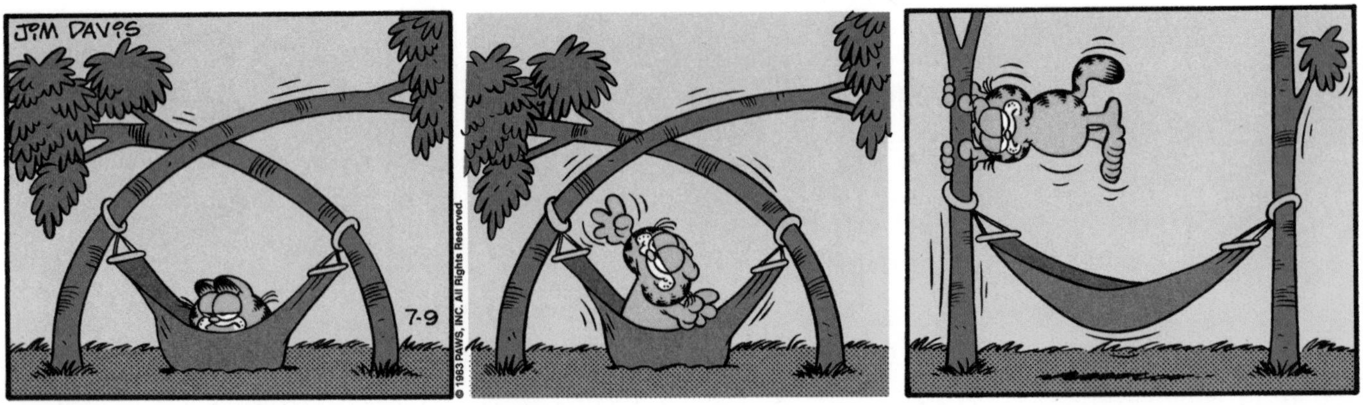
JIM DAVIS
7-9
© 1983 PAWS, INC. All Rights Reserved.

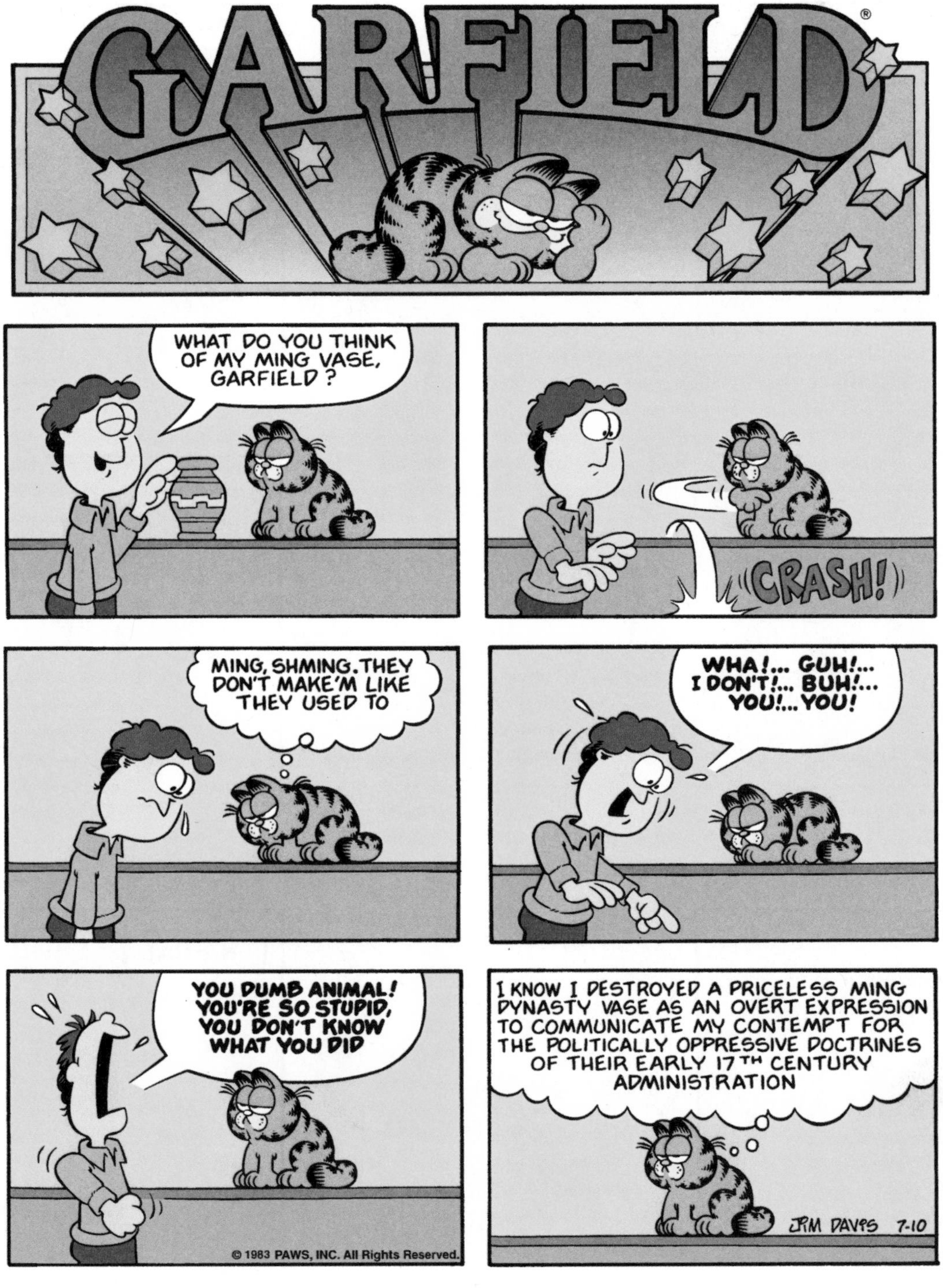
GARFIELD®
WHAT DO YOU THINK OF MY MING VASE, GARFIELD?
CRASH!
MING, SHMING. THEY DON'T MAKE'M LIKE THEY USED TO
WHA!... GUH!... I DON'T!... BUH!... YOU!... YOU!
YOU DUMB ANIMAL! YOU'RE SO STUPID, YOU DON'T KNOW WHAT YOU DID
I KNOW I DESTROYED A PRICELESS MING DYNASTY VASE AS AN OVERT EXPRESSION TO COMMUNICATE MY CONTEMPT FOR THE POLITICALLY OPPRESSIVE DOCTRINES OF THEIR EARLY 17TH CENTURY ADMINISTRATION
JIM DAVIS 7-10
© 1983 PAWS, INC. All Rights Reserved.

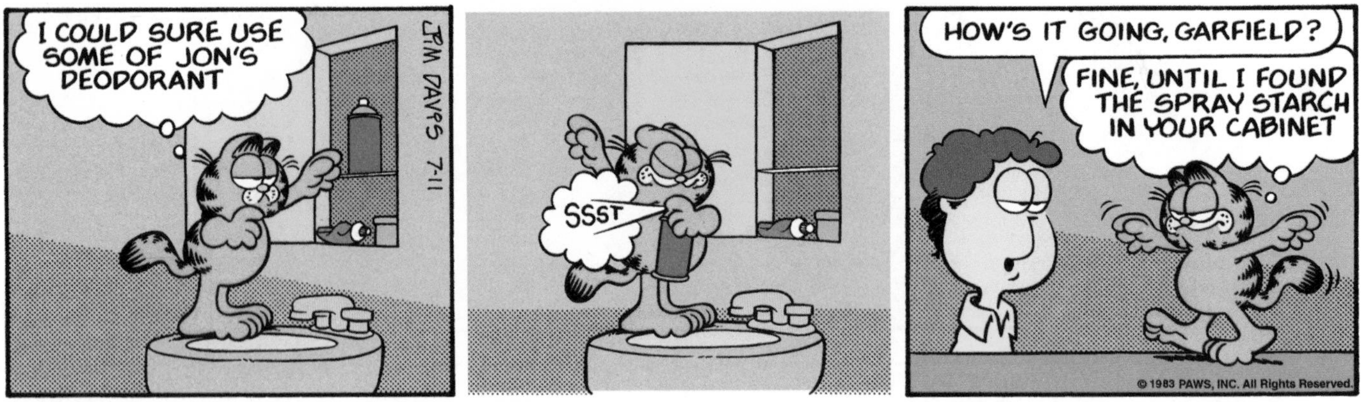
I COULD SURE USE SOME OF JON'S DEODORANT
JIM DAVIS 7-11
SSST
HOW'S IT GOING, GARFIELD?
FINE, UNTIL I FOUND THE SPRAY STARCH IN YOUR CABINET
© 1983 PAWS, INC. All Rights Reserved.

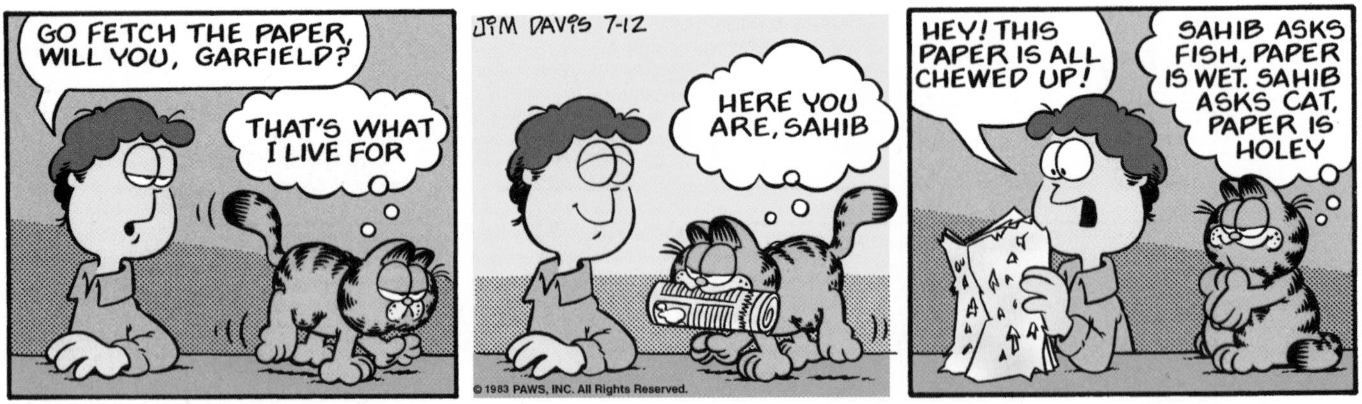
GO FETCH THE PAPER, WILL YOU, GARFIELD?
THAT'S WHAT I LIVE FOR
JIM DAVIS 7-12
HERE YOU ARE, SAHIB
© 1983 PAWS, INC. All Rights Reserved.
HEY! THIS PAPER IS ALL CHEWED UP!
SAHIB ASKS FISH, PAPER IS WET. SAHIB ASKS CAT, PAPER IS HOLEY

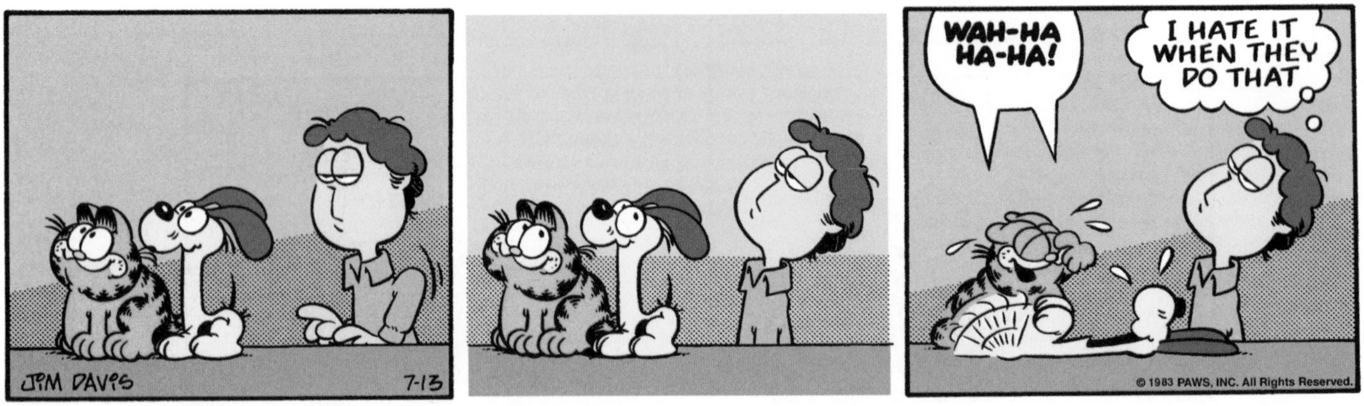
JIM DAVIS
7-13
WAH-HA HA-HA!
I HATE IT WHEN THEY DO THAT
© 1983 PAWS, INC. All Rights Reserved.

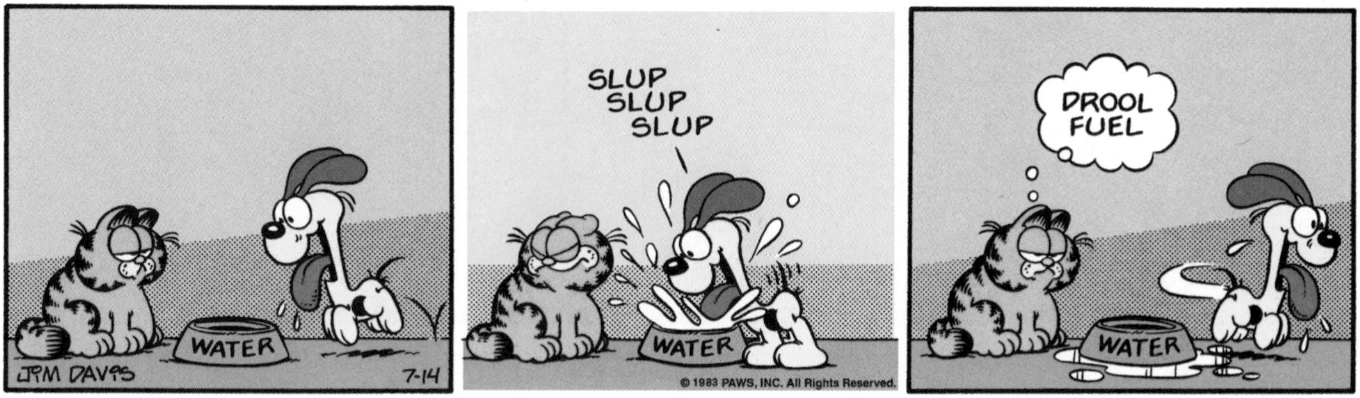
JIM DAVIS
7-14
SLUP
SLUP
SLUP
WATER
© 1983 PAWS, INC. All Rights Reserved.
DROOL FUEL

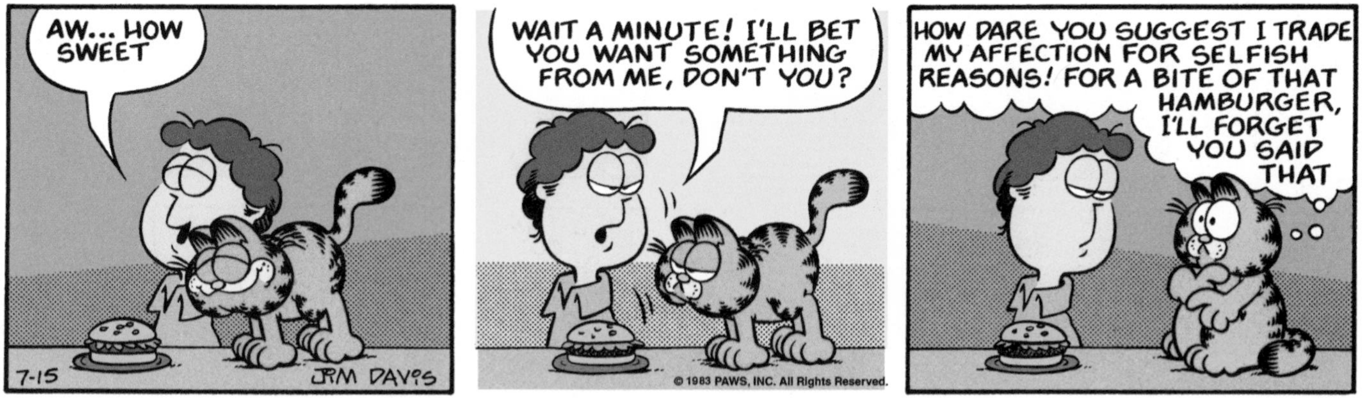
AW... HOW SWEET
7-15
JIM DAVIS
WAIT A MINUTE! I'LL BET YOU WANT SOMETHING FROM ME, DON'T YOU?
© 1983 PAWS, INC. All Rights Reserved.
HOW DARE YOU SUGGEST I TRADE MY AFFECTION FOR SELFISH REASONS! FOR A BITE OF THAT HAMBURGER, I'LL FORGET YOU SAID THAT

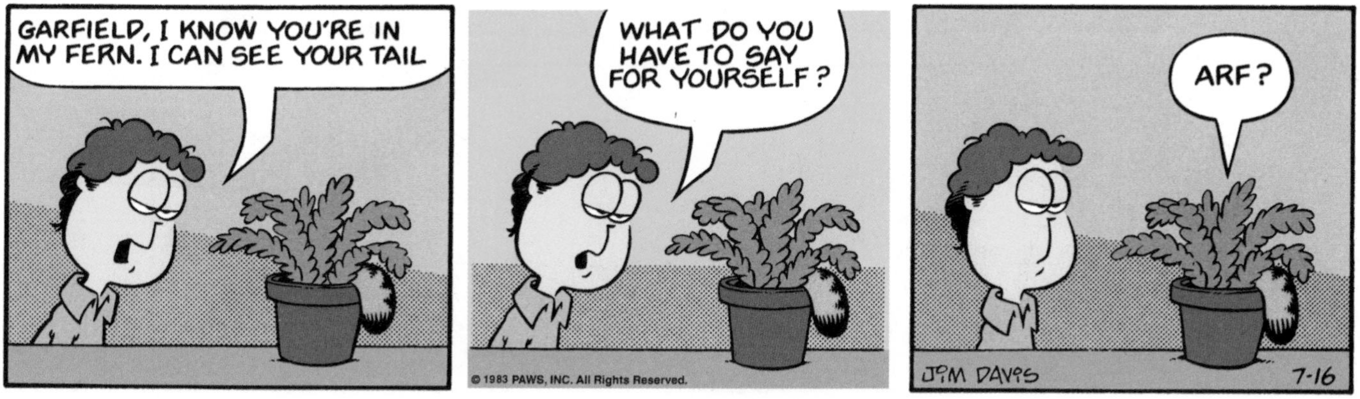
GARFIELD, I KNOW YOU'RE IN MY FERN. I CAN SEE YOUR TAIL
WHAT DO YOU HAVE TO SAY FOR YOURSELF?
© 1983 PAWS, INC. All Rights Reserved.
ARF?
JIM DAVIS
7-16

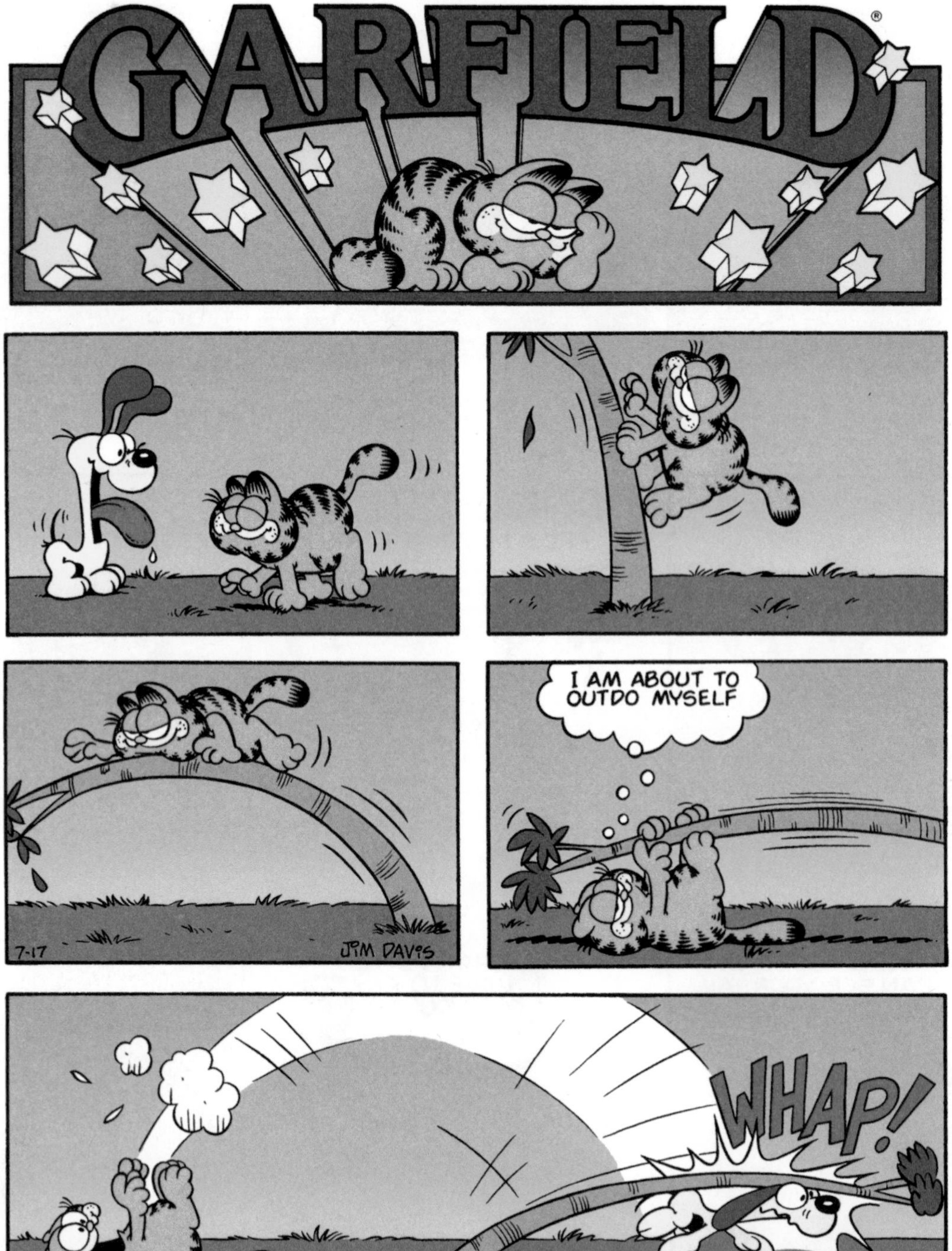
GARFIELD
I AM ABOUT TO OUTDO MYSELF
7-17
JIM DAVIS
WHAP!
© 1983 PAWS, INC. All Rights Reserved.

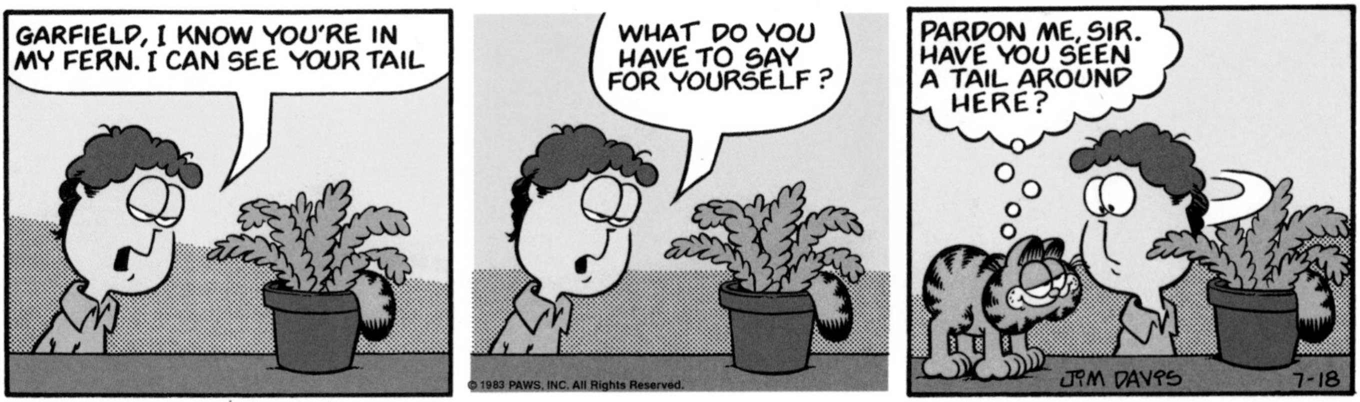
GARFIELD, I KNOW YOU'RE IN MY FERN. I CAN SEE YOUR TAIL
WHAT DO YOU HAVE TO SAY FOR YOURSELF?
© 1983 PAWS, INC. All Rights Reserved.
PARDON ME, SIR. HAVE YOU SEEN A TAIL AROUND HERE?
JIM DAVIS
7-18

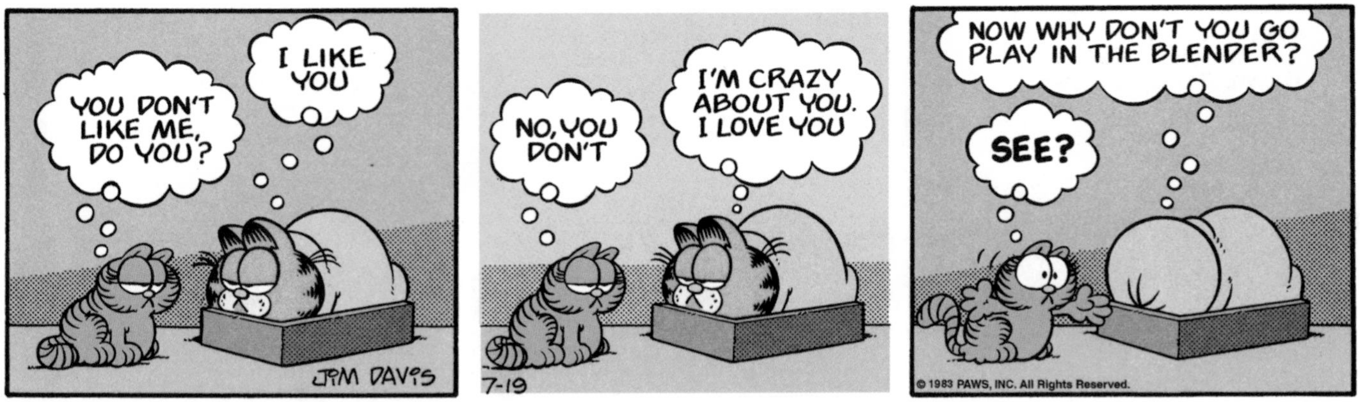
YOU DON'T LIKE ME, DO YOU?
I LIKE YOU
JIM DAVIS
NO, YOU DON'T
I'M CRAZY ABOUT YOU. I LOVE YOU
7-19
NOW WHY DON'T YOU GO PLAY IN THE BLENDER?
SEE?
© 1983 PAWS, INC. All Rights Reserved.

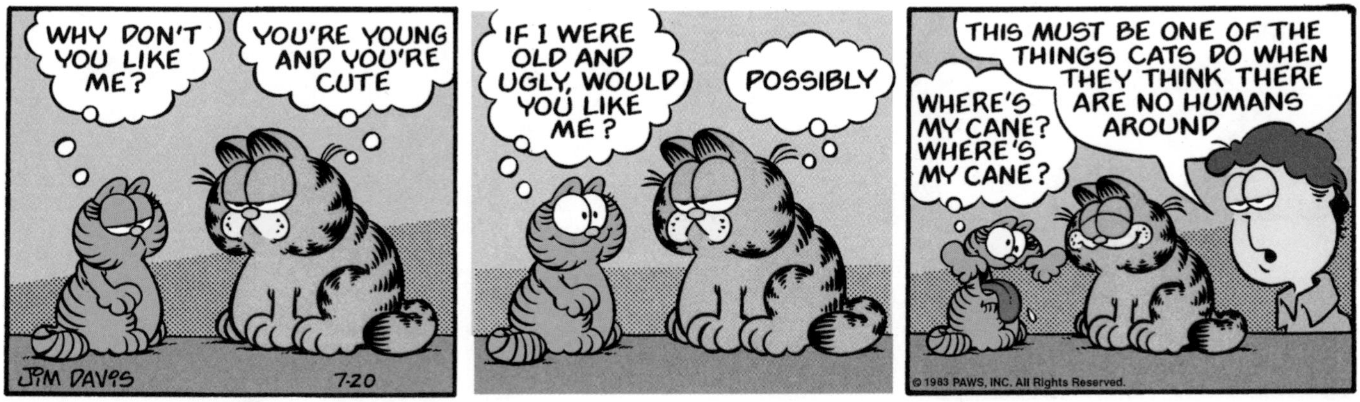
WHY DON'T YOU LIKE ME?
YOU'RE YOUNG AND YOU'RE CUTE
JIM DAVIS
7-20
IF I WERE OLD AND UGLY, WOULD YOU LIKE ME?
POSSIBLY
THIS MUST BE ONE OF THE THINGS CATS DO WHEN THEY THINK THERE ARE NO HUMANS AROUND
WHERE'S MY CANE? WHERE'S MY CANE?
© 1983 PAWS, INC. All Rights Reserved.

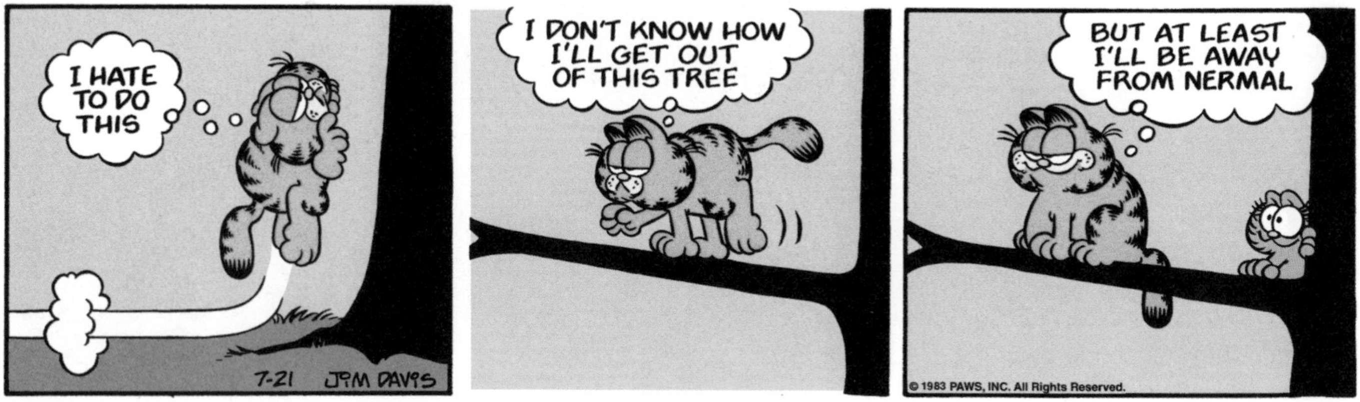
I HATE TO DO THIS
7-21 JIM DAVIS
I DON'T KNOW HOW I'LL GET OUT OF THIS TREE
BUT AT LEAST I'LL BE AWAY FROM NERMAL
© 1983 PAWS, INC. All Rights Reserved.

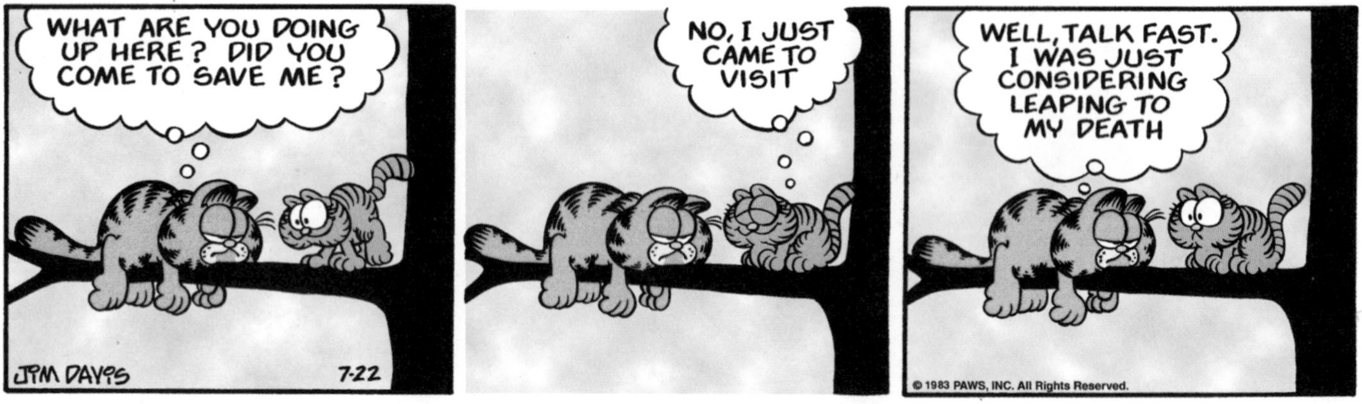
WHAT ARE YOU DOING UP HERE? DID YOU COME TO SAVE ME?
JIM DAVIS 7-22
NO, I JUST CAME TO VISIT
WELL, TALK FAST. I WAS JUST CONSIDERING LEAPING TO MY DEATH
© 1983 PAWS, INC. All Rights Reserved.

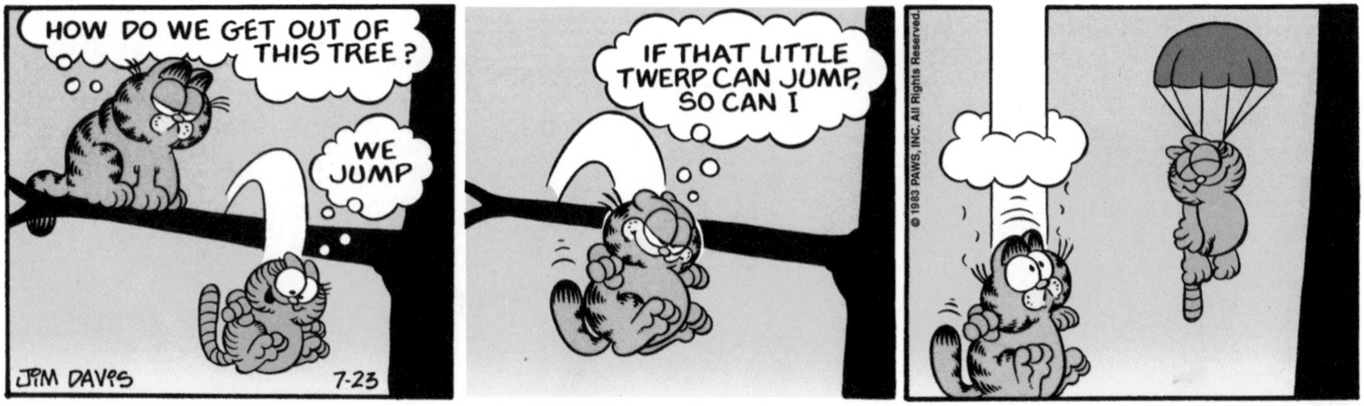
HOW DO WE GET OUT OF THIS TREE?
WE JUMP
JIM DAVIS 7-23
IF THAT LITTLE TWERP CAN JUMP, SO CAN I
© 1983 PAWS, INC. All Rights Reserved.

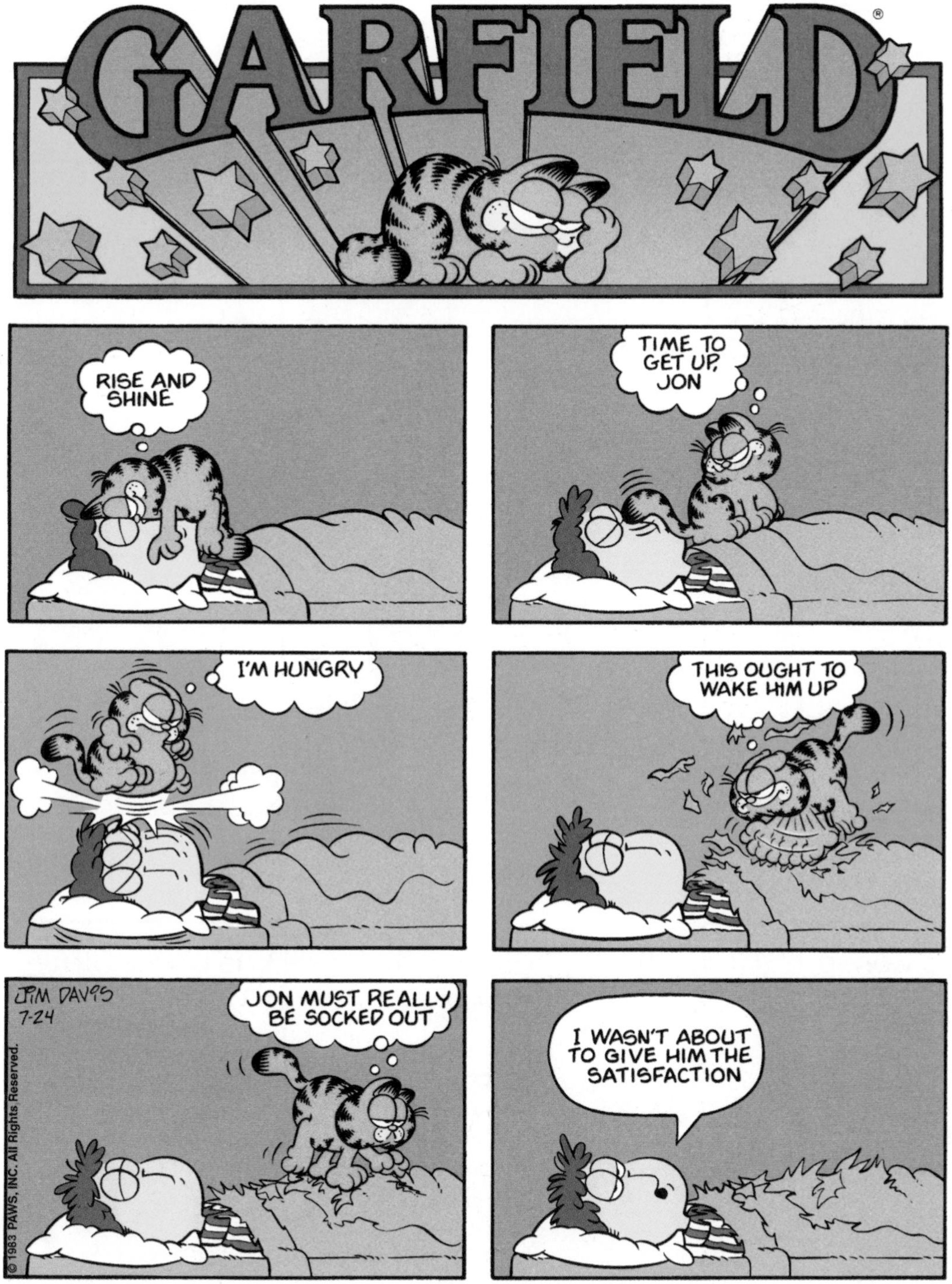
GARFIELD®
RISE AND SHINE
TIME TO GET UP, JON
I'M HUNGRY
THIS OUGHT TO WAKE HIM UP
JIM DAVIS 7-24
© 1983 PAWS, INC. All Rights Reserved.
JON MUST REALLY BE SOCKED OUT
I WASN'T ABOUT TO GIVE HIM THE SATISFACTION

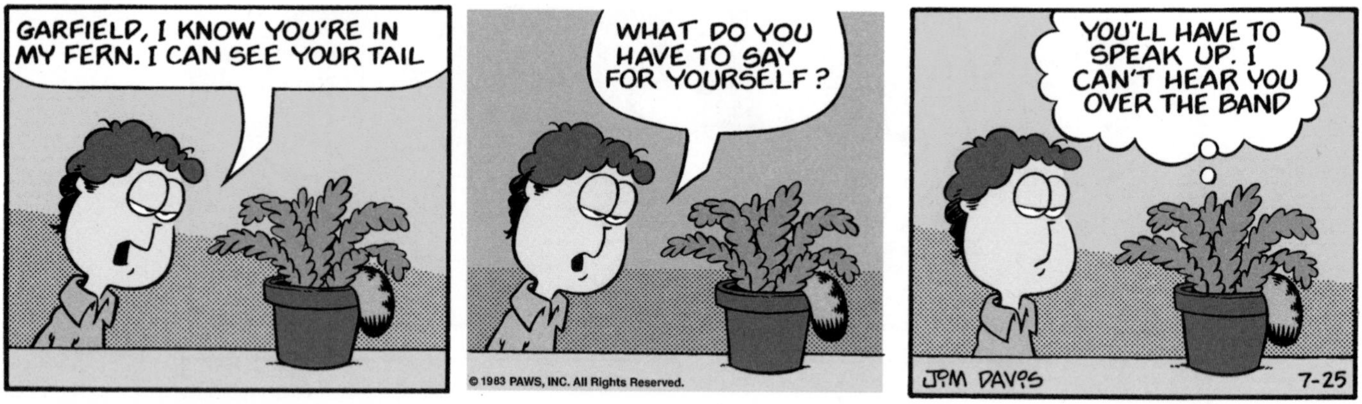
GARFIELD, I KNOW YOU'RE IN MY FERN. I CAN SEE YOUR TAIL
WHAT DO YOU HAVE TO SAY FOR YOURSELF?
© 1983 PAWS, INC. All Rights Reserved.
YOU'LL HAVE TO SPEAK UP. I CAN'T HEAR YOU OVER THE BAND
JIM DAVIS
7-25

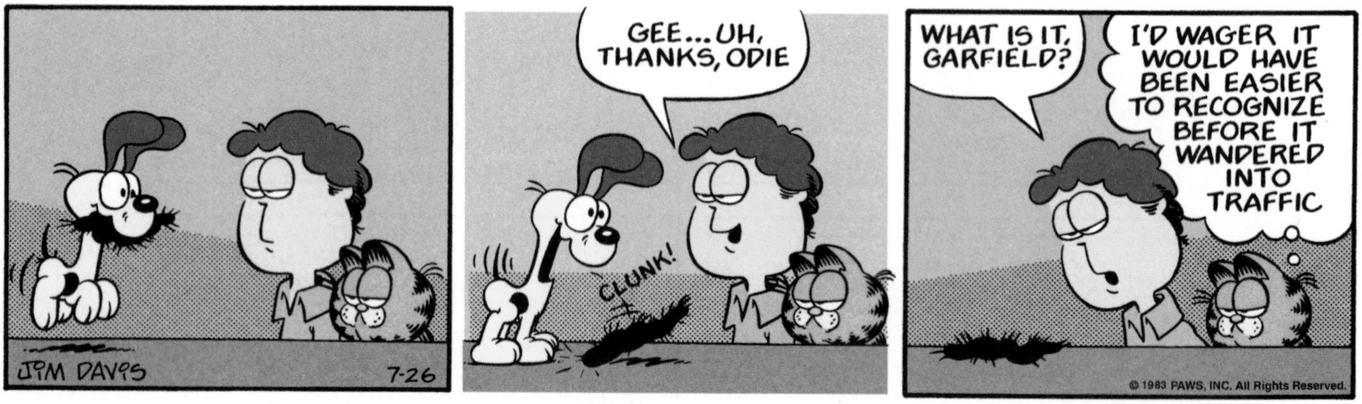
JIM DAVIS
7-26
GEE... UH, THANKS, ODIE
CLUNK!
WHAT IS IT, GARFIELD?
I'D WAGER IT WOULD HAVE BEEN EASIER TO RECOGNIZE BEFORE IT WANDERED INTO TRAFFIC
© 1983 PAWS, INC. All Rights Reserved.

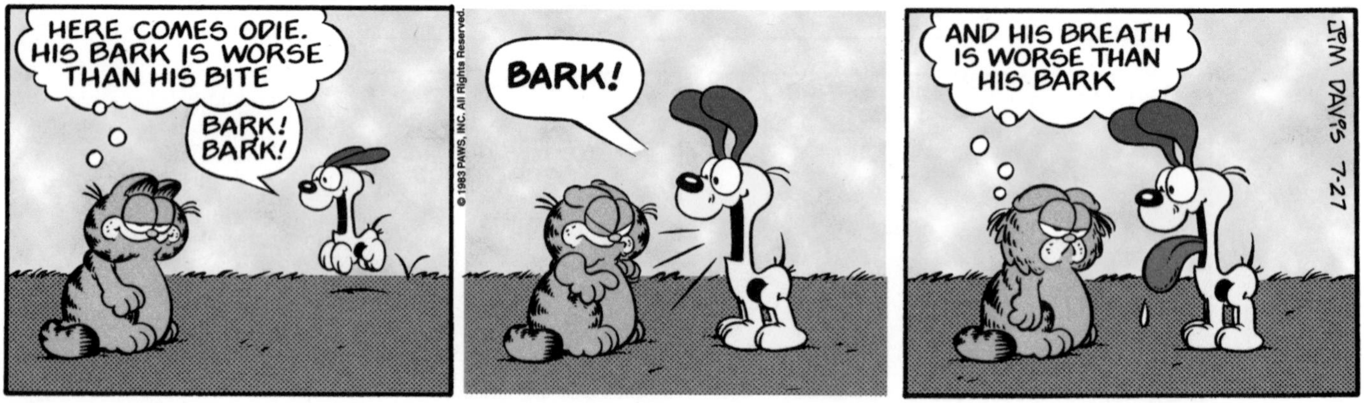
HERE COMES ODIE. HIS BARK IS WORSE THAN HIS BITE
BARK! BARK!
© 1983 PAWS, INC. All Rights Reserved.
BARK!
AND HIS BREATH IS WORSE THAN HIS BARK
JIM DAVIS 7-27

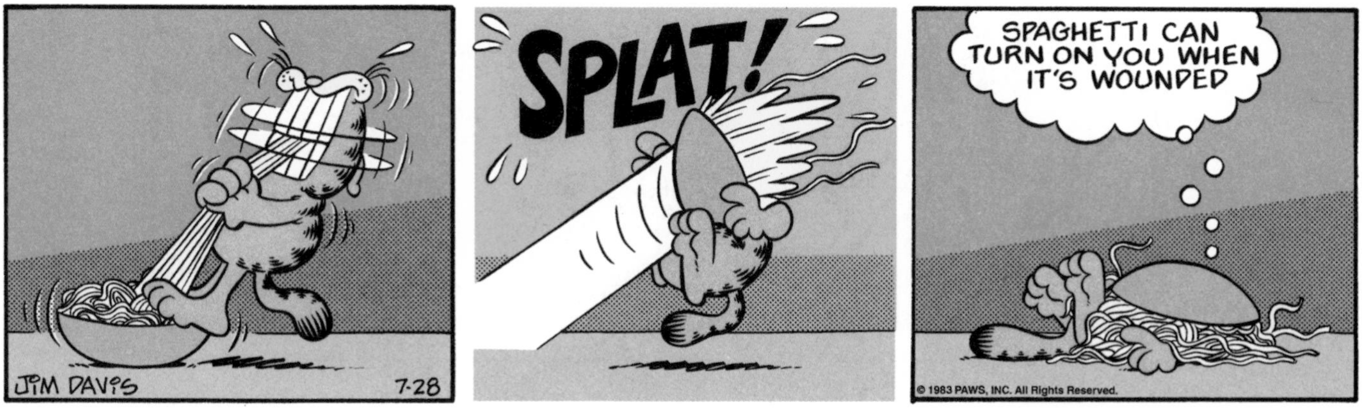
SPLAT!
SPAGHETTI CAN TURN ON YOU WHEN IT'S WOUNDED
JIM DAVIS
7-28
© 1983 PAWS, INC. All Rights Reserved.

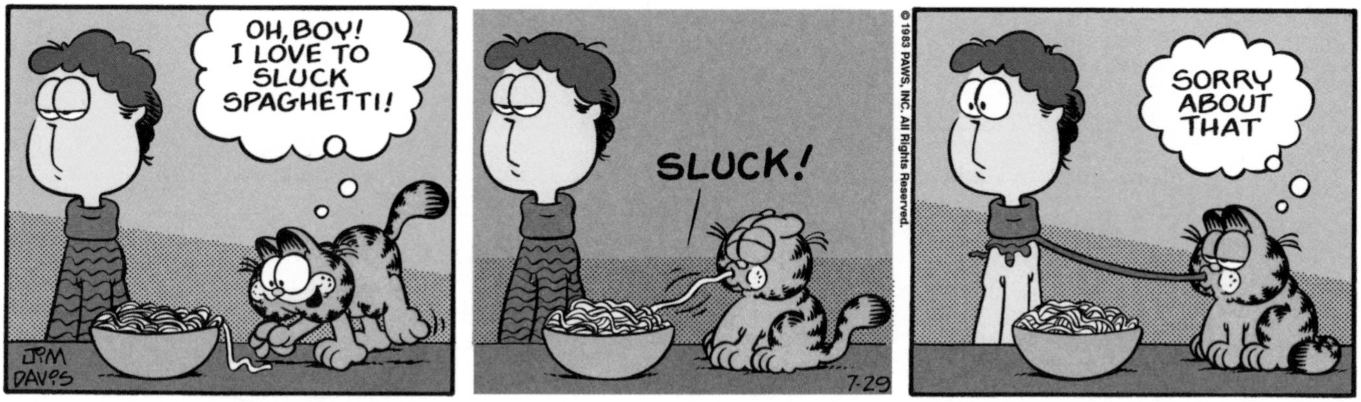
OH, BOY! I LOVE TO SLUCK SPAGHETTI!
SLUCK!
SORRY ABOUT THAT
JIM DAVIS
7-29
© 1983 PAWS, INC. All Rights Reserved.

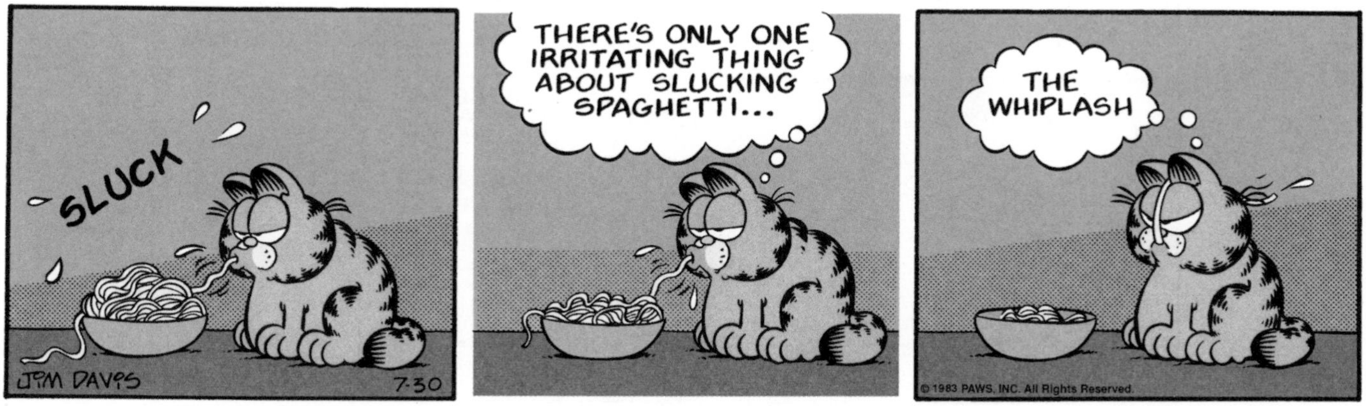
SLUCK
THERE'S ONLY ONE IRRITATING THING ABOUT SLUCKING SPAGHETTI...
THE WHIPLASH
JIM DAVIS
7-30
© 1983 PAWS, INC. All Rights Reserved.

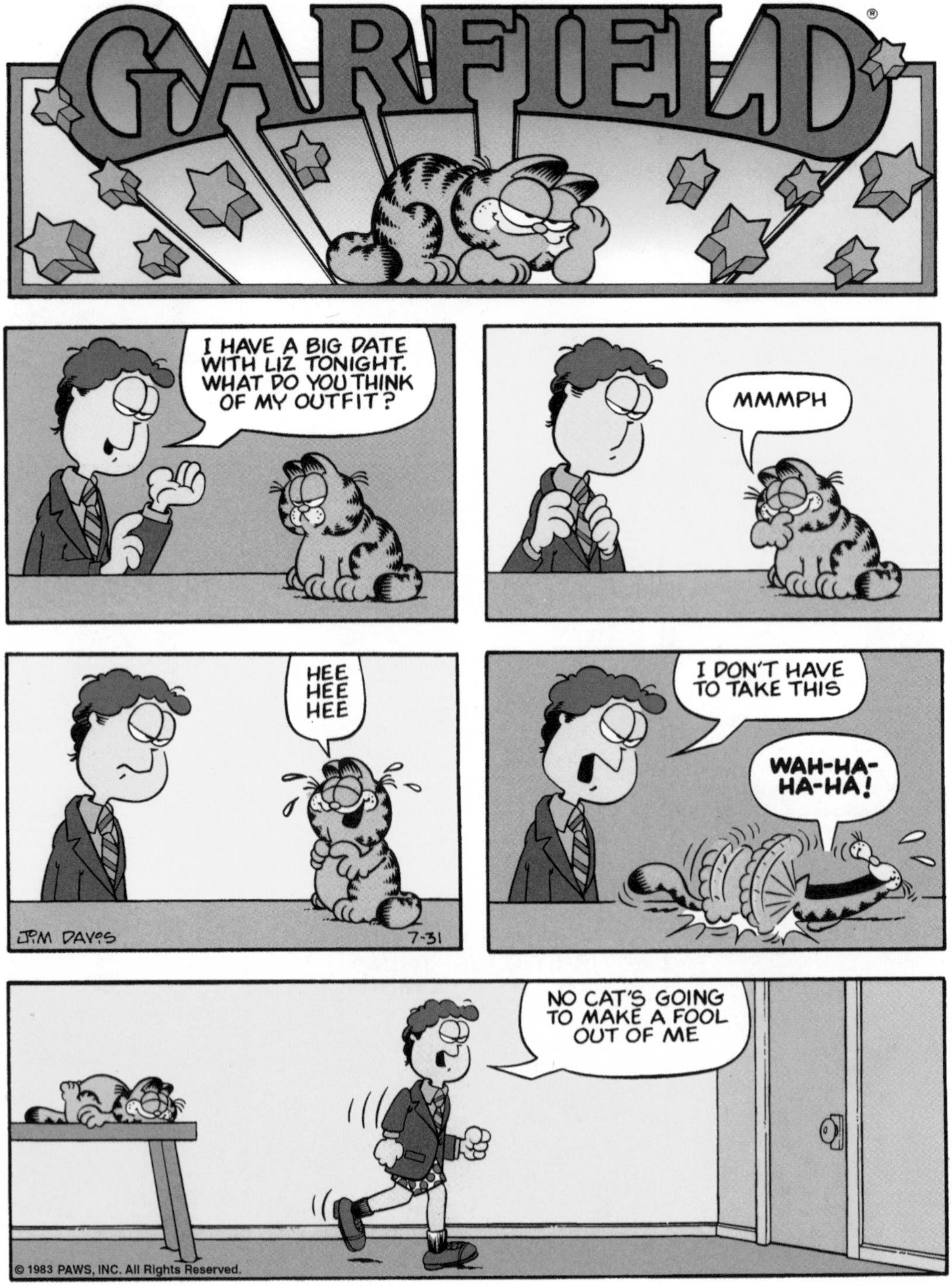
GARFIELD®
I HAVE A BIG DATE WITH LIZ TONIGHT. WHAT DO YOU THINK OF MY OUTFIT?
MMMPH
HEE HEE HEE
JIM DAVIS
7-31
I DON'T HAVE TO TAKE THIS
WAH-HA-HA-HA!
NO CAT'S GOING TO MAKE A FOOL OUT OF ME
© 1983 PAWS, INC. All Rights Reserved.

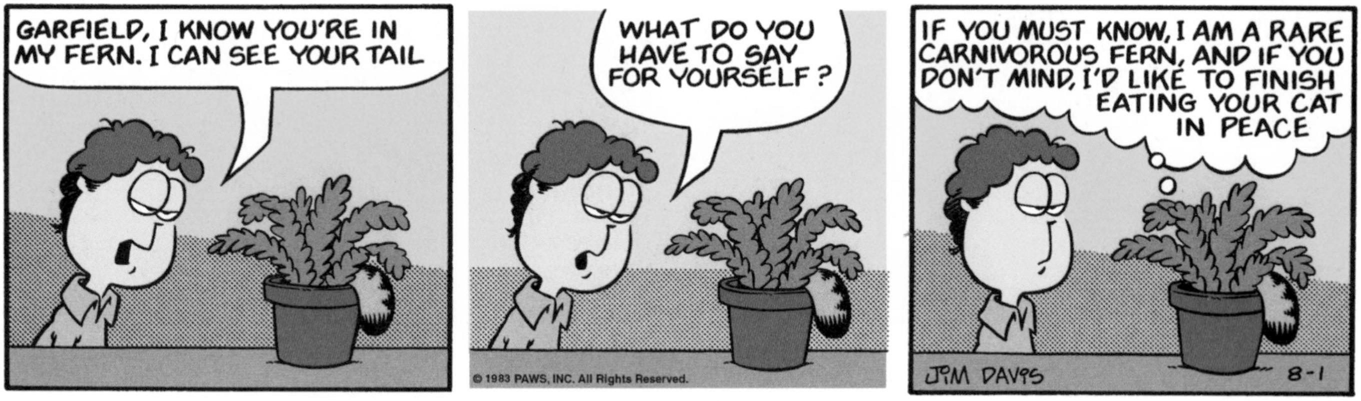
GARFIELD, I KNOW YOU'RE IN MY FERN. I CAN SEE YOUR TAIL
WHAT DO YOU HAVE TO SAY FOR YOURSELF?
© 1983 PAWS, INC. All Rights Reserved.
IF YOU MUST KNOW, I AM A RARE CARNIVOROUS FERN, AND IF YOU DON'T MIND, I'D LIKE TO FINISH EATING YOUR CAT IN PEACE
JIM DAVIS
8-1

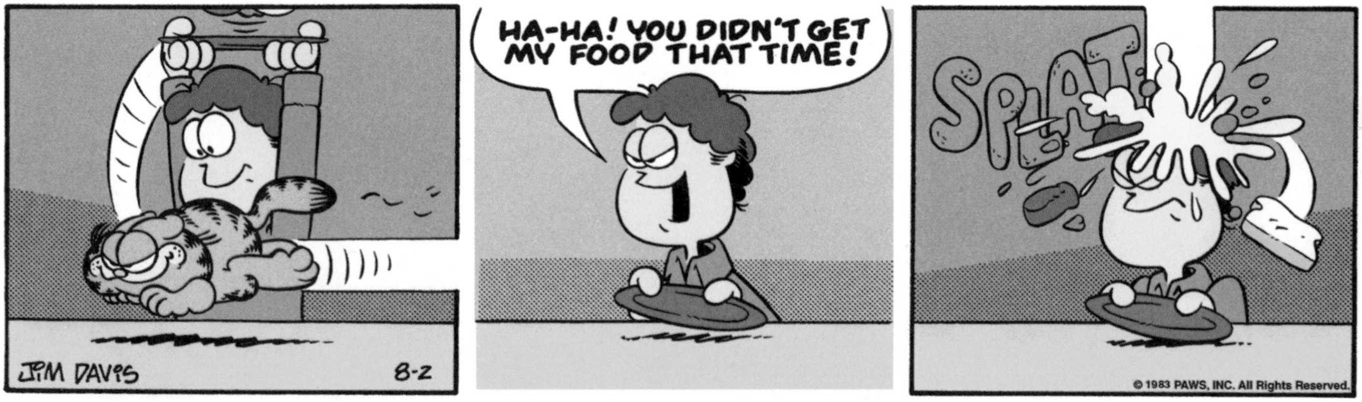
JIM DAVIS
8-2
HA-HA! YOU DIDN'T GET MY FOOD THAT TIME!
SPLAT!
© 1983 PAWS, INC. All Rights Reserved.

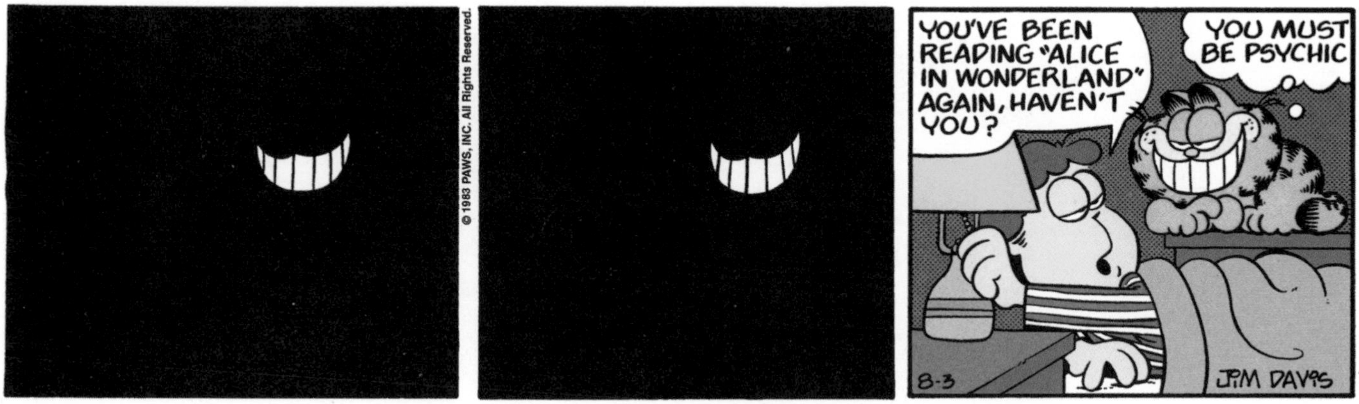
© 1983 PAWS, INC. All Rights Reserved.
YOU'VE BEEN READING "ALICE IN WONDERLAND" AGAIN, HAVEN'T YOU?
YOU MUST BE PSYCHIC
8-3
JIM DAVIS

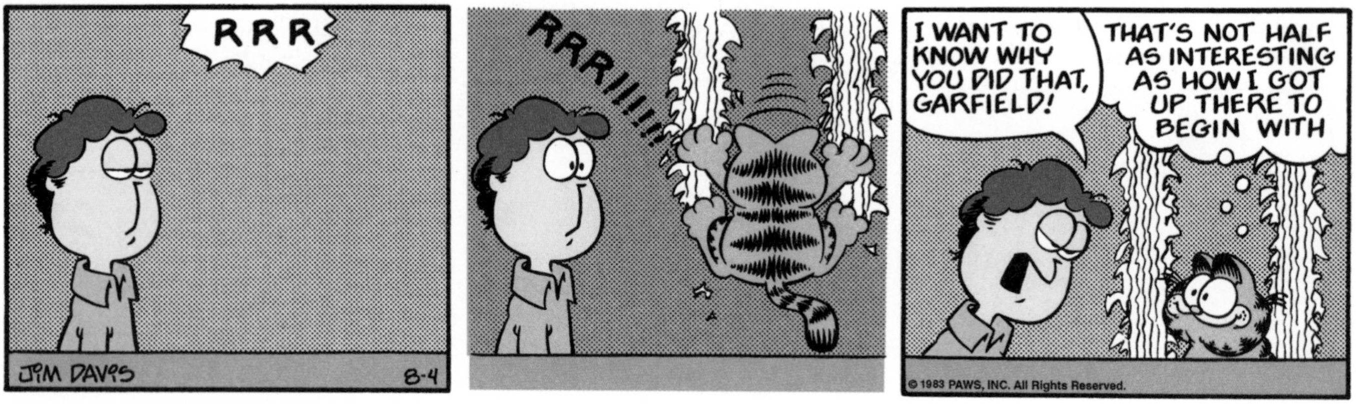
RRR
RRR!!!!!!
I WANT TO KNOW WHY YOU DID THAT, GARFIELD!
THAT'S NOT HALF AS INTERESTING AS HOW I GOT UP THERE TO BEGIN WITH
JIM DAVIS 8-4
© 1983 PAWS, INC. All Rights Reserved.

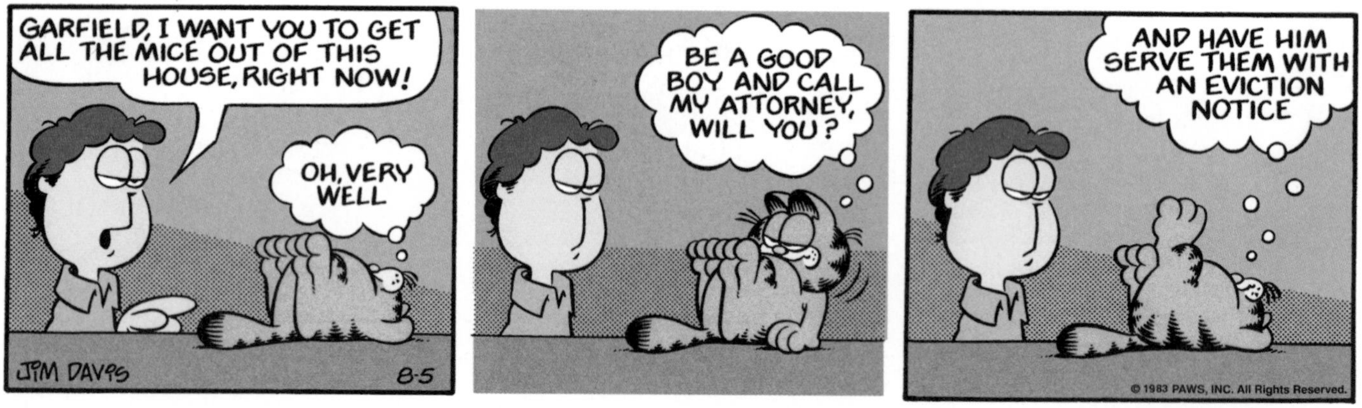
GARFIELD, I WANT YOU TO GET ALL THE MICE OUT OF THIS HOUSE, RIGHT NOW!
OH, VERY WELL
BE A GOOD BOY AND CALL MY ATTORNEY, WILL YOU?
AND HAVE HIM SERVE THEM WITH AN EVICTION NOTICE
JIM DAVIS 8-5
© 1983 PAWS, INC. All Rights Reserved.

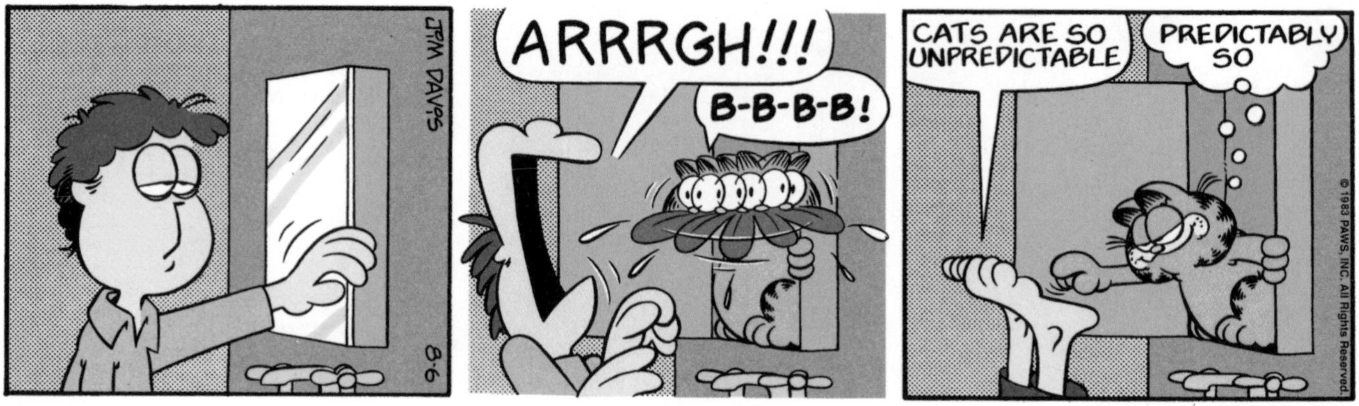
JIM DAVIS 8-6
ARRRGH!!!
B-B-B-B!
CATS ARE SO UNPREDICTABLE
PREDICTABLY SO
© 1983 PAWS, INC. All Rights Reserved.

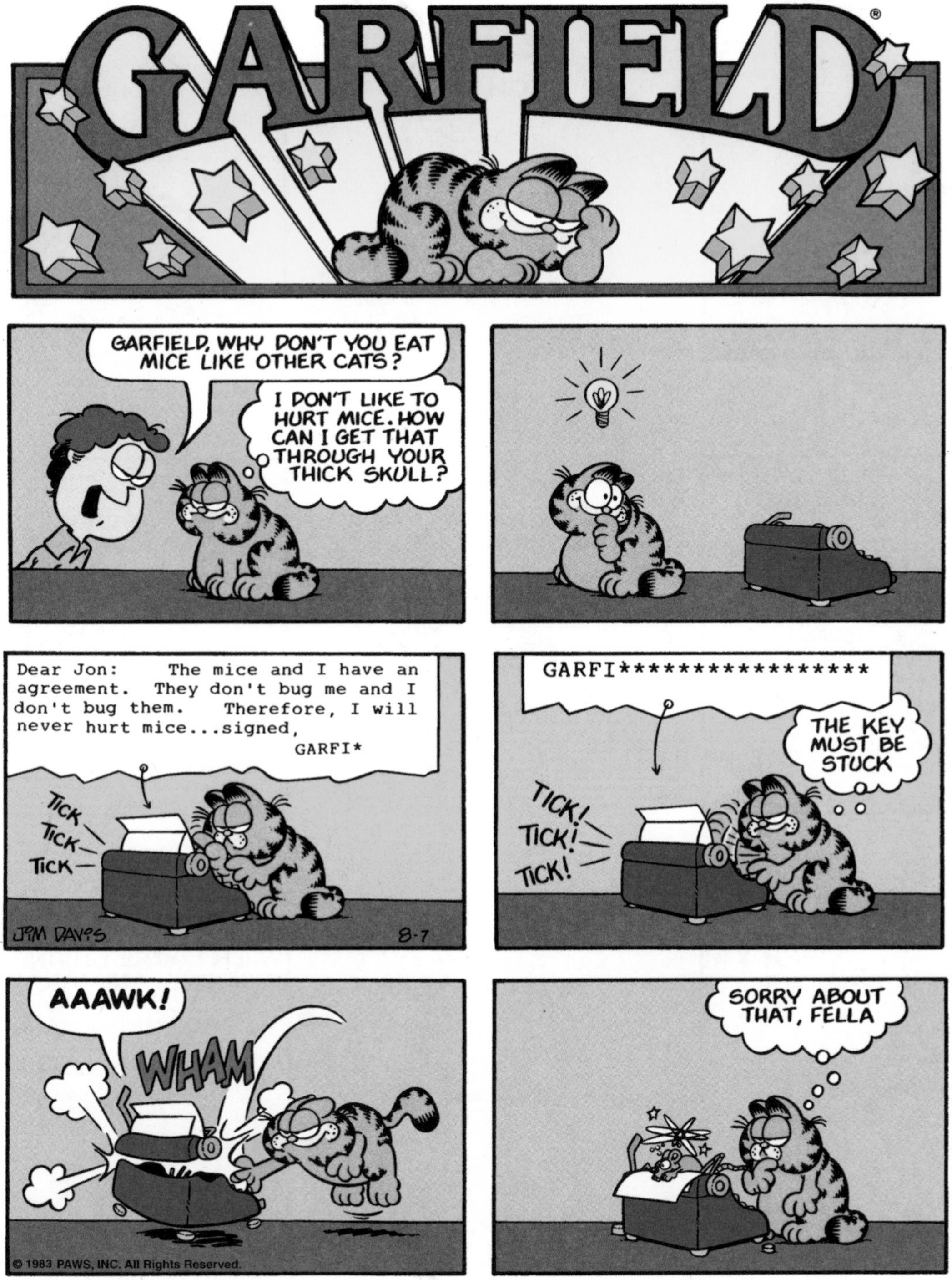
GARFIELD
GARFIELD, WHY DON'T YOU EAT MICE LIKE OTHER CATS?
I DON'T LIKE TO HURT MICE. HOW CAN I GET THAT THROUGH YOUR THICK SKULL?
Dear Jon: The mice and I have an agreement. They don't bug me and I don't bug them. Therefore, I will never hurt mice...signed, GARFI*
TICK TICK TICK
JIM DAVIS
8-7
GARFI******************
THE KEY MUST BE STUCK
TICK! TICK! TICK!
AAAWK!
WHAM
© 1983 PAWS, INC. All Rights Reserved.
SORRY ABOUT THAT, FELLA

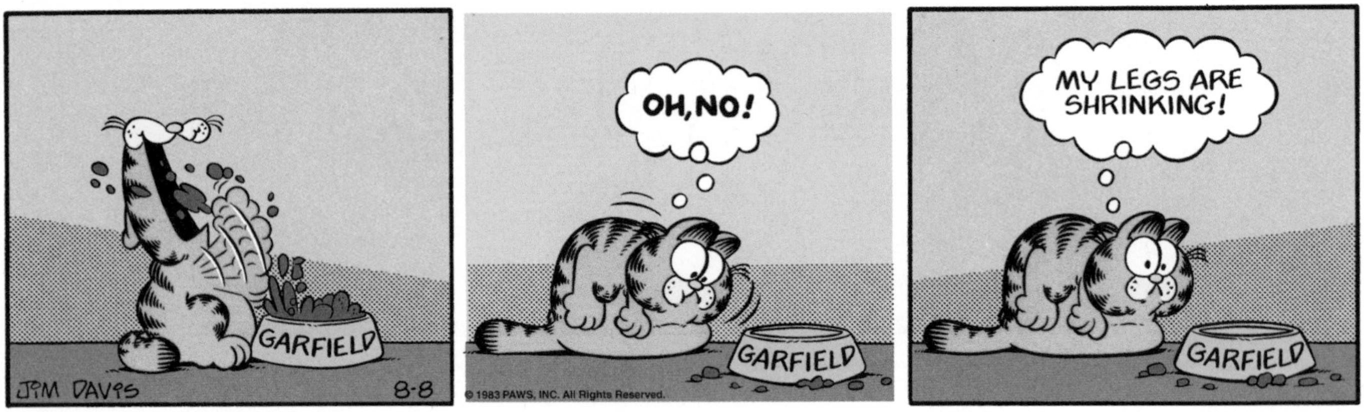
GARFIELD
JIM DAVIS
8-8
OH, NO!
GARFIELD
© 1983 PAWS, INC. All Rights Reserved.
MY LEGS ARE SHRINKING!
GARFIELD

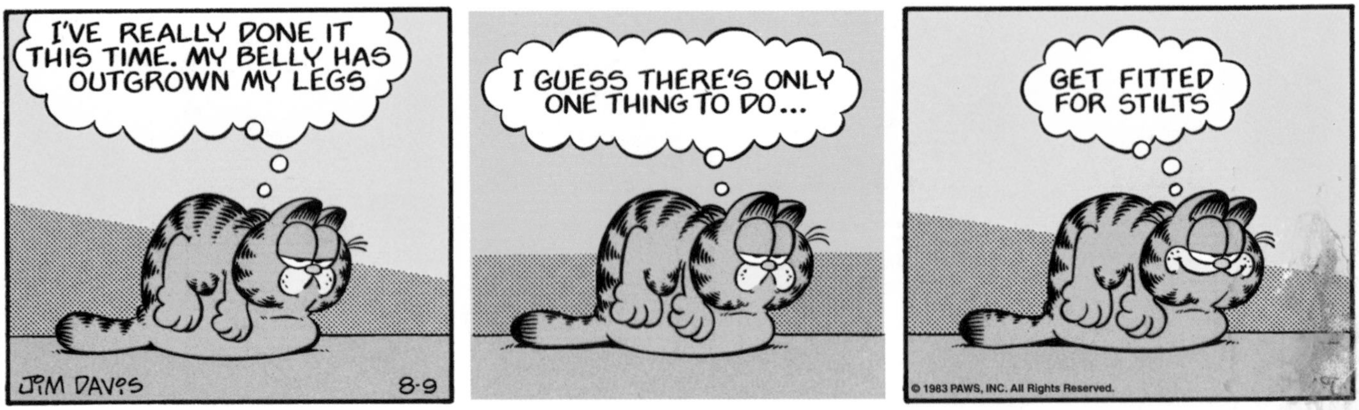
I'VE REALLY DONE IT THIS TIME. MY BELLY HAS OUTGROWN MY LEGS
JIM DAVIS
8-9
I GUESS THERE'S ONLY ONE THING TO DO...
GET FITTED FOR STILTS
© 1983 PAWS, INC. All Rights Reserved.

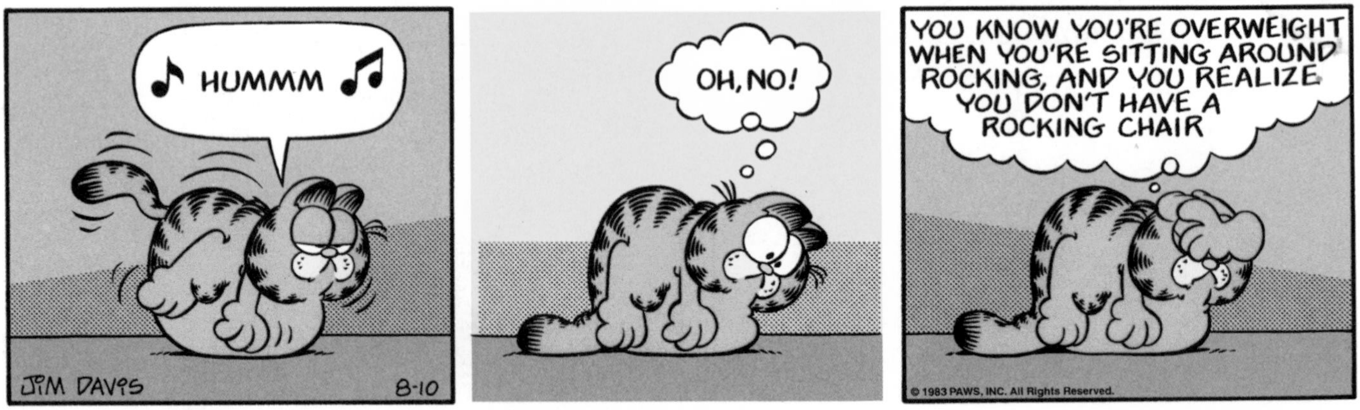
♪ HUMMM ♫
JIM DAVIS
8-10
OH, NO!
YOU KNOW YOU'RE OVERWEIGHT WHEN YOU'RE SITTING AROUND ROCKING, AND YOU REALIZE YOU DON'T HAVE A ROCKING CHAIR
© 1983 PAWS, INC. All Rights Reserved.

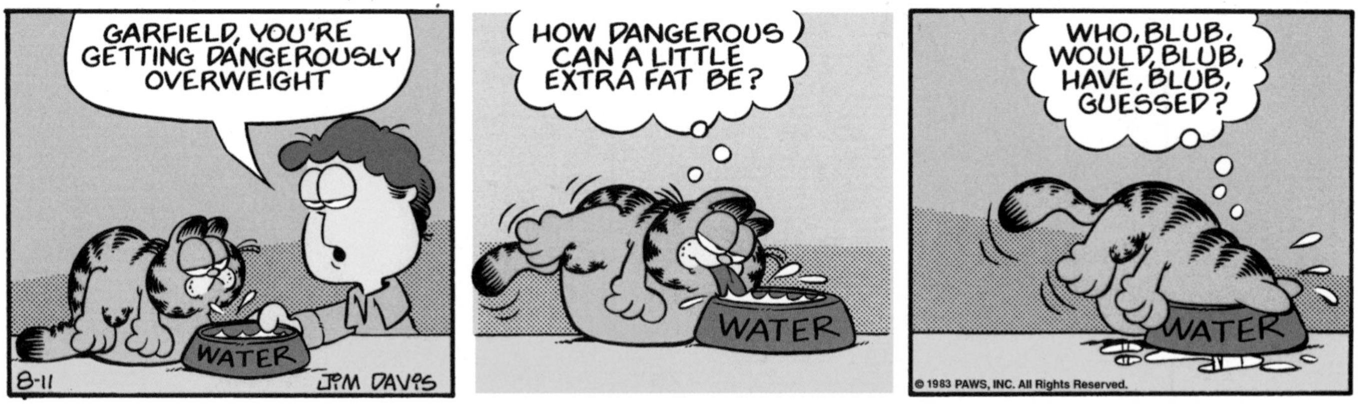
GARFIELD, YOU'RE GETTING DANGEROUSLY OVERWEIGHT
WATER
8-11
JIM DAVIS
HOW DANGEROUS CAN A LITTLE EXTRA FAT BE?
WATER
WHO, BLUB, WOULD, BLUB, HAVE, BLUB, GUESSED?
WATER
© 1983 PAWS, INC. All Rights Reserved.

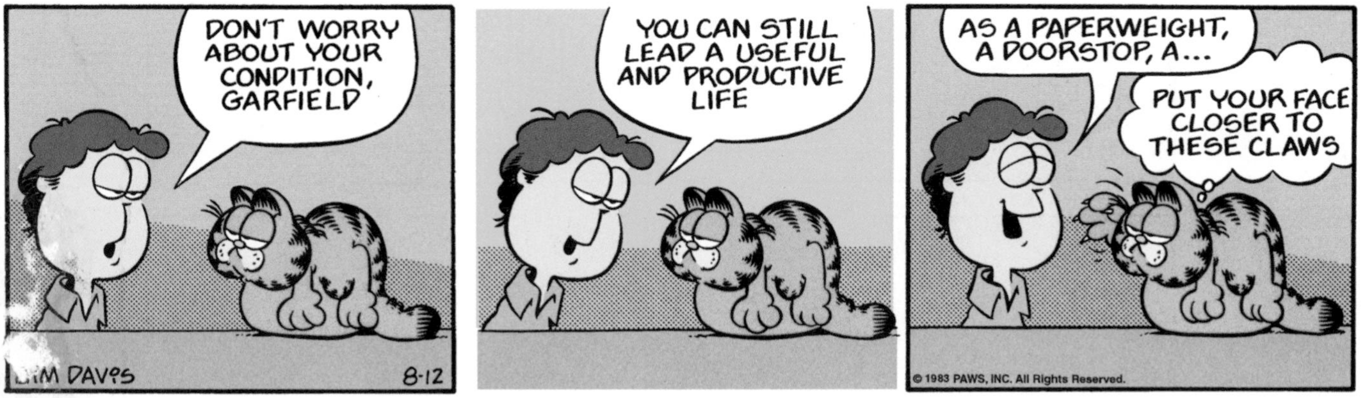
DON'T WORRY ABOUT YOUR CONDITION, GARFIELD
8-12
YOU CAN STILL LEAD A USEFUL AND PRODUCTIVE LIFE
AS A PAPERWEIGHT, A DOORSTOP, A...
PUT YOUR FACE CLOSER TO THESE CLAWS
© 1983 PAWS, INC. All Rights Reserved.

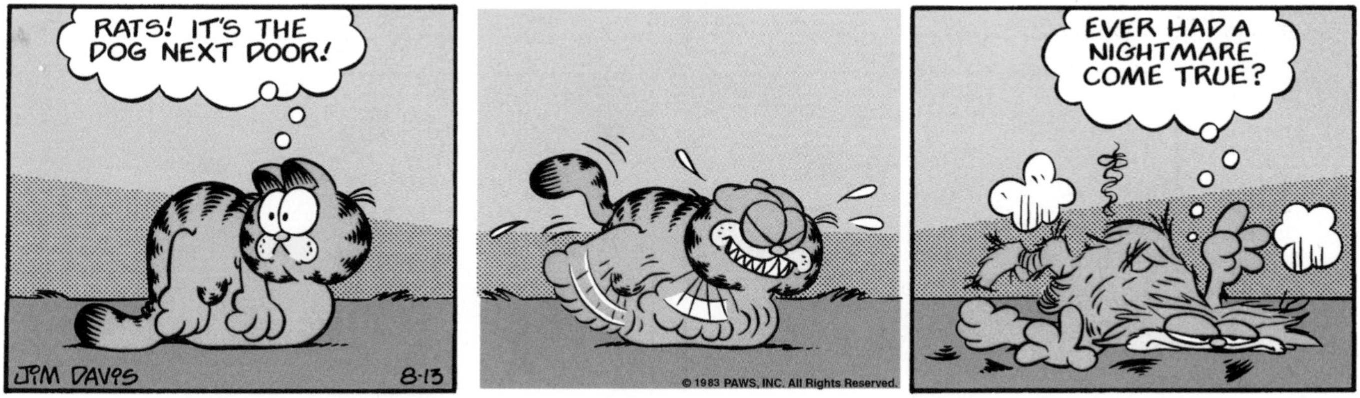
RATS! IT'S THE DOG NEXT DOOR!
JIM DAVIS
8-13
© 1983 PAWS, INC. All Rights Reserved.
EVER HAD A NIGHTMARE COME TRUE?

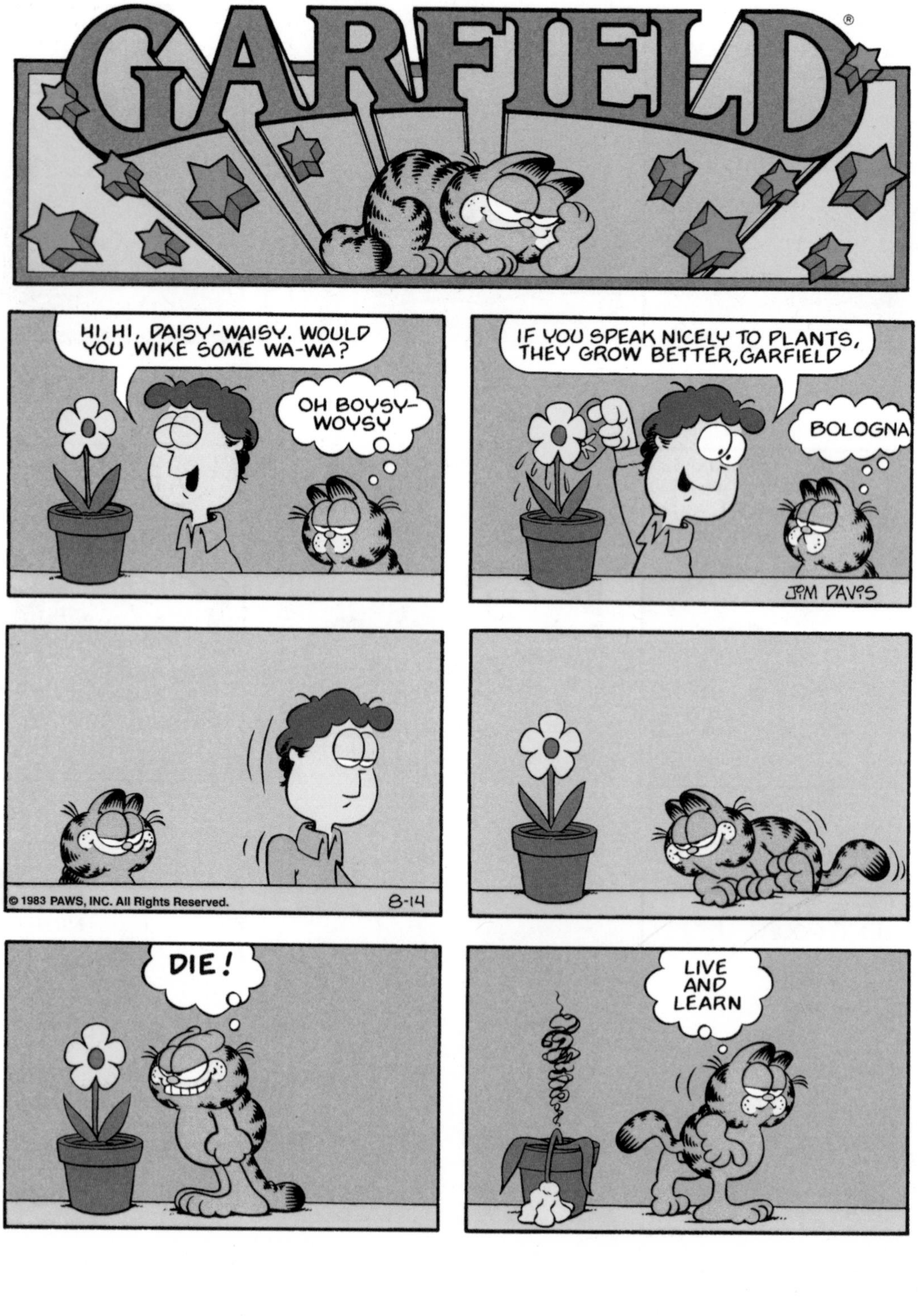
GARFIELD®
HI, HI, DAISY-WAISY. WOULD YOU WIKE SOME WA-WA?
OH BOYSY-WOYSY
IF YOU SPEAK NICELY TO PLANTS, THEY GROW BETTER, GARFIELD
BOLOGNA
JIM DAVIS
© 1983 PAWS, INC. All Rights Reserved.
8-14
DIE!
LIVE AND LEARN

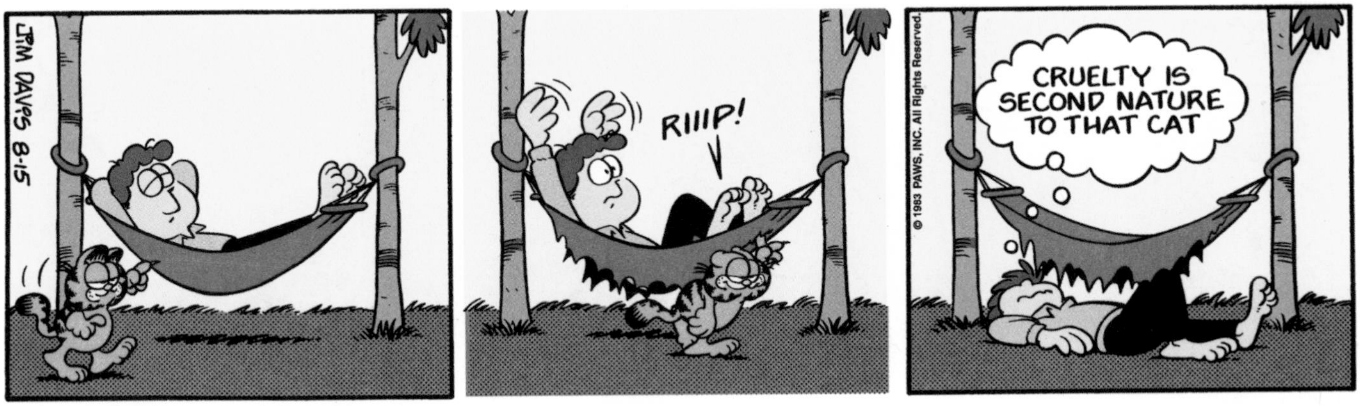
JIM DAVIS 8-15
RIIIP!
CRUELTY IS SECOND NATURE TO THAT CAT
© 1983 PAWS, INC. All Rights Reserved.

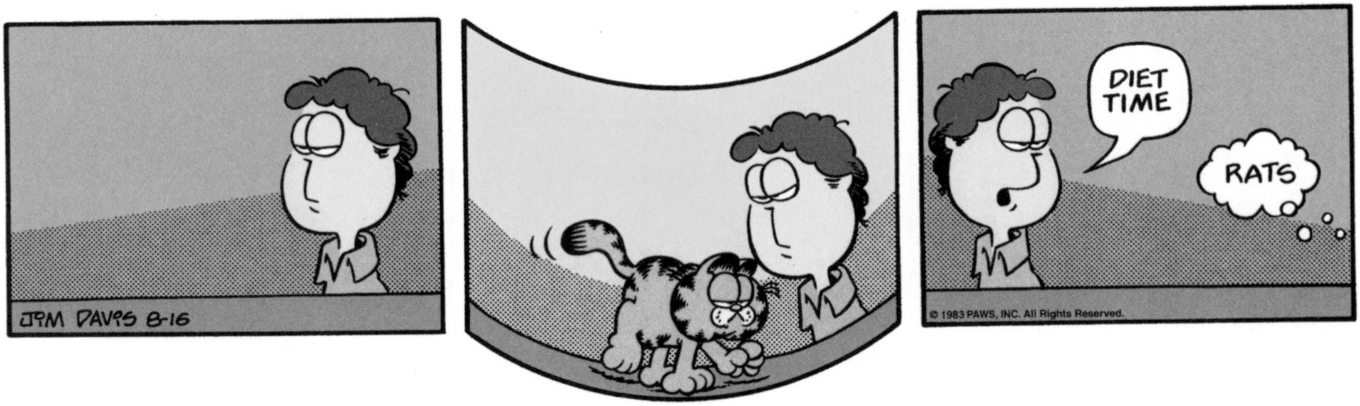
JIM DAVIS 8-16
DIET TIME
RATS
© 1983 PAWS, INC. All Rights Reserved.

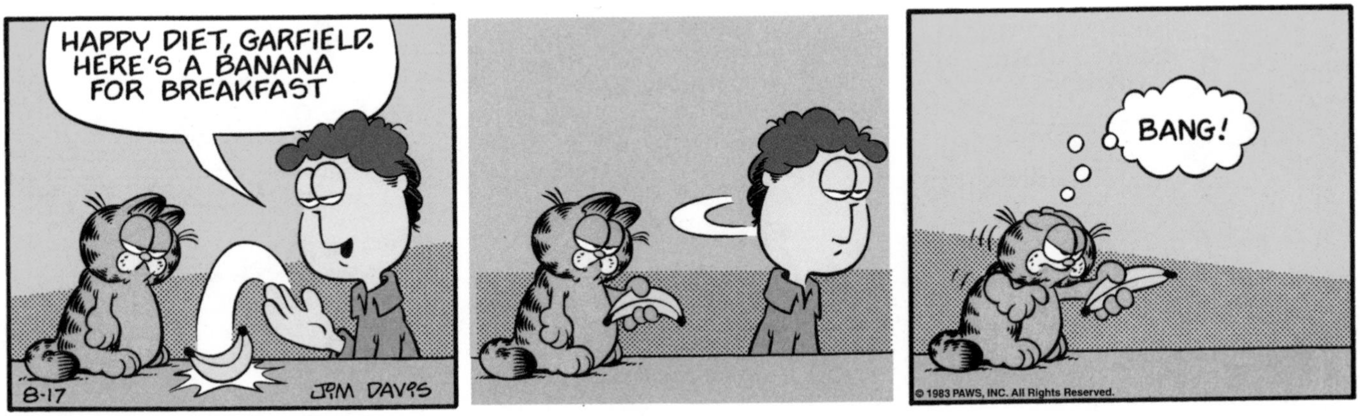
HAPPY DIET, GARFIELD. HERE'S A BANANA FOR BREAKFAST
8-17
JIM DAVIS
BANG!
© 1983 PAWS, INC. All Rights Reserved.

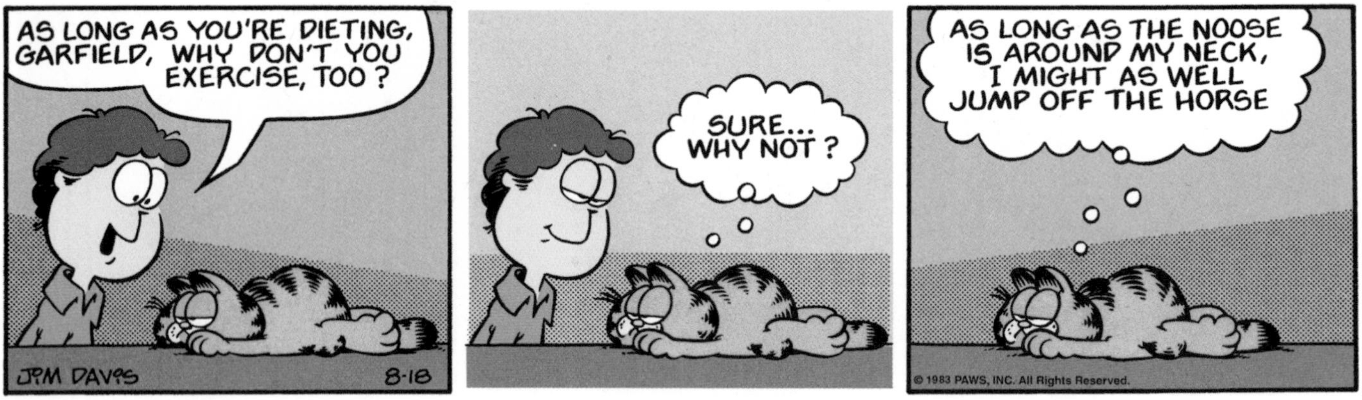
AS LONG AS YOU'RE DIETING, GARFIELD, WHY DON'T YOU EXERCISE, TOO?
SURE... WHY NOT?
AS LONG AS THE NOOSE IS AROUND MY NECK, I MIGHT AS WELL JUMP OFF THE HORSE
JIM DAVIS
8-18
© 1983 PAWS, INC. All Rights Reserved.

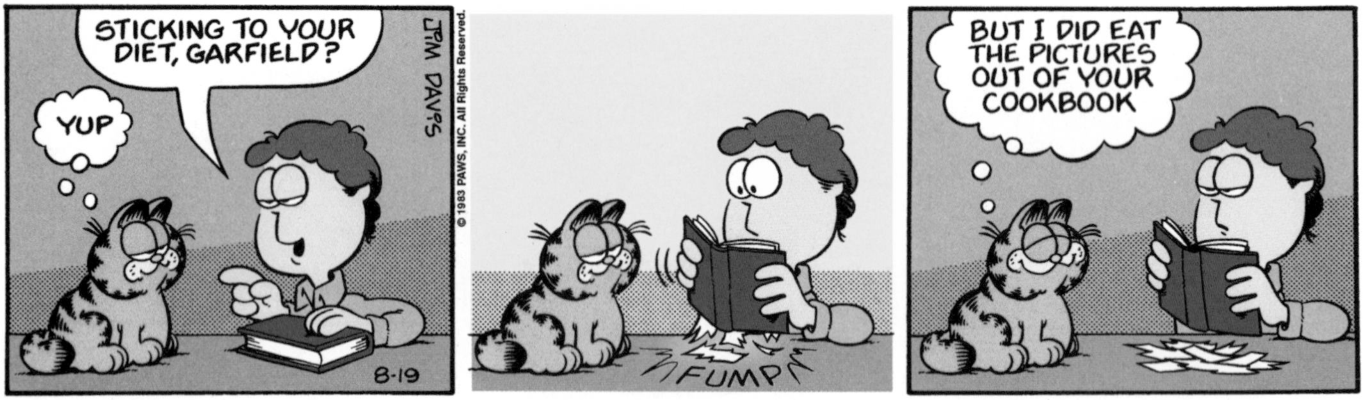
STICKING TO YOUR DIET, GARFIELD?
YUP
JIM DAVIS
8-19
© 1983 PAWS, INC. All Rights Reserved.
FUMP
BUT I DID EAT THE PICTURES OUT OF YOUR COOKBOOK

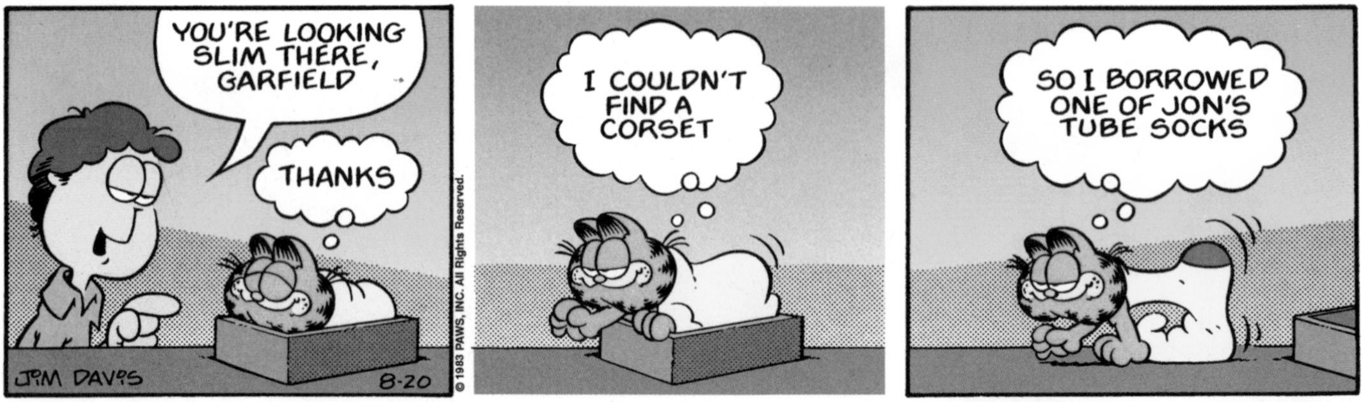
YOU'RE LOOKING SLIM THERE, GARFIELD
THANKS
JIM DAVIS
8-20
© 1983 PAWS, INC. All Rights Reserved.
I COULDN'T FIND A CORSET
SO I BORROWED ONE OF JON'S TUBE SOCKS

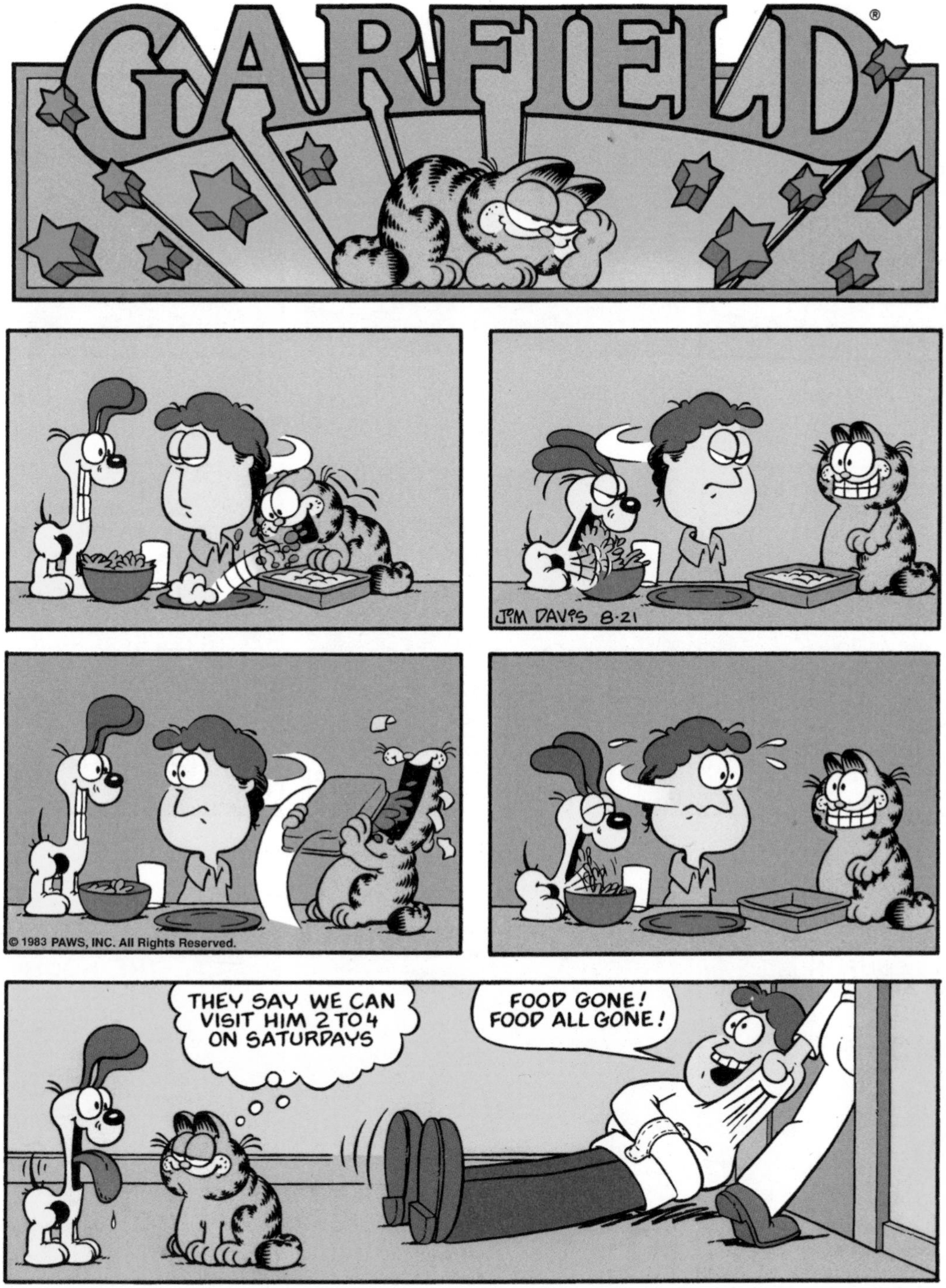
GARFIELD
JIM DAVIS 8·21
© 1983 PAWS, INC. All Rights Reserved.
THEY SAY WE CAN VISIT HIM 2 TO 4 ON SATURDAYS
FOOD GONE! FOOD ALL GONE!

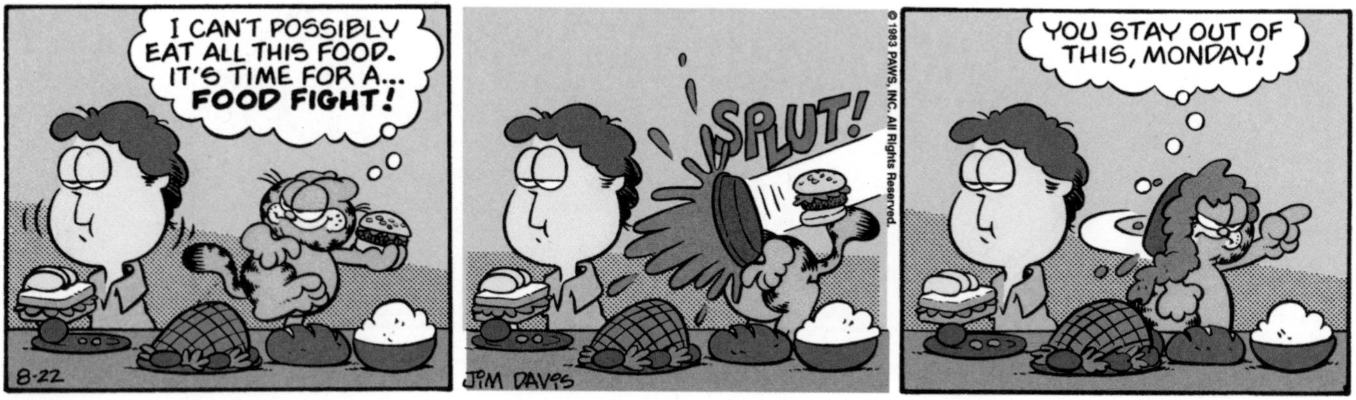
I CAN'T POSSIBLY EAT ALL THIS FOOD. IT'S TIME FOR A... **FOOD FIGHT!**
8-22
SPLUT!
JIM DAVIS
© 1983 PAWS, INC. All Rights Reserved.
YOU STAY OUT OF THIS, MONDAY!

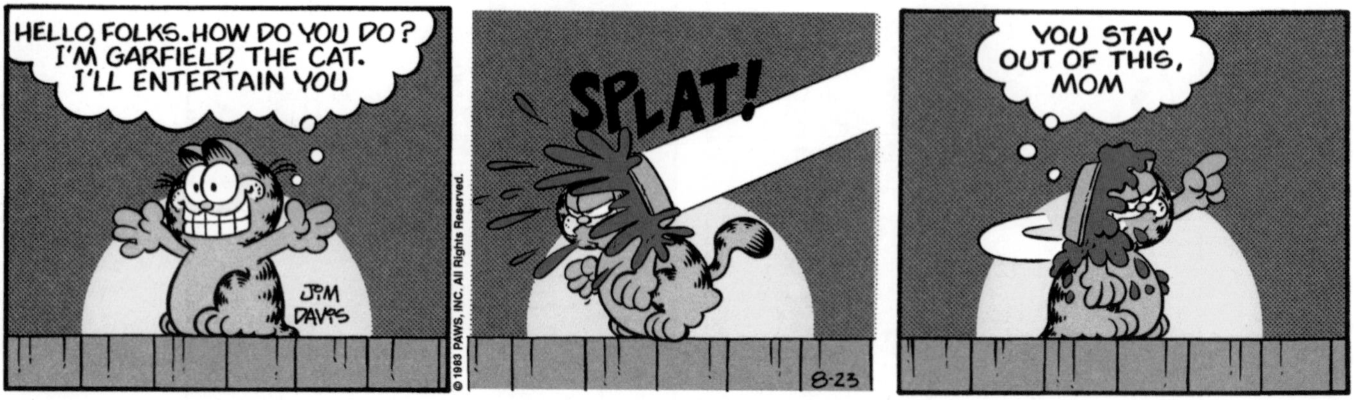
HELLO, FOLKS. HOW DO YOU DO? I'M GARFIELD, THE CAT. I'LL ENTERTAIN YOU
JIM DAVIS
© 1983 PAWS, INC. All Rights Reserved.
SPLAT!
8-23
YOU STAY OUT OF THIS, MOM

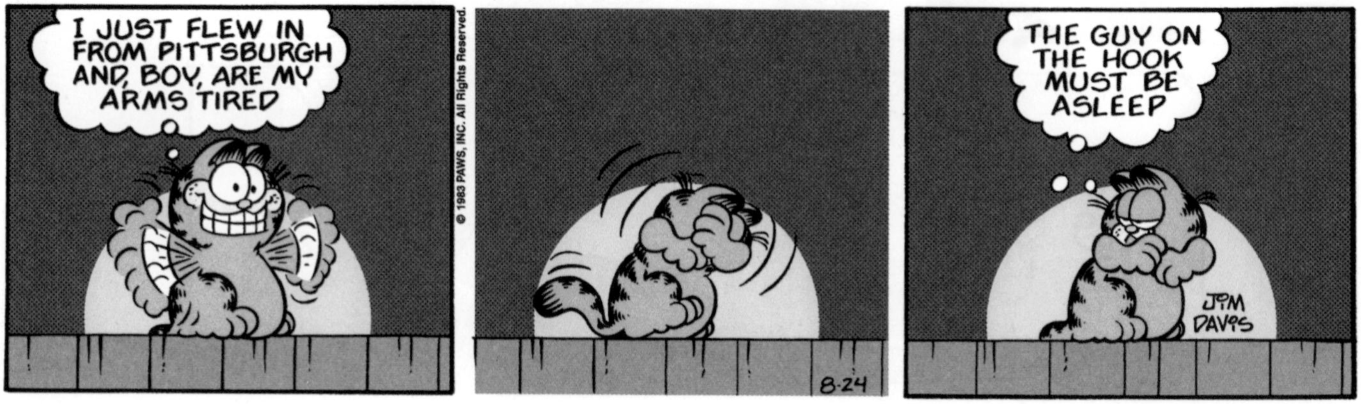
I JUST FLEW IN FROM PITTSBURGH AND, BOY, ARE MY ARMS TIRED
© 1983 PAWS, INC. All Rights Reserved.
8-24
THE GUY ON THE HOOK MUST BE ASLEEP
JIM DAVIS

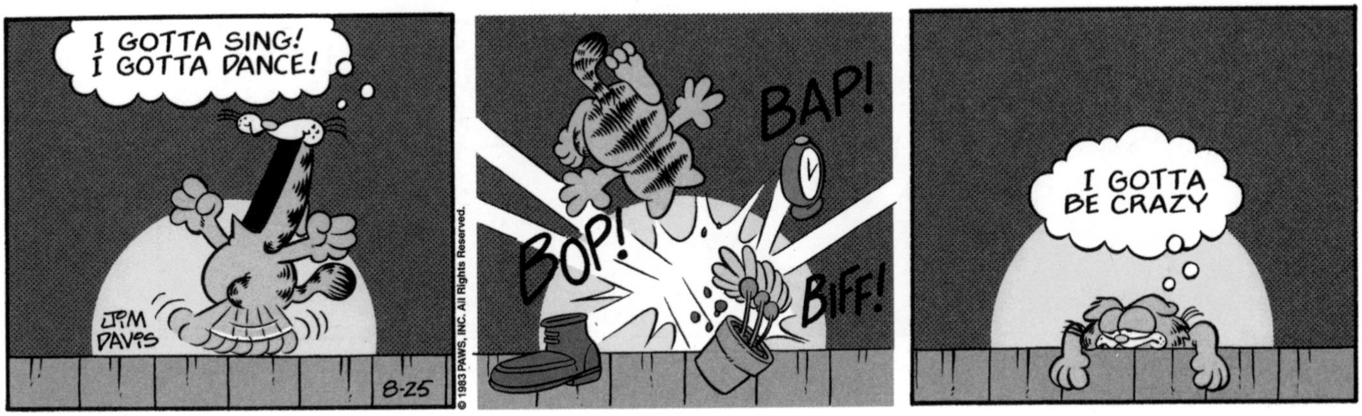
I GOTTA SING! I GOTTA DANCE!
JIM DAVIS
8-25
© 1983 PAWS, INC. All Rights Reserved.
BAP!
BOP!
BIFF!
I GOTTA BE CRAZY

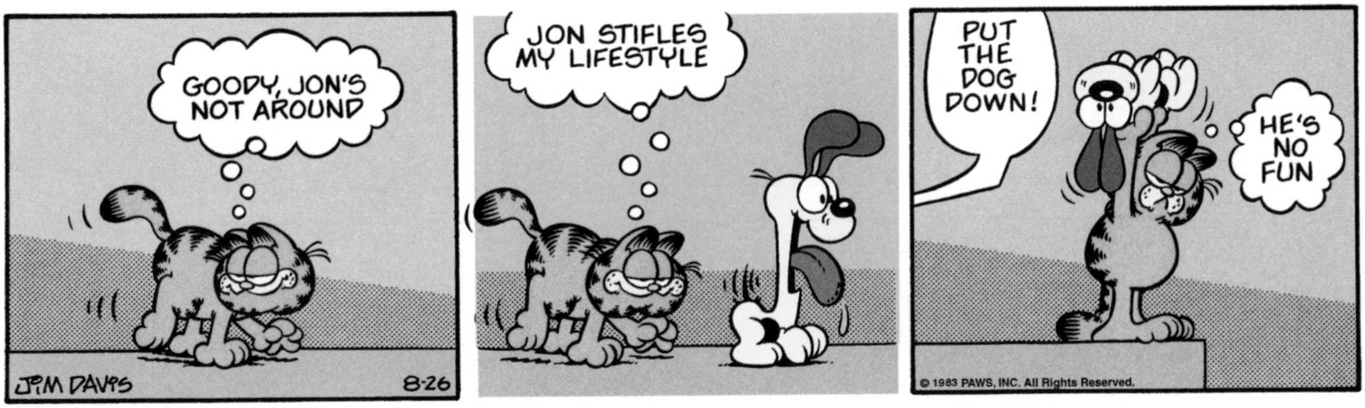
GOODY, JON'S NOT AROUND
JIM DAVIS
8-26
JON STIFLES MY LIFESTYLE
PUT THE DOG DOWN!
HE'S NO FUN
© 1983 PAWS, INC. All Rights Reserved.

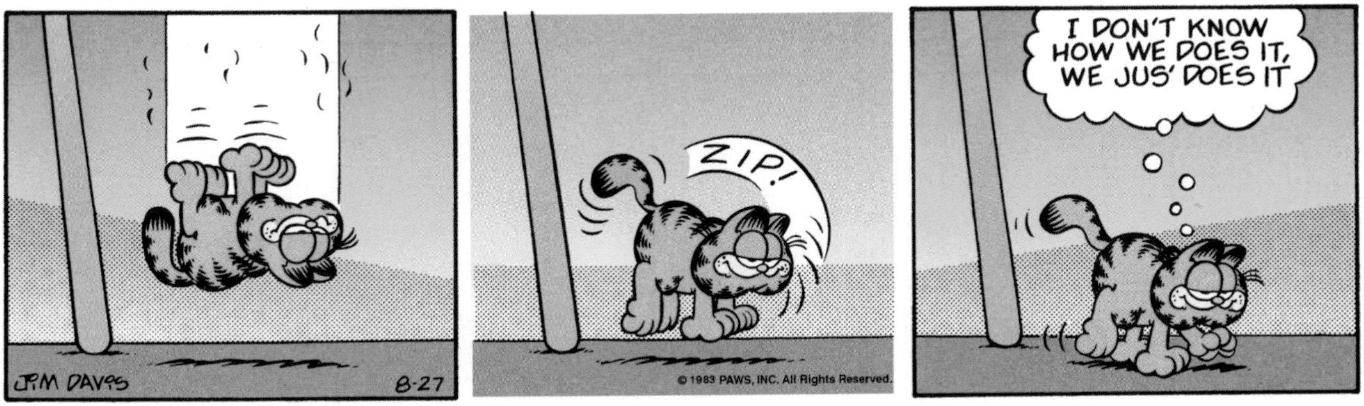
JIM DAVIS
8-27
ZIP!
© 1983 PAWS, INC. All Rights Reserved.
I DON'T KNOW HOW WE DOES IT, WE JUS' DOES IT

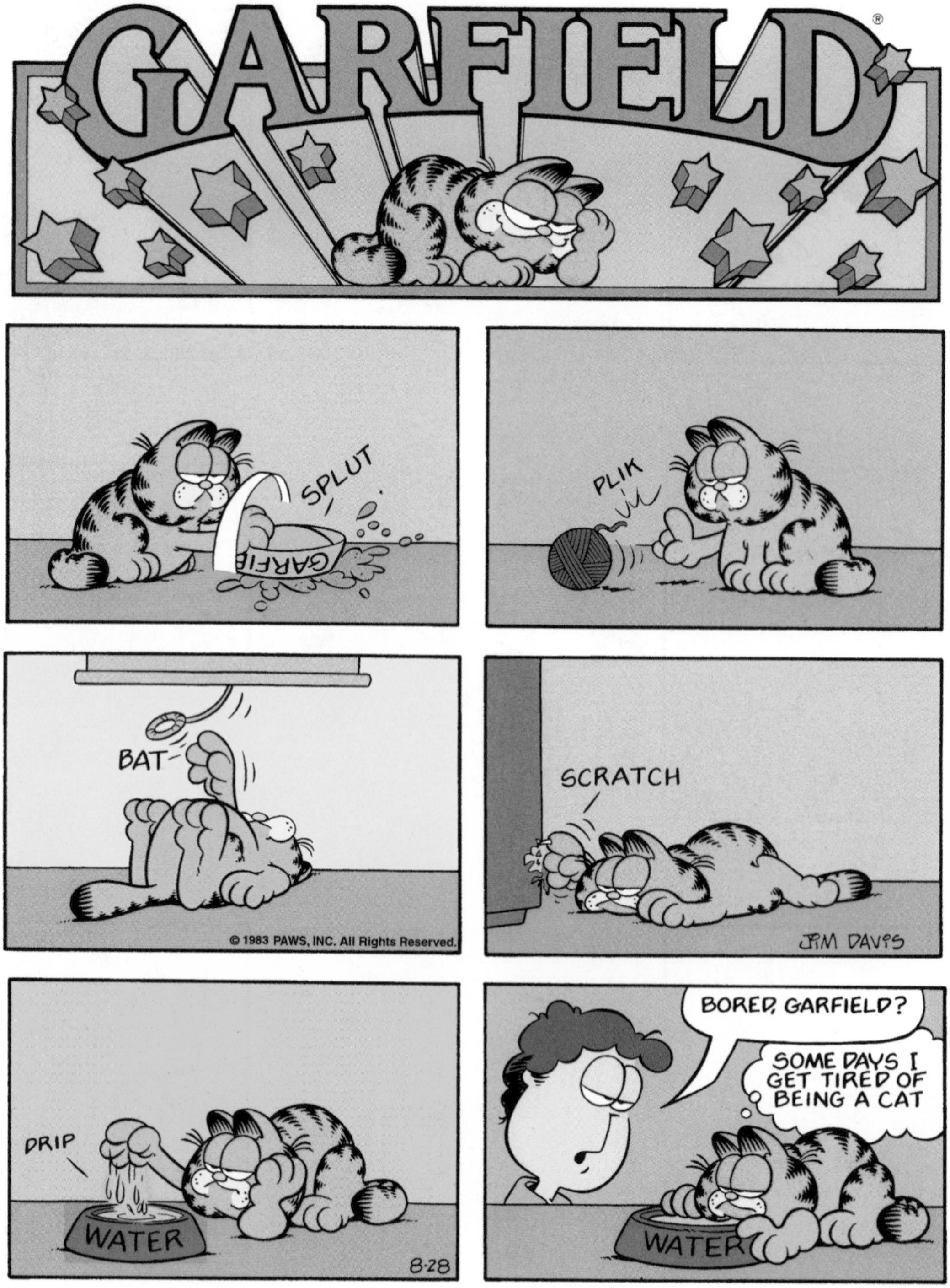
GARFIELD®
SPLUT
GARFIELD
PLIK
BAT
SCRATCH
© 1983 PAWS, INC. All Rights Reserved.
JIM DAVIS
DRIP
WATER
8-28
BORED, GARFIELD?
SOME DAYS I GET TIRED OF BEING A CAT
WATER

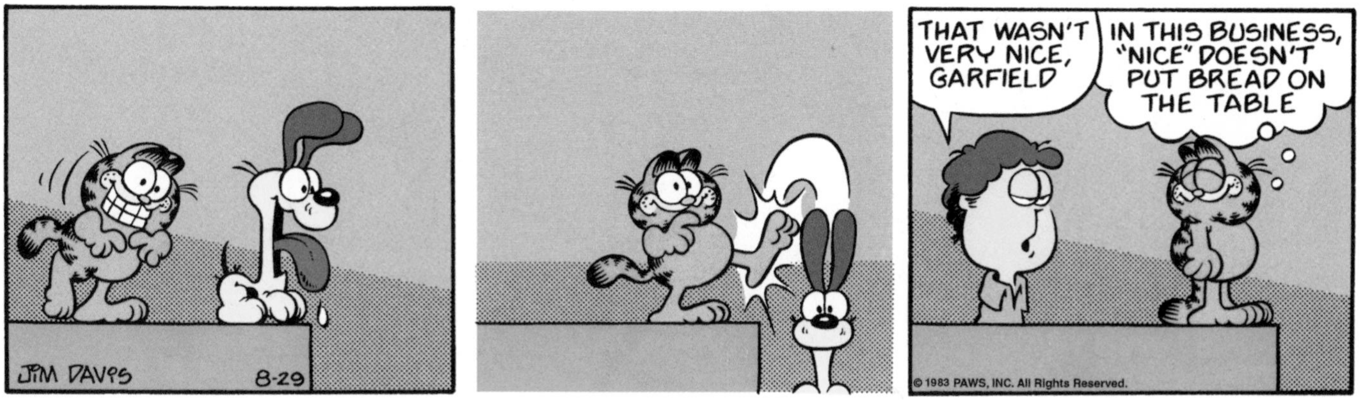
JIM DAVIS
8-29
THAT WASN'T VERY NICE, GARFIELD
IN THIS BUSINESS, "NICE" DOESN'T PUT BREAD ON THE TABLE
© 1983 PAWS, INC. All Rights Reserved.

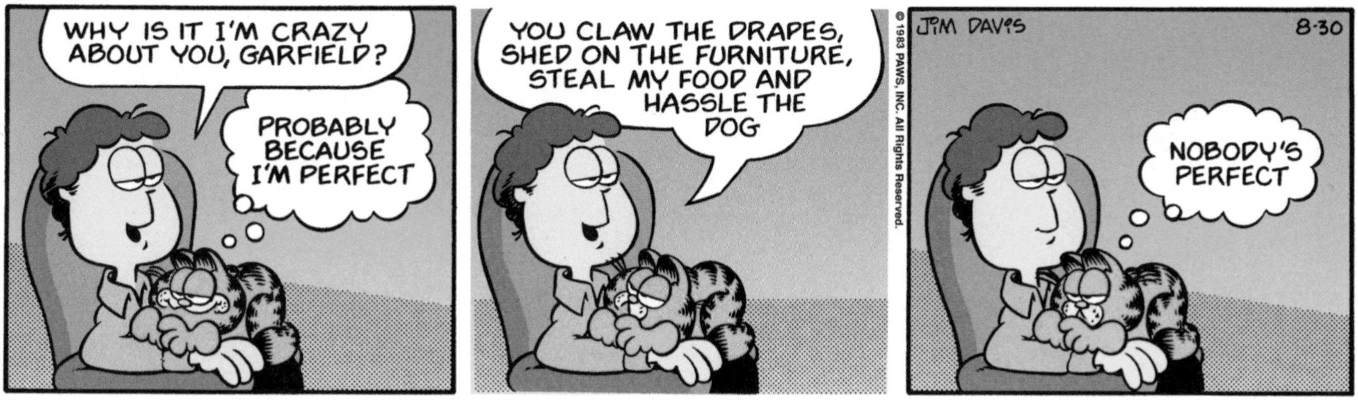
WHY IS IT I'M CRAZY ABOUT YOU, GARFIELD?
PROBABLY BECAUSE I'M PERFECT
YOU CLAW THE DRAPES, SHED ON THE FURNITURE, STEAL MY FOOD AND HASSLE THE DOG
© 1983 PAWS, INC. All Rights Reserved.
JIM DAVIS
8-30
NOBODY'S PERFECT

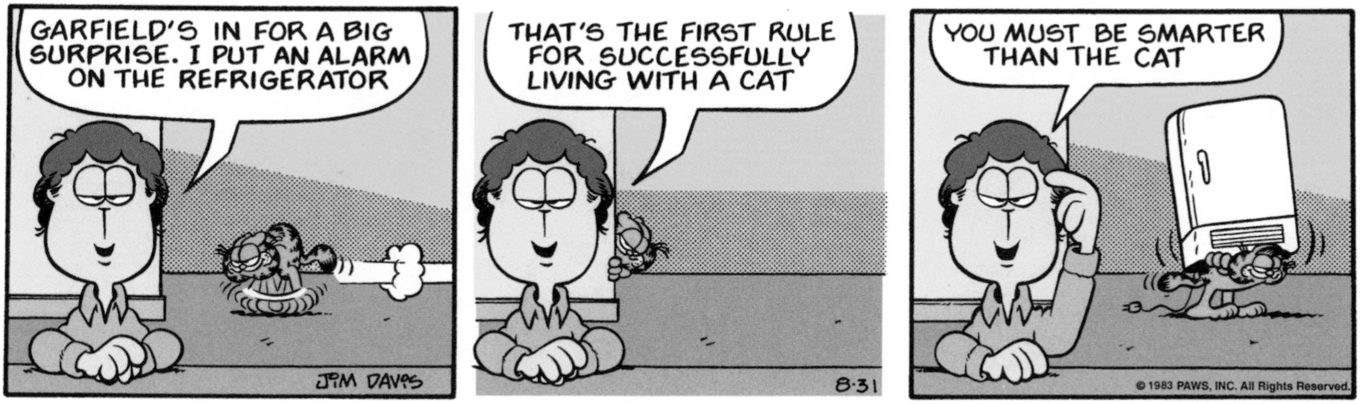
GARFIELD'S IN FOR A BIG SURPRISE. I PUT AN ALARM ON THE REFRIGERATOR
JIM DAVIS
THAT'S THE FIRST RULE FOR SUCCESSFULLY LIVING WITH A CAT
8-31
YOU MUST BE SMARTER THAN THE CAT
© 1983 PAWS, INC. All Rights Reserved.

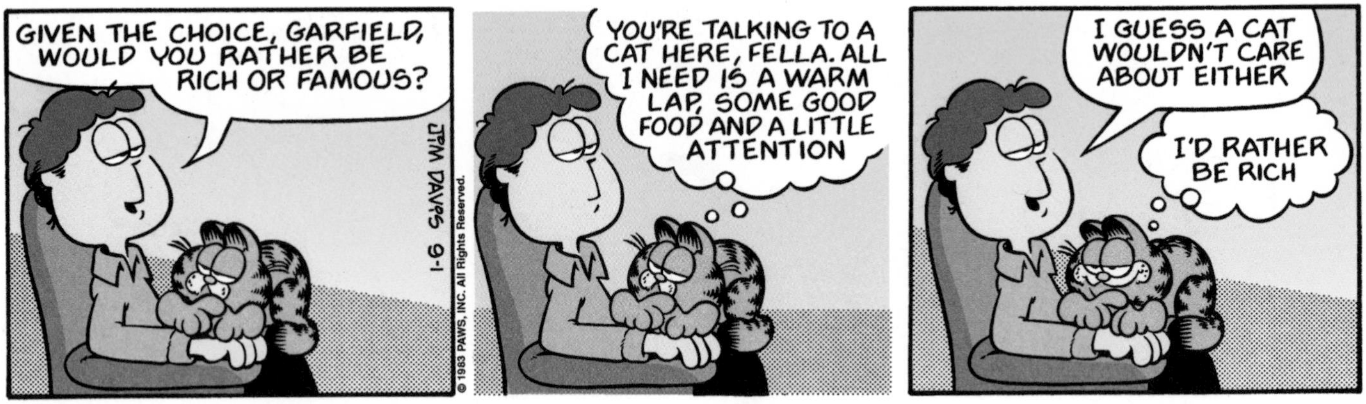
GIVEN THE CHOICE, GARFIELD, WOULD YOU RATHER BE RICH OR FAMOUS?
JIM DAVIS 9-1
© 1983 PAWS, INC. All Rights Reserved.
YOU'RE TALKING TO A CAT HERE, FELLA. ALL I NEED IS A WARM LAP, SOME GOOD FOOD AND A LITTLE ATTENTION
I GUESS A CAT WOULDN'T CARE ABOUT EITHER
I'D RATHER BE RICH

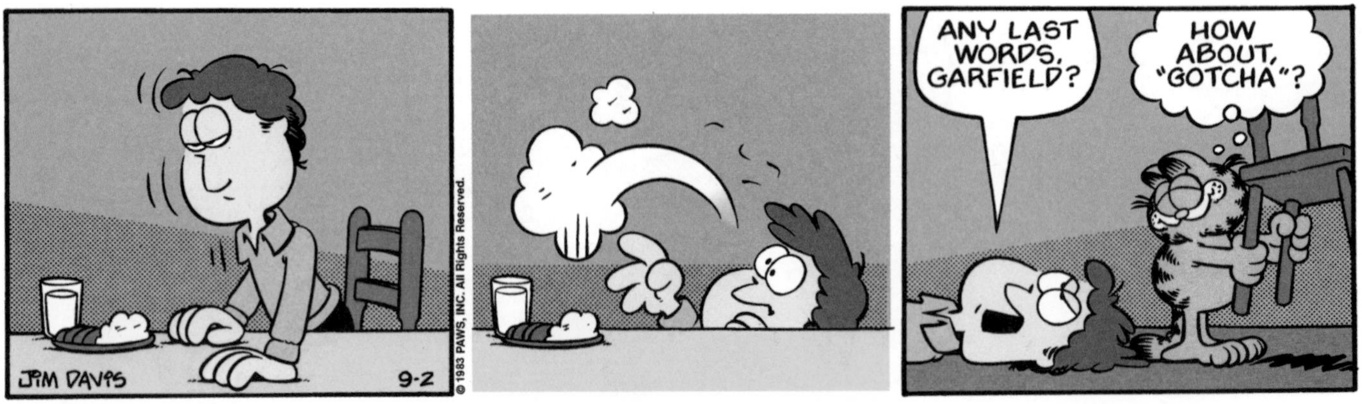
JIM DAVIS
9-2
© 1983 PAWS, INC. All Rights Reserved.
ANY LAST WORDS, GARFIELD?
HOW ABOUT, "GOTCHA"?

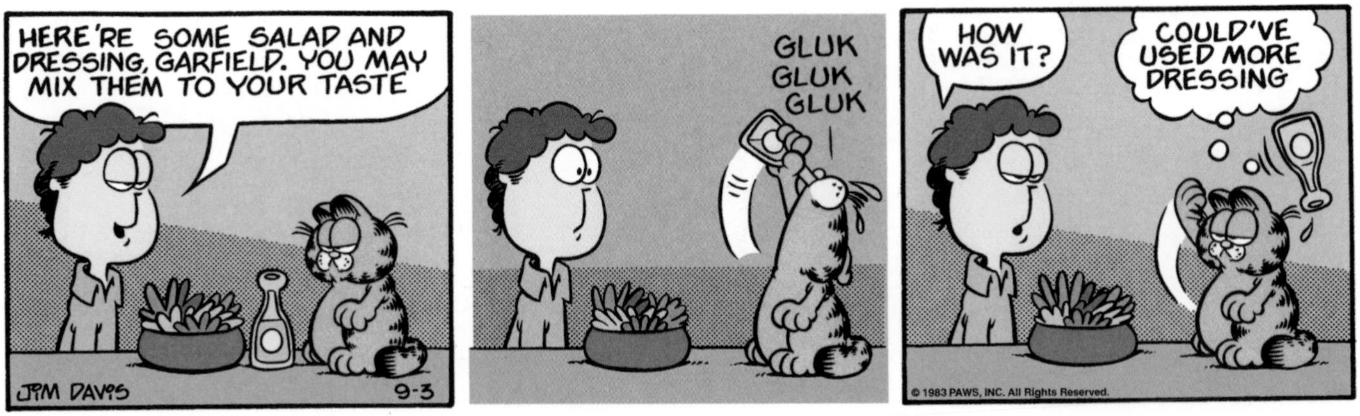
HERE'RE SOME SALAD AND DRESSING, GARFIELD. YOU MAY MIX THEM TO YOUR TASTE
JIM DAVIS
9-3
GLUK GLUK GLUK
HOW WAS IT?
COULD'VE USED MORE DRESSING
© 1983 PAWS, INC. All Rights Reserved.

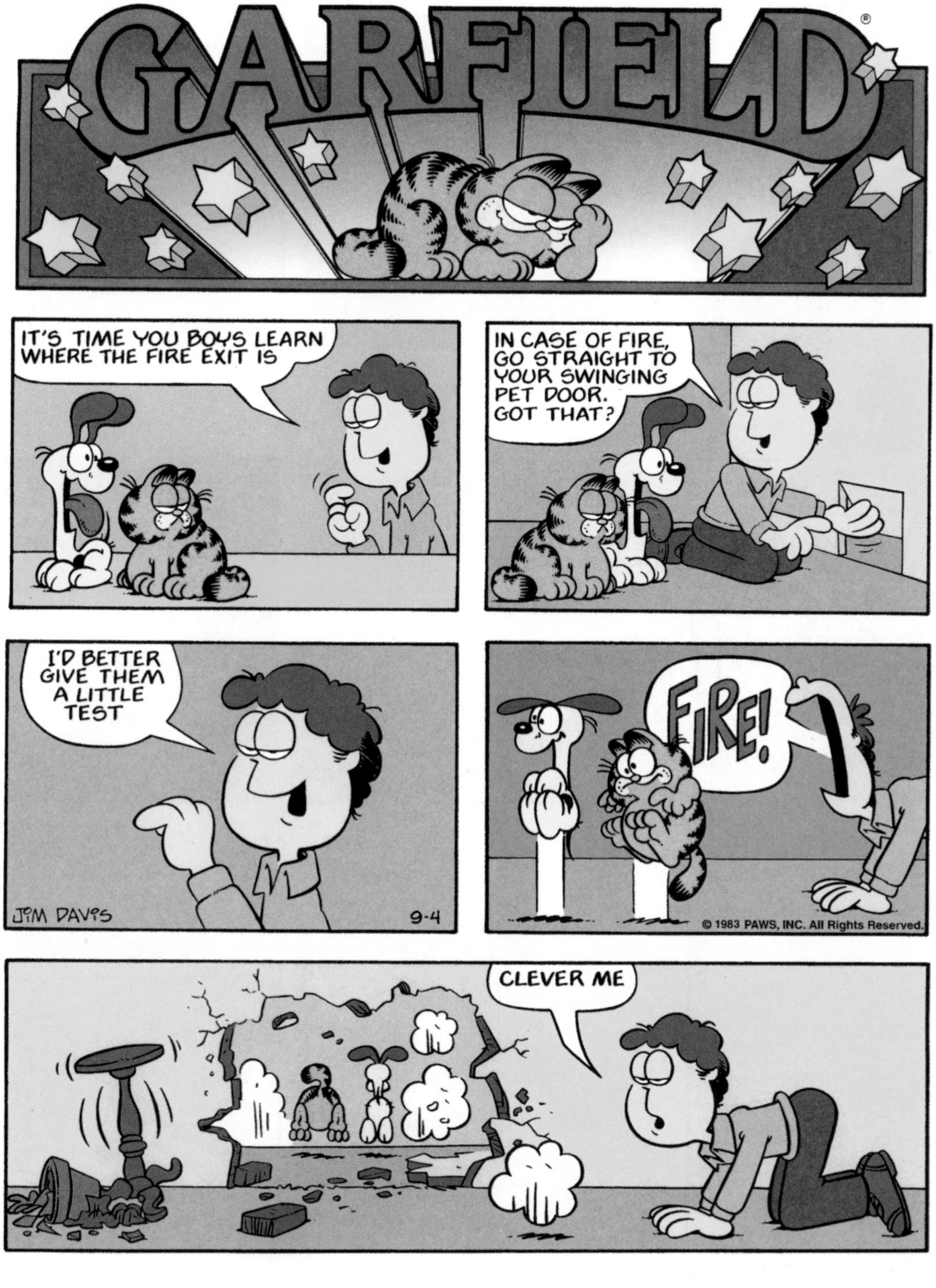
GARFIELD®
IT'S TIME YOU BOYS LEARN WHERE THE FIRE EXIT IS
IN CASE OF FIRE, GO STRAIGHT TO YOUR SWINGING PET DOOR. GOT THAT?
I'D BETTER GIVE THEM A LITTLE TEST
JIM DAVIS
9-4
FIRE!
© 1983 PAWS, INC. All Rights Reserved.
CLEVER ME

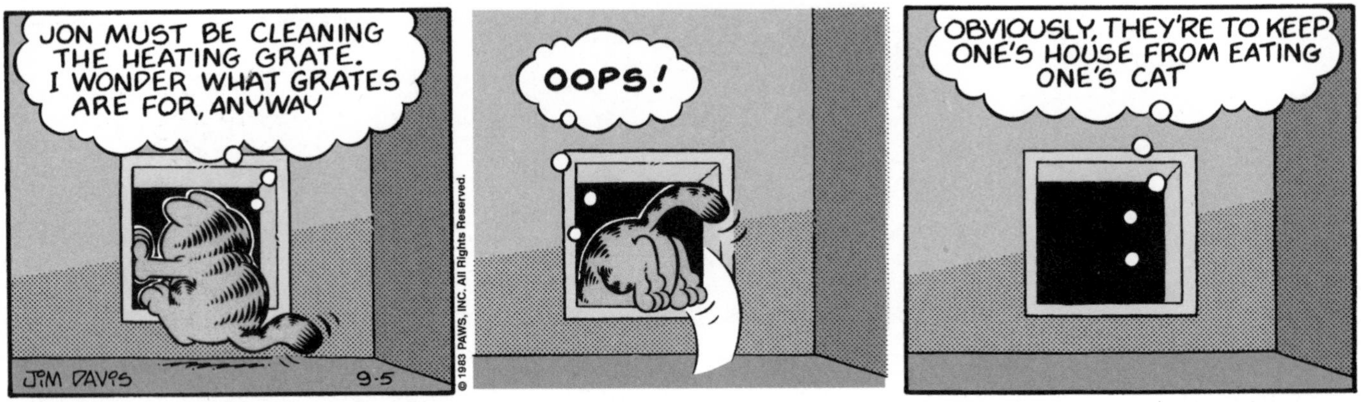
JON MUST BE CLEANING THE HEATING GRATE. I WONDER WHAT GRATES ARE FOR, ANYWAY
OOPS!
OBVIOUSLY, THEY'RE TO KEEP ONE'S HOUSE FROM EATING ONE'S CAT
JIM DAVIS 9-5
© 1983 PAWS, INC. All Rights Reserved.

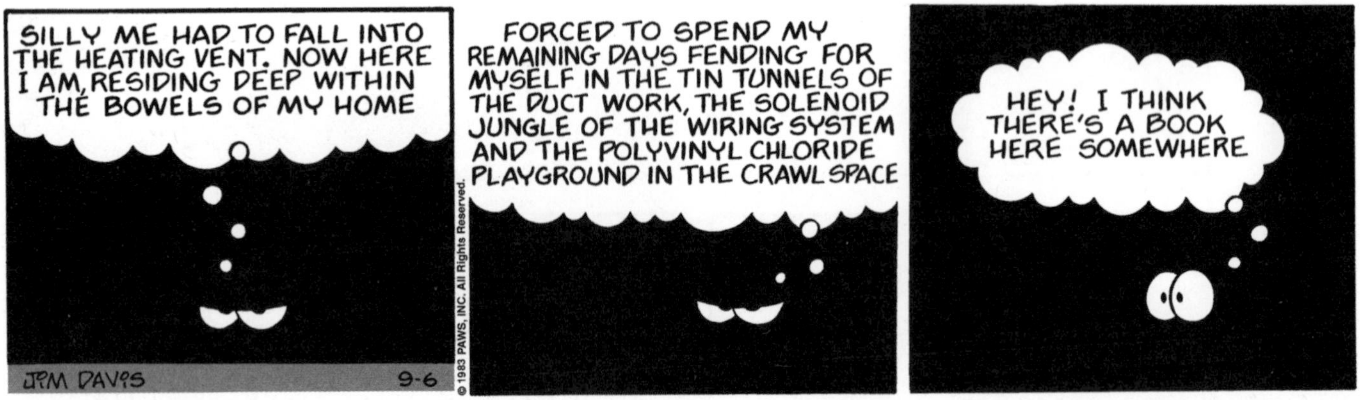
SILLY ME HAD TO FALL INTO THE HEATING VENT. NOW HERE I AM, RESIDING DEEP WITHIN THE BOWELS OF MY HOME
FORCED TO SPEND MY REMAINING DAYS FENDING FOR MYSELF IN THE TIN TUNNELS OF THE DUCT WORK, THE SOLENOID JUNGLE OF THE WIRING SYSTEM AND THE POLYVINYL CHLORIDE PLAYGROUND IN THE CRAWL SPACE
HEY! I THINK THERE'S A BOOK HERE SOMEWHERE
JIM DAVIS 9-6
© 1983 PAWS, INC. All Rights Reserved.

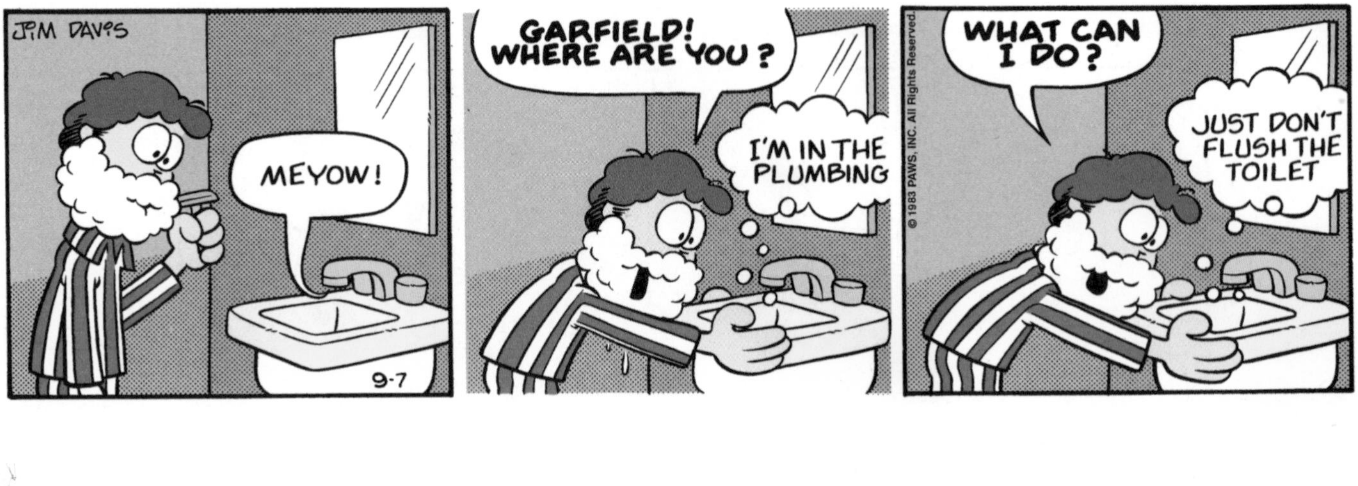
JIM DAVIS
MEYOW!
9-7
GARFIELD! WHERE ARE YOU?
I'M IN THE PLUMBING
WHAT CAN I DO?
JUST DON'T FLUSH THE TOILET
© 1983 PAWS, INC. All Rights Reserved.

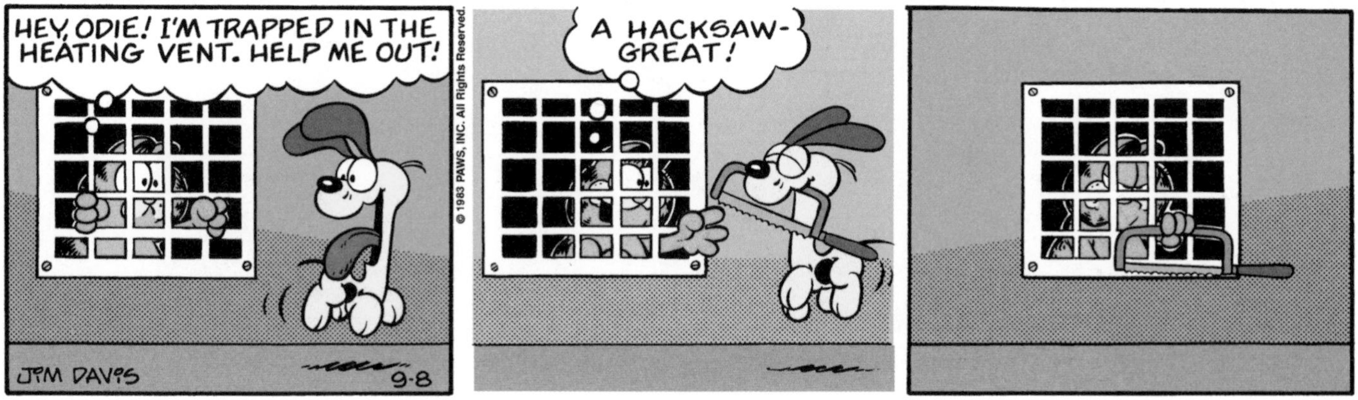
HEY, ODIE! I'M TRAPPED IN THE HEATING VENT. HELP ME OUT!
JIM DAVIS
9-8
© 1983 PAWS, INC. All Rights Reserved.
A HACKSAW-GREAT!

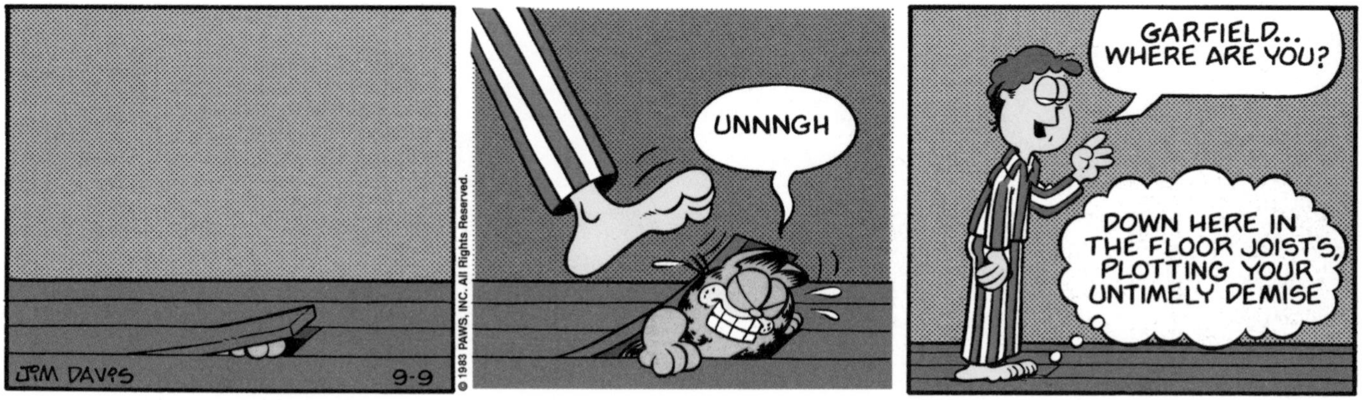
JIM DAVIS
9-9
© 1983 PAWS, INC. All Rights Reserved.
UNNNGH
GARFIELD... WHERE ARE YOU?
DOWN HERE IN THE FLOOR JOISTS, PLOTTING YOUR UNTIMELY DEMISE

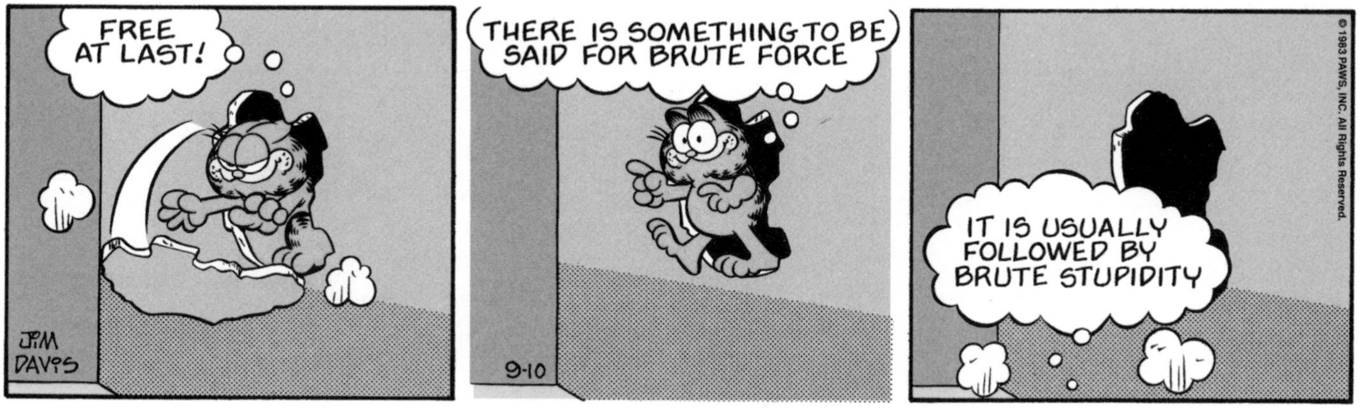
FREE AT LAST!
JIM DAVIS
THERE IS SOMETHING TO BE SAID FOR BRUTE FORCE
9-10
IT IS USUALLY FOLLOWED BY BRUTE STUPIDITY
© 1983 PAWS, INC. All Rights Reserved.

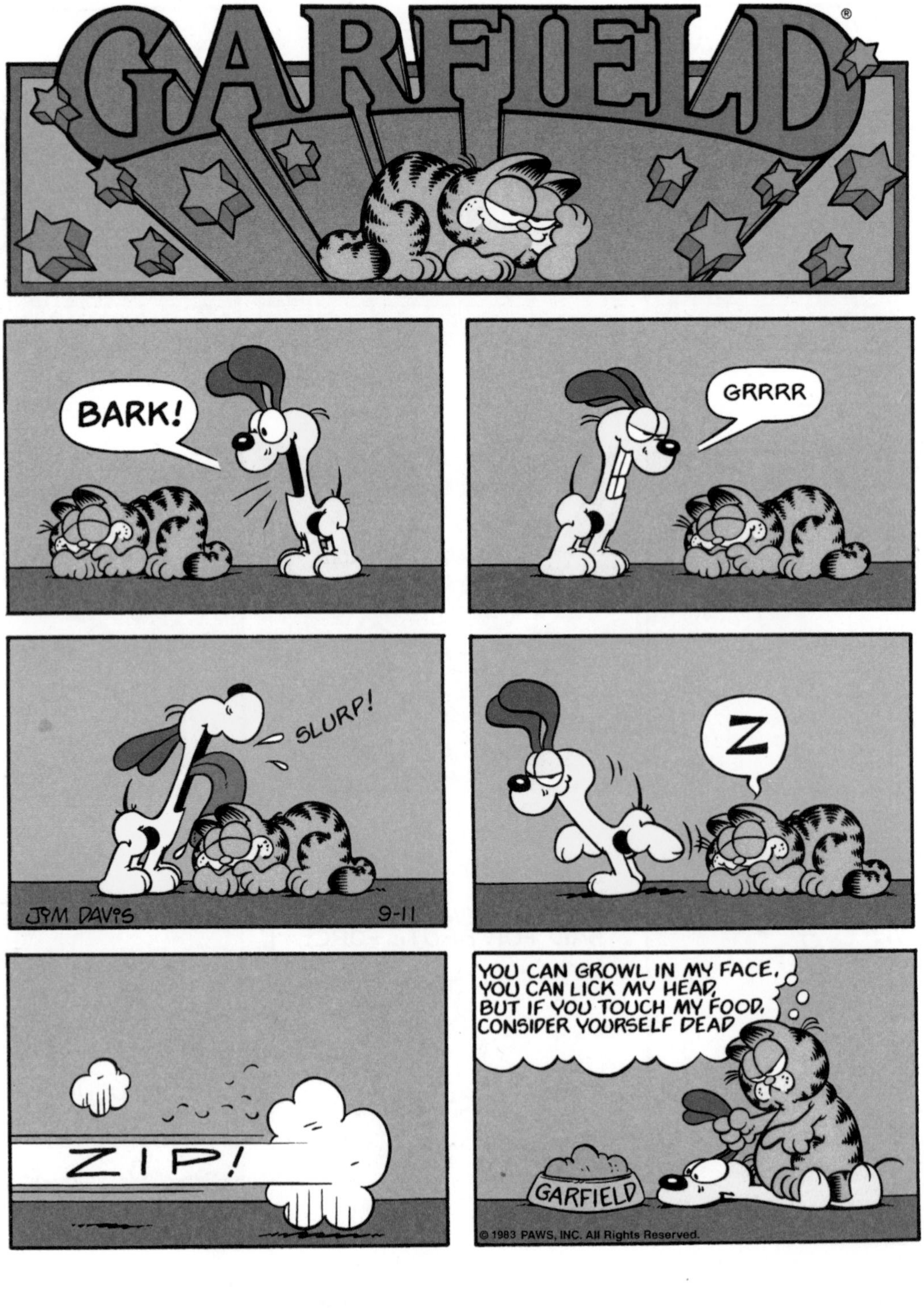
GARFIELD
BARK!
GRRRR
SLURP!
JIM DAVIS
9-11
Z
ZIP!
YOU CAN GROWL IN MY FACE,
YOU CAN LICK MY HEAD,
BUT IF YOU TOUCH MY FOOD,
CONSIDER YOURSELF DEAD
GARFIELD
© 1983 PAWS, INC. All Rights Reserved.

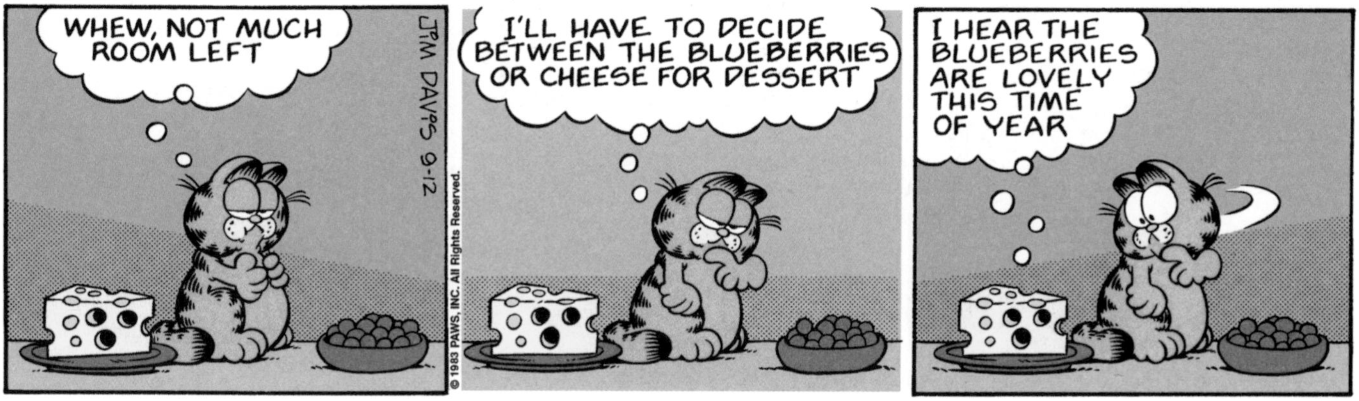
WHEW, NOT MUCH ROOM LEFT
JIM DAVIS 9-12
© 1983 PAWS, INC. All Rights Reserved.
I'LL HAVE TO DECIDE BETWEEN THE BLUEBERRIES OR CHEESE FOR DESSERT
I HEAR THE BLUEBERRIES ARE LOVELY THIS TIME OF YEAR

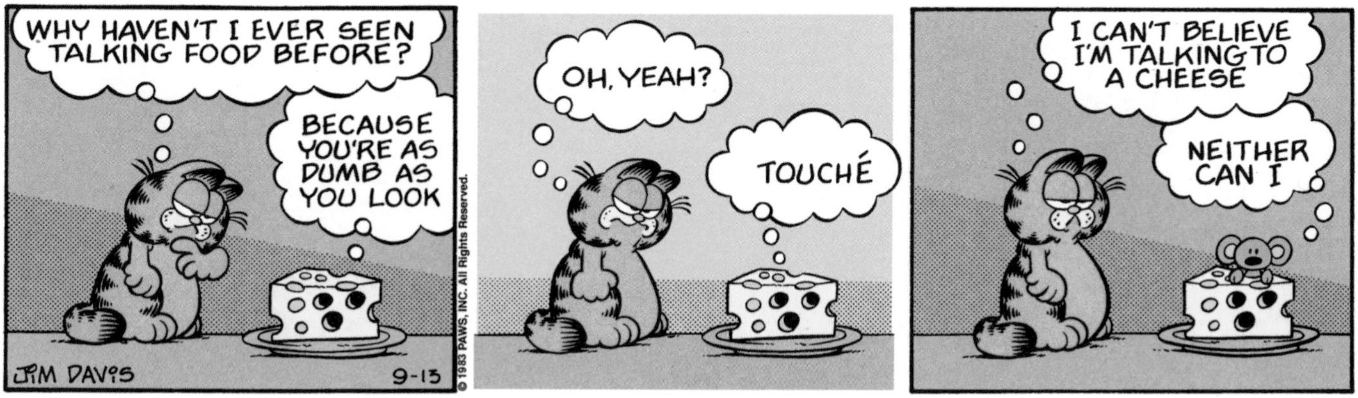
WHY HAVEN'T I EVER SEEN TALKING FOOD BEFORE?
BECAUSE YOU'RE AS DUMB AS YOU LOOK
JIM DAVIS
9-13
© 1983 PAWS, INC. All Rights Reserved.
OH, YEAH?
TOUCHÉ
I CAN'T BELIEVE I'M TALKING TO A CHEESE
NEITHER CAN I

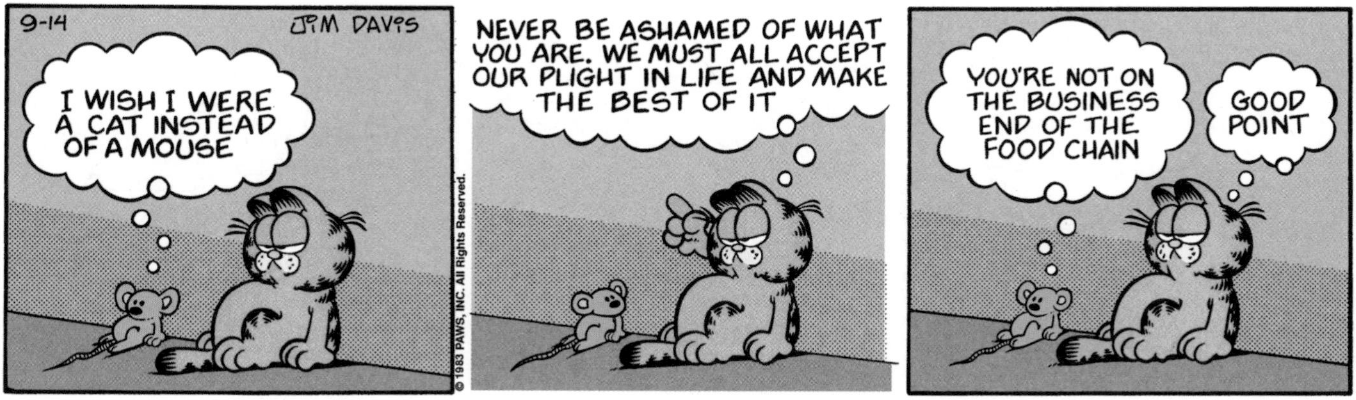
9-14
JIM DAVIS
I WISH I WERE A CAT INSTEAD OF A MOUSE
© 1983 PAWS, INC. All Rights Reserved.
NEVER BE ASHAMED OF WHAT YOU ARE. WE MUST ALL ACCEPT OUR PLIGHT IN LIFE AND MAKE THE BEST OF IT
YOU'RE NOT ON THE BUSINESS END OF THE FOOD CHAIN
GOOD POINT

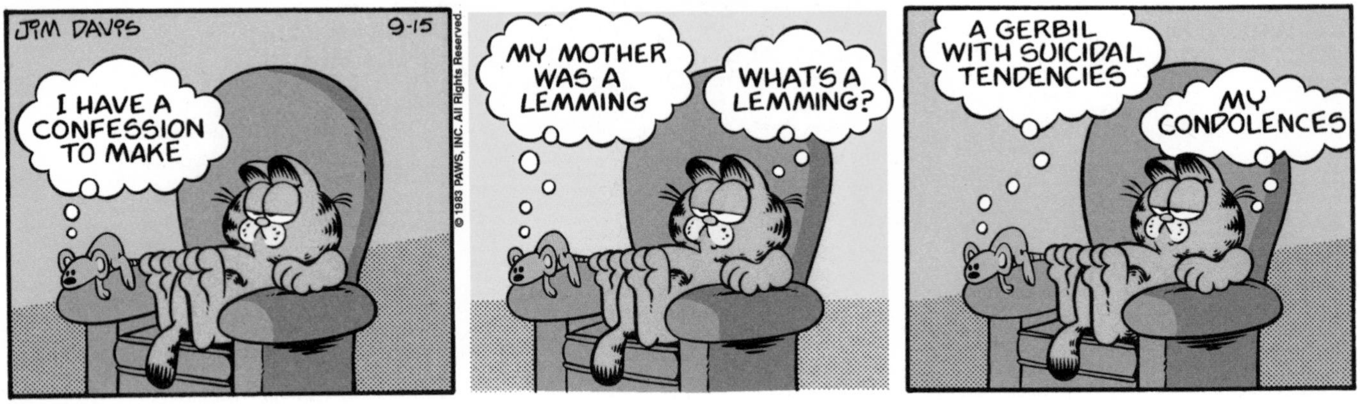
JIM DAVIS 9-15
I HAVE A CONFESSION TO MAKE
© 1983 PAWS, INC. All Rights Reserved.
MY MOTHER WAS A LEMMING
WHAT'S A LEMMING?
A GERBIL WITH SUICIDAL TENDENCIES
MY CONDOLENCES

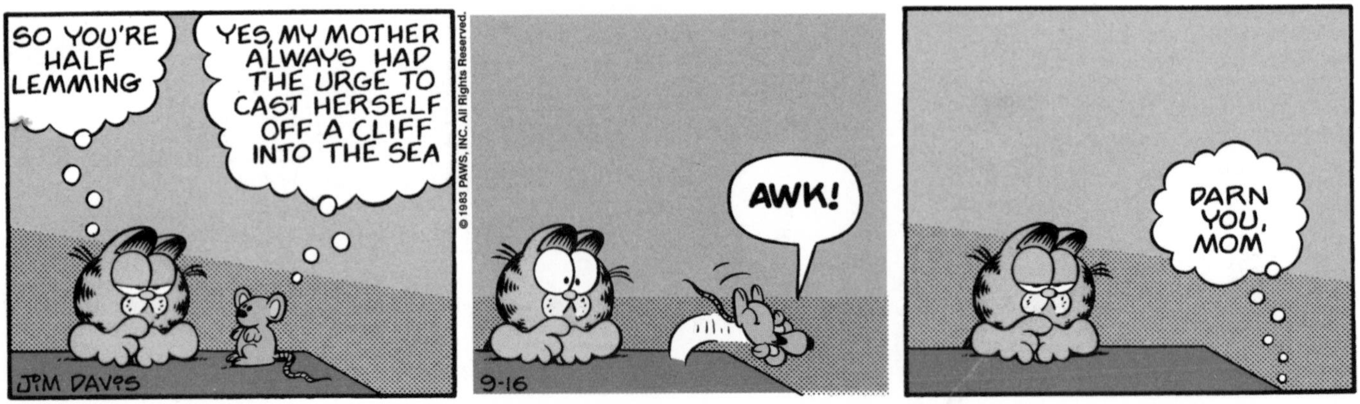
SO YOU'RE HALF LEMMING
YES, MY MOTHER ALWAYS HAD THE URGE TO CAST HERSELF OFF A CLIFF INTO THE SEA
JIM DAVIS
© 1983 PAWS, INC. All Rights Reserved.
AWK!
9-16
DARN YOU, MOM

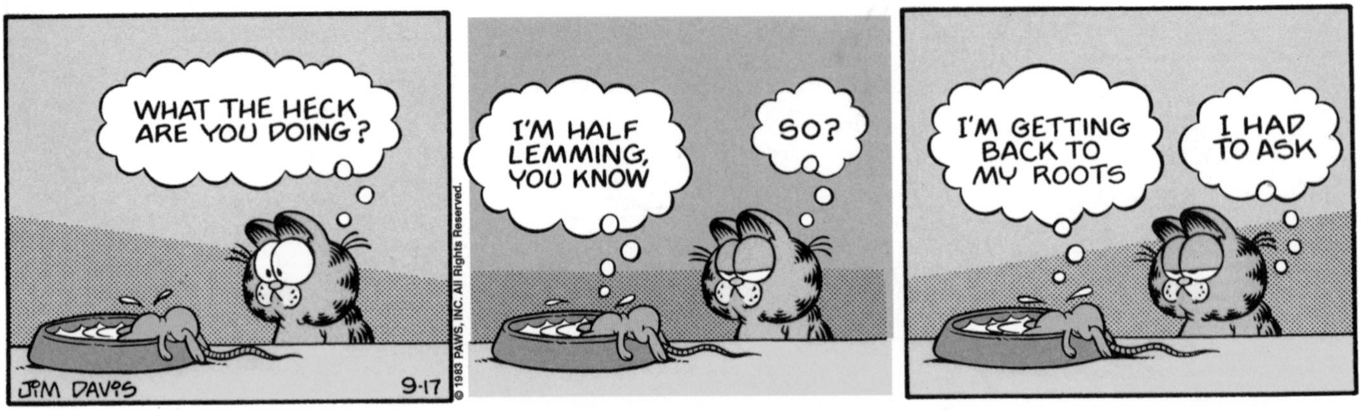
WHAT THE HECK ARE YOU DOING?
JIM DAVIS 9-17
© 1983 PAWS, INC. All Rights Reserved.
I'M HALF LEMMING, YOU KNOW
SO?
I'M GETTING BACK TO MY ROOTS
I HAD TO ASK

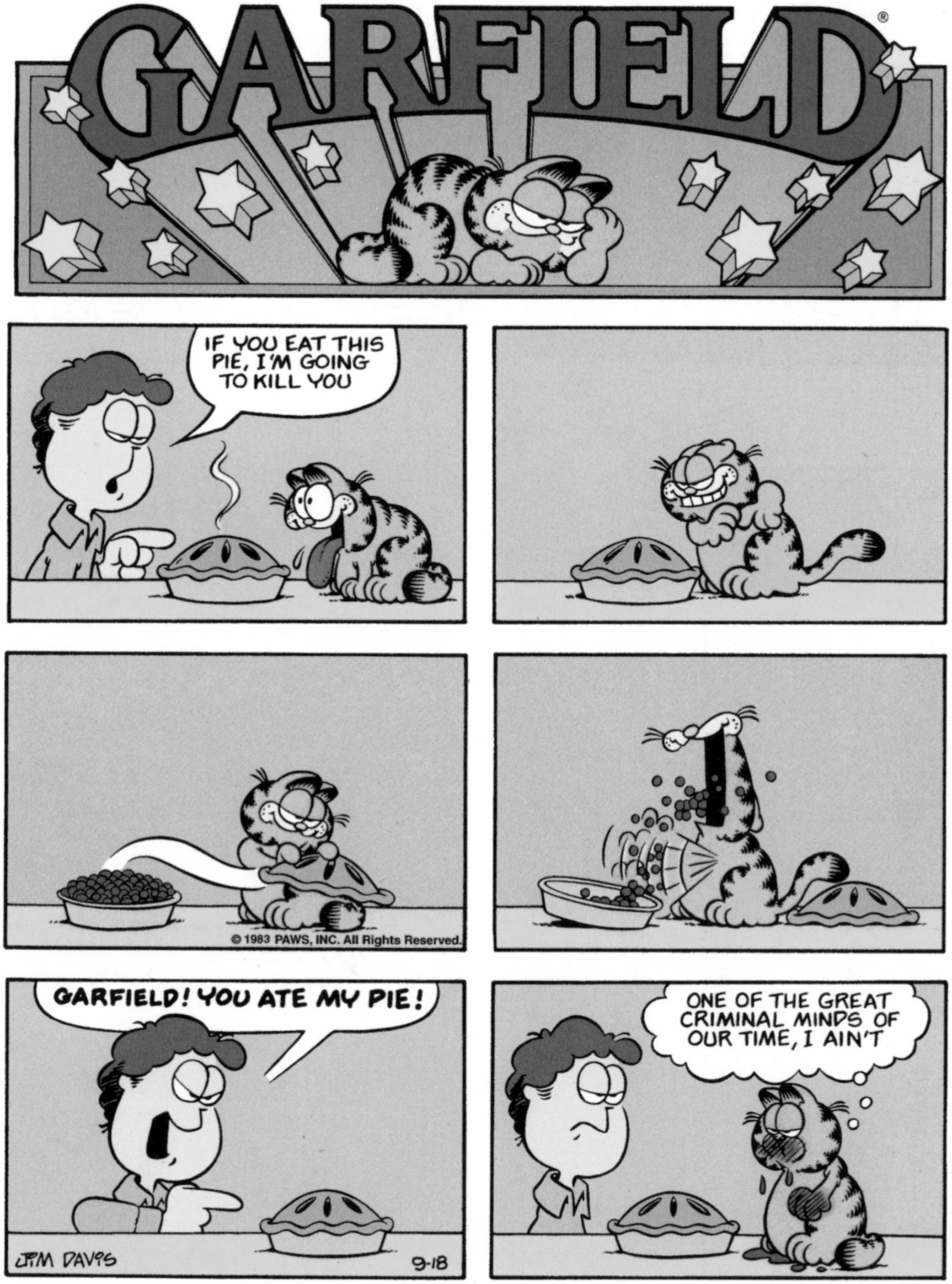
GARFIELD
IF YOU EAT THIS PIE, I'M GOING TO KILL YOU
© 1983 PAWS, INC. All Rights Reserved.
GARFIELD! YOU ATE MY PIE!
JIM DAVIS
9-18
ONE OF THE GREAT CRIMINAL MINDS OF OUR TIME, I AIN'T

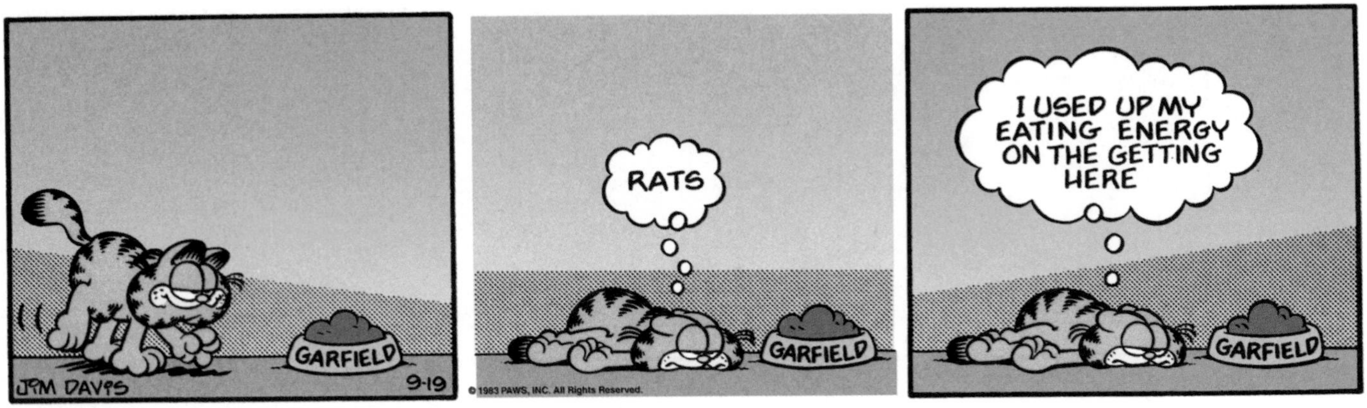
JIM DAVIS
9-19
GARFIELD
© 1983 PAWS, INC. All Rights Reserved.
RATS
I USED UP MY EATING ENERGY ON THE GETTING HERE

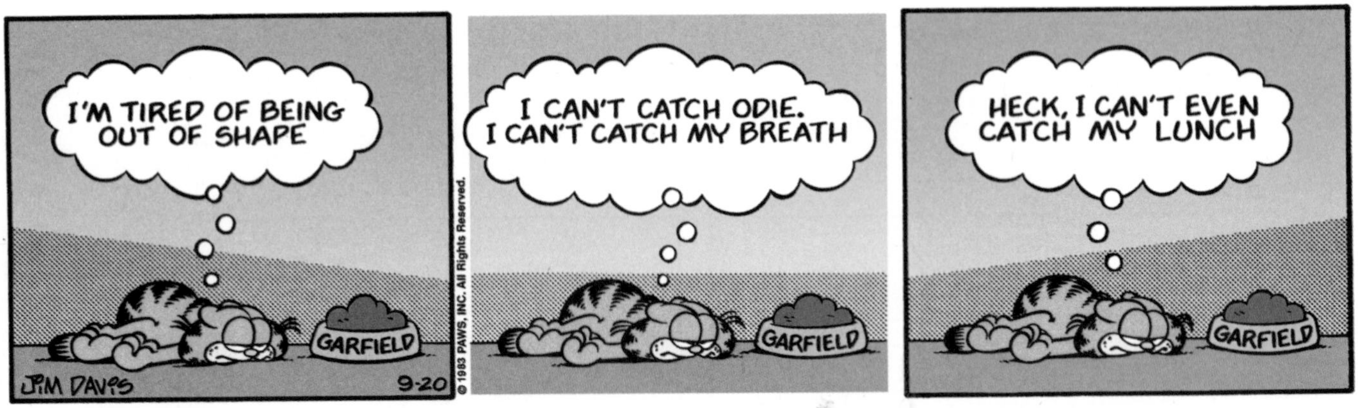
I'M TIRED OF BEING OUT OF SHAPE
JIM DAVIS
9-20
GARFIELD
© 1983 PAWS, INC. All Rights Reserved.
I CAN'T CATCH ODIE. I CAN'T CATCH MY BREATH
HECK, I CAN'T EVEN CATCH MY LUNCH

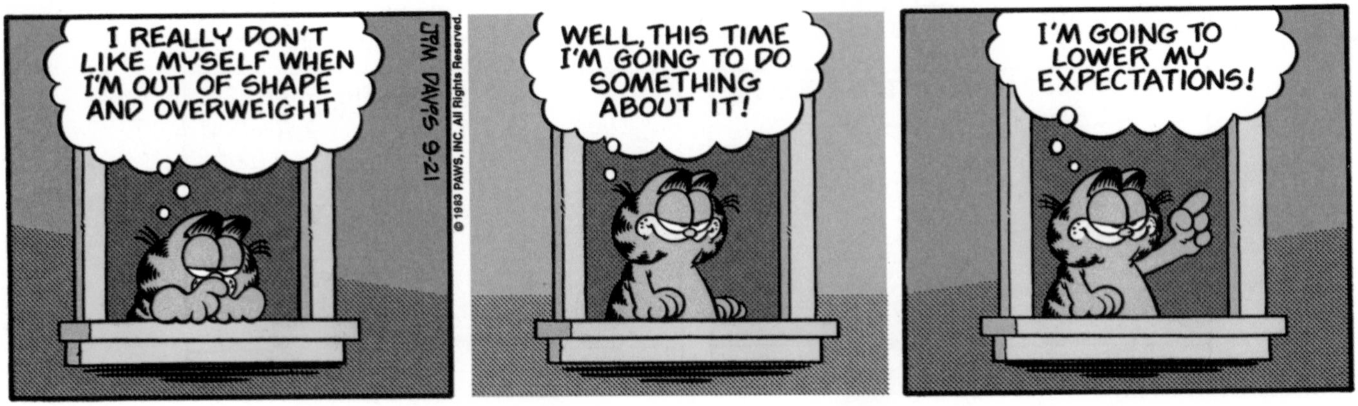
I REALLY DON'T LIKE MYSELF WHEN I'M OUT OF SHAPE AND OVERWEIGHT
JIM DAVIS 9-21
© 1983 PAWS, INC. All Rights Reserved.
WELL, THIS TIME I'M GOING TO DO SOMETHING ABOUT IT!
I'M GOING TO LOWER MY EXPECTATIONS!

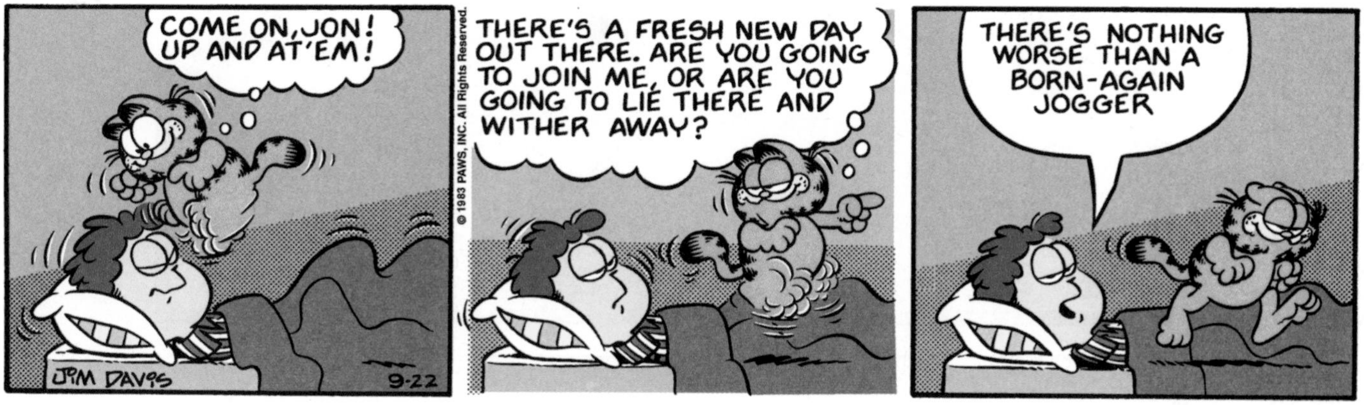
COME ON, JON! UP AND AT 'EM!
JIM DAVIS
9-22
© 1983 PAWS, INC. All Rights Reserved.
THERE'S A FRESH NEW DAY OUT THERE. ARE YOU GOING TO JOIN ME, OR ARE YOU GOING TO LIE THERE AND WITHER AWAY?
THERE'S NOTHING WORSE THAN A BORN-AGAIN JOGGER

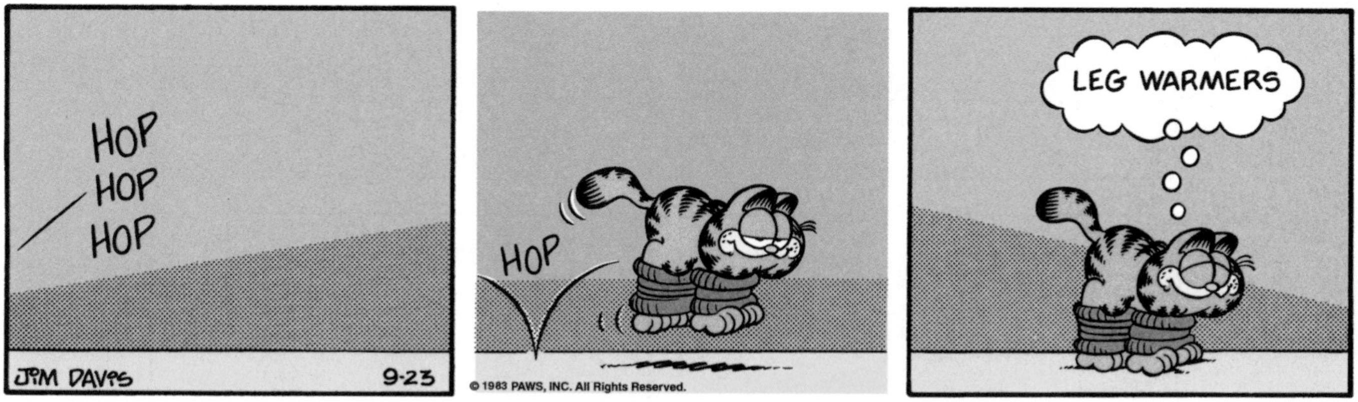
HOP
HOP
HOP
JIM DAVIS
9-23
HOP
© 1983 PAWS, INC. All Rights Reserved.
LEG WARMERS

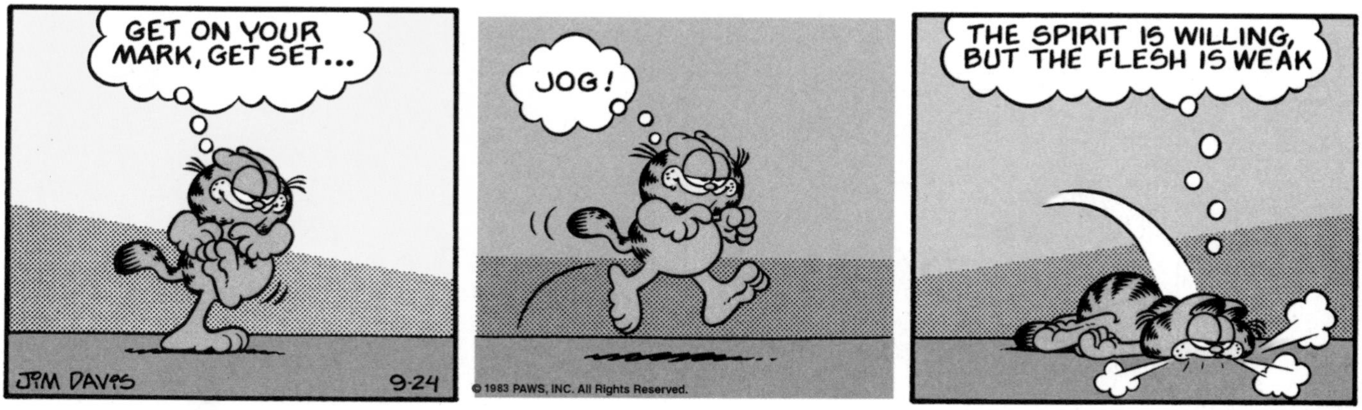
GET ON YOUR MARK, GET SET...
JIM DAVIS
9-24
JOG!
© 1983 PAWS, INC. All Rights Reserved.
THE SPIRIT IS WILLING, BUT THE FLESH IS WEAK

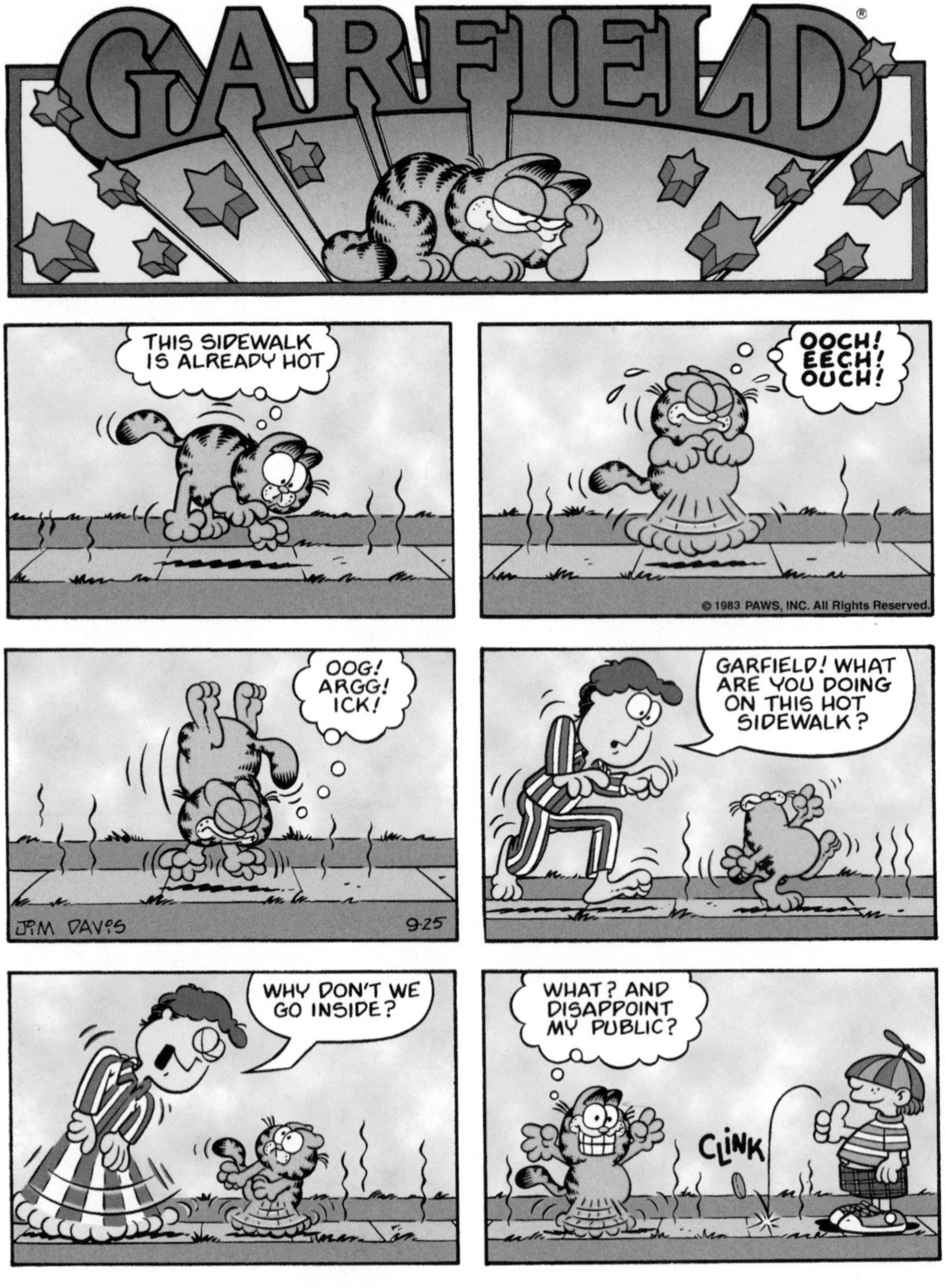
GARFIELD®
THIS SIDEWALK IS ALREADY HOT
OOCH! EECH! OUCH!
© 1983 PAWS, INC. All Rights Reserved.
OOG! ARGG! ICK!
JIM DAVIS
9-25
GARFIELD! WHAT ARE YOU DOING ON THIS HOT SIDEWALK?
WHY DON'T WE GO INSIDE?
WHAT? AND DISAPPOINT MY PUBLIC?
CLINK

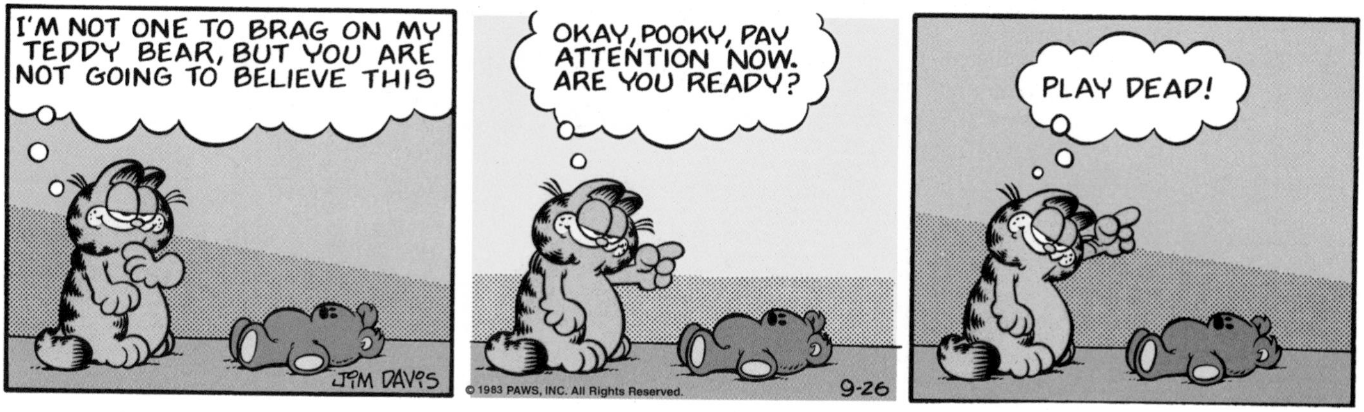
I'M NOT ONE TO BRAG ON MY TEDDY BEAR, BUT YOU ARE NOT GOING TO BELIEVE THIS
JIM DAVIS
OKAY, POOKY, PAY ATTENTION NOW. ARE YOU READY?
© 1983 PAWS, INC. All Rights Reserved.
9-26
PLAY DEAD!

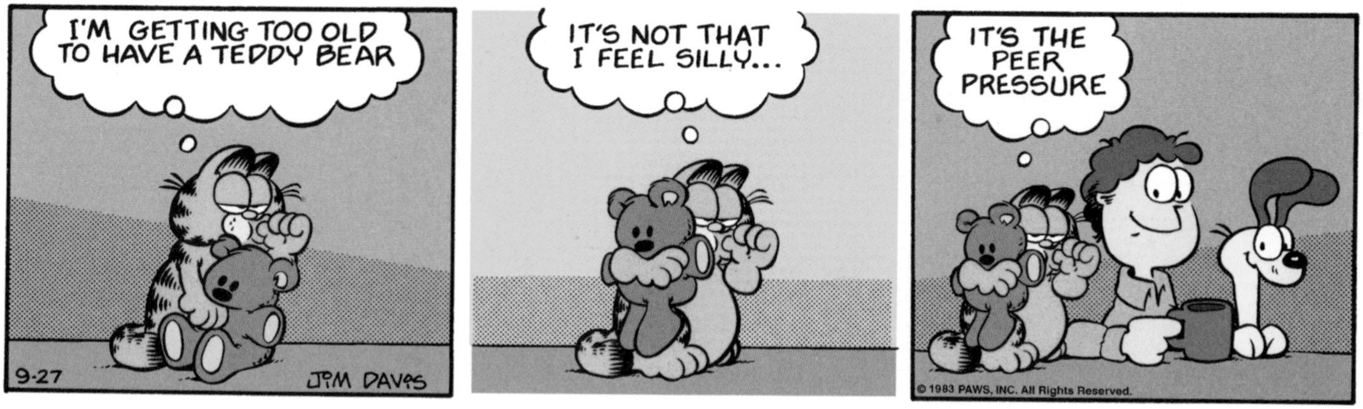
I'M GETTING TOO OLD TO HAVE A TEDDY BEAR
9-27
JIM DAVIS
IT'S NOT THAT I FEEL SILLY...
IT'S THE PEER PRESSURE
© 1983 PAWS, INC. All Rights Reserved.

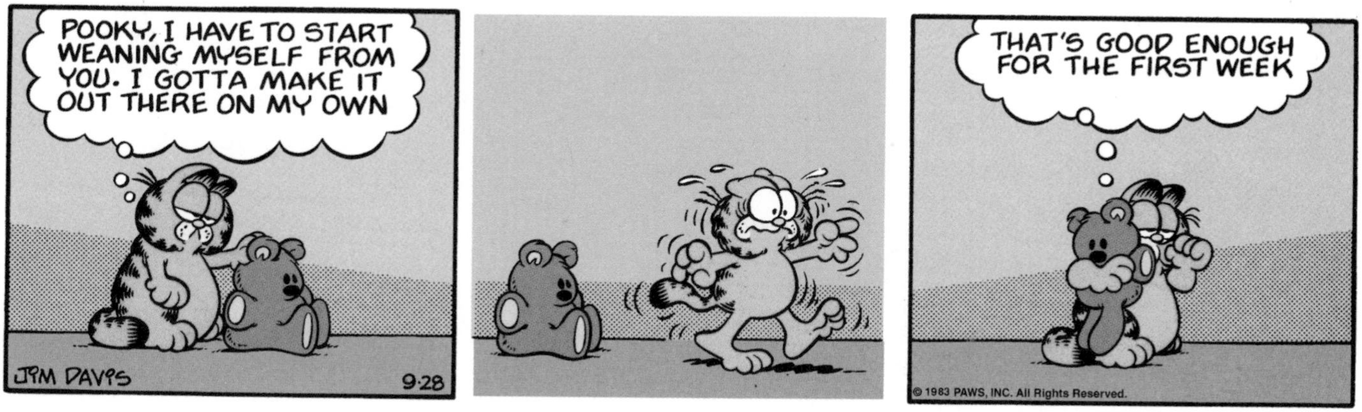
POOKY, I HAVE TO START WEANING MYSELF FROM YOU. I GOTTA MAKE IT OUT THERE ON MY OWN
JIM DAVIS
9-28
THAT'S GOOD ENOUGH FOR THE FIRST WEEK
© 1983 PAWS, INC. All Rights Reserved.

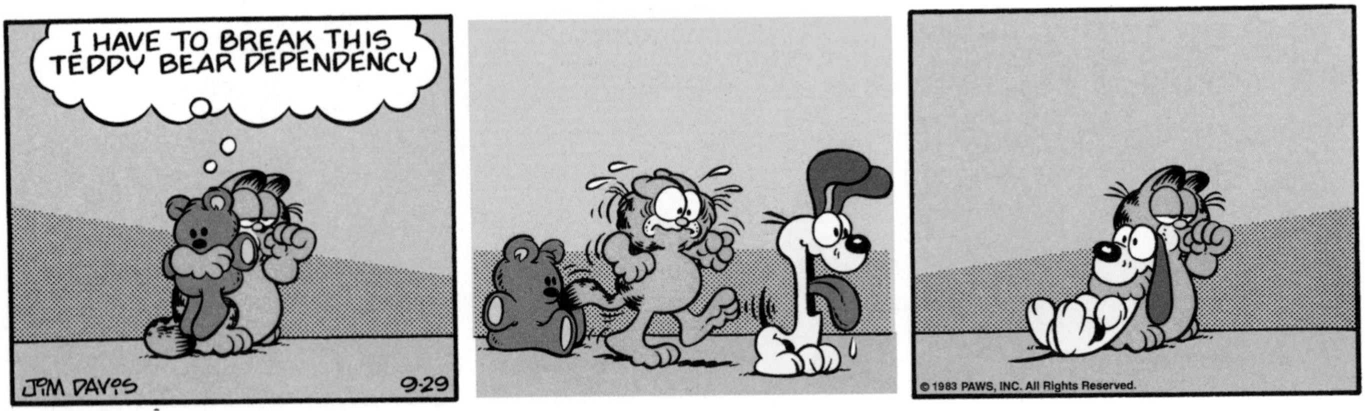
I HAVE TO BREAK THIS TEDDY BEAR DEPENDENCY
JIM DAVIS
9-29
© 1983 PAWS, INC. All Rights Reserved.

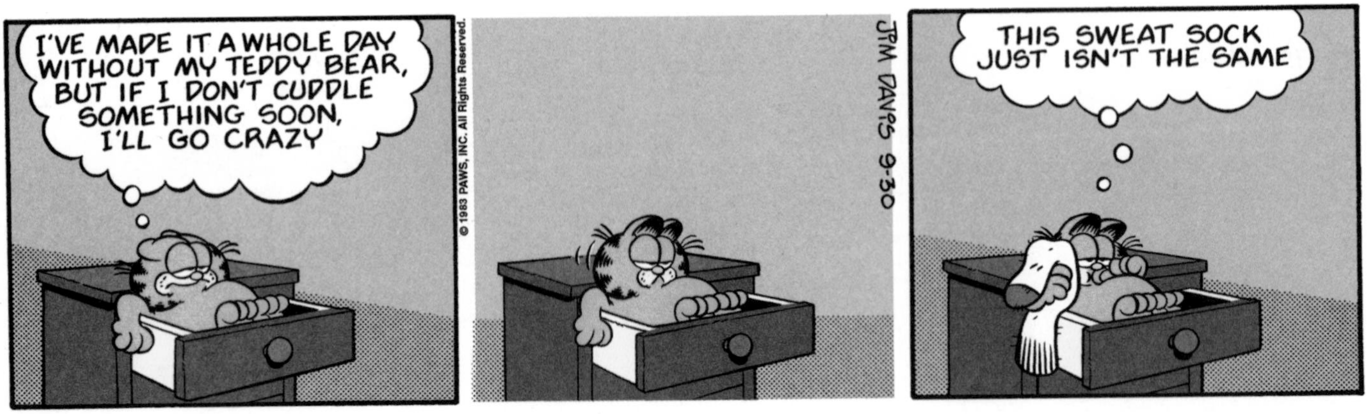
I'VE MADE IT A WHOLE DAY WITHOUT MY TEDDY BEAR, BUT IF I DON'T CUDDLE SOMETHING SOON, I'LL GO CRAZY
© 1983 PAWS, INC. All Rights Reserved.
JIM DAVIS 9-30
THIS SWEAT SOCK JUST ISN'T THE SAME

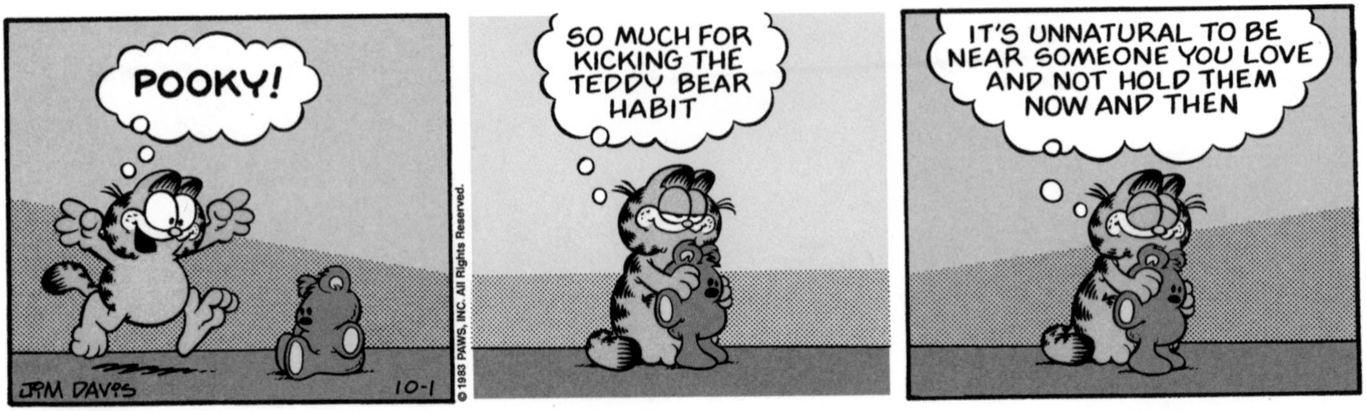
POOKY!
JIM DAVIS
10-1
© 1983 PAWS, INC. All Rights Reserved.
SO MUCH FOR KICKING THE TEDDY BEAR HABIT
IT'S UNNATURAL TO BE NEAR SOMEONE YOU LOVE AND NOT HOLD THEM NOW AND THEN

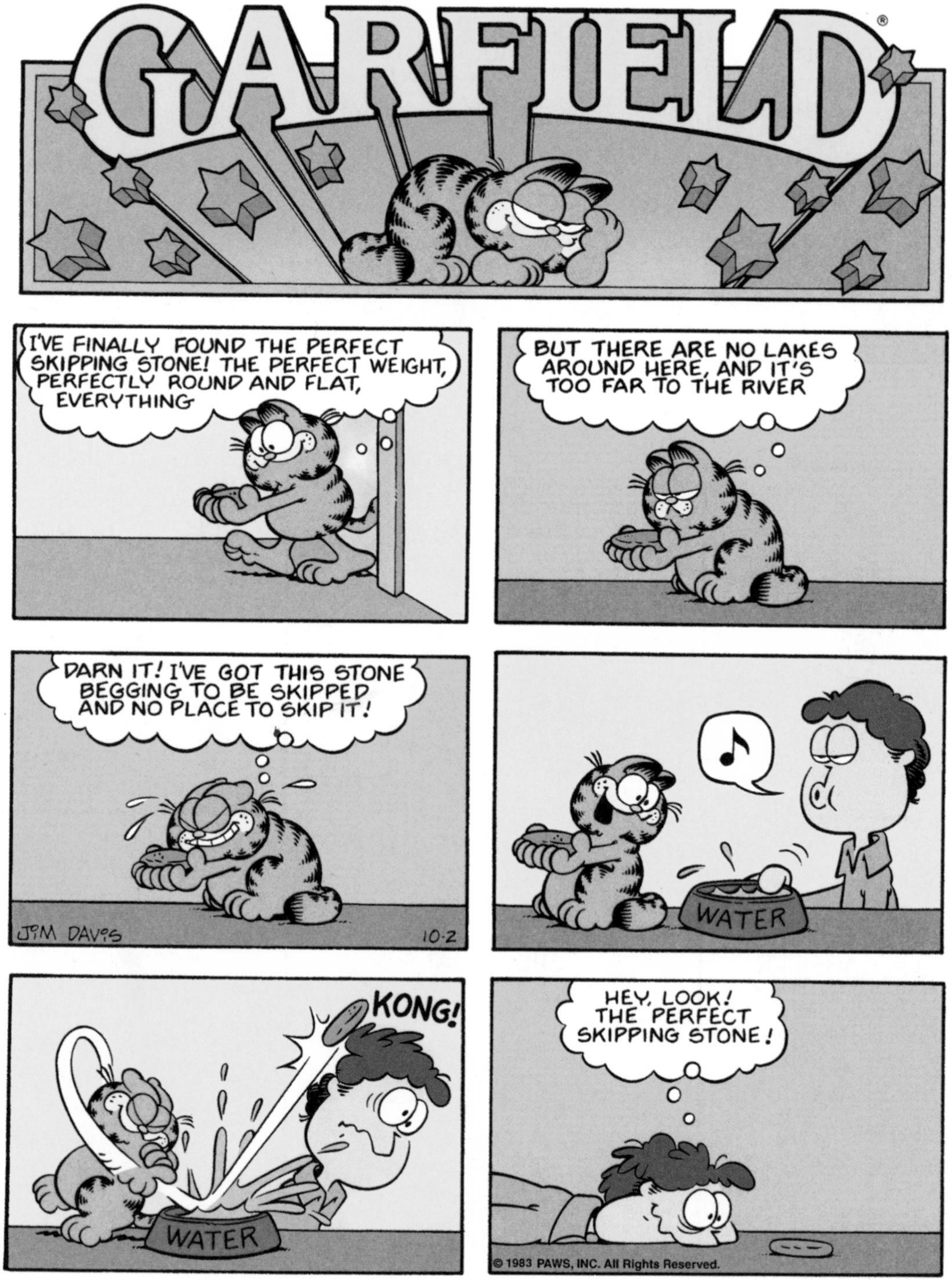
GARFIELD
I'VE FINALLY FOUND THE PERFECT SKIPPING STONE! THE PERFECT WEIGHT, PERFECTLY ROUND AND FLAT, EVERYTHING
BUT THERE ARE NO LAKES AROUND HERE, AND IT'S TOO FAR TO THE RIVER
DARN IT! I'VE GOT THIS STONE BEGGING TO BE SKIPPED AND NO PLACE TO SKIP IT!
JIM DAVIS
10-2
♪
WATER
KONG!
WATER
HEY, LOOK! THE PERFECT SKIPPING STONE!
© 1983 PAWS, INC. All Rights Reserved.

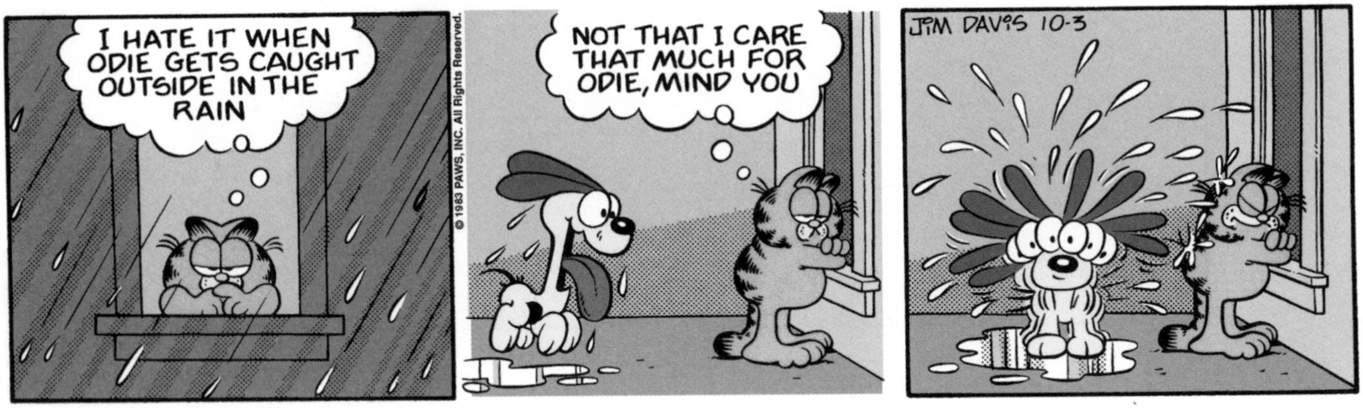
I HATE IT WHEN ODIE GETS CAUGHT OUTSIDE IN THE RAIN
© 1983 PAWS, INC. All Rights Reserved.
NOT THAT I CARE THAT MUCH FOR ODIE, MIND YOU
JIM DAVIS 10-3

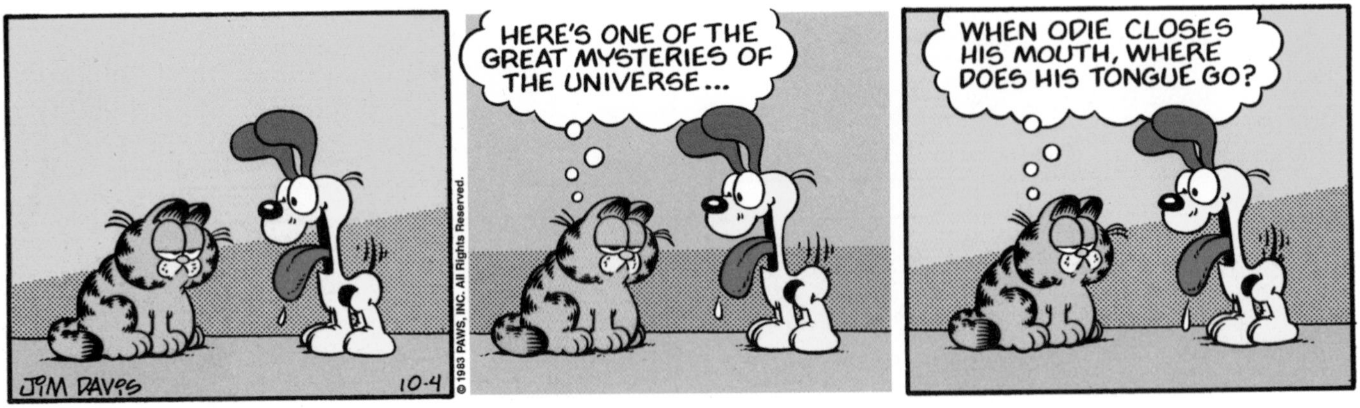
JIM DAVIS
10-4
© 1983 PAWS, INC. All Rights Reserved.
HERE'S ONE OF THE GREAT MYSTERIES OF THE UNIVERSE...
WHEN ODIE CLOSES HIS MOUTH, WHERE DOES HIS TONGUE GO?

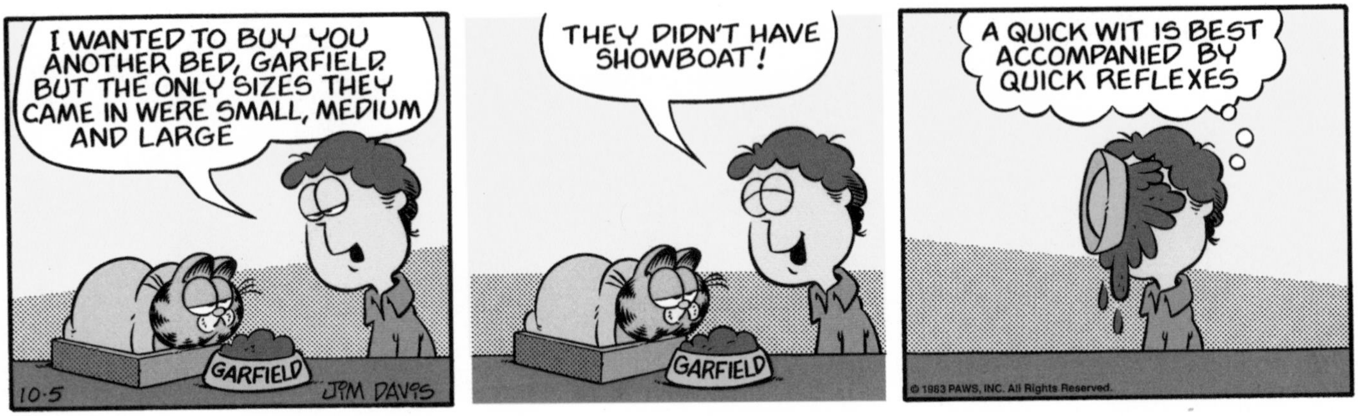
I WANTED TO BUY YOU ANOTHER BED, GARFIELD, BUT THE ONLY SIZES THEY CAME IN WERE SMALL, MEDIUM AND LARGE
GARFIELD
10-5
JIM DAVIS
THEY DIDN'T HAVE SHOWBOAT!
GARFIELD
A QUICK WIT IS BEST ACCOMPANIED BY QUICK REFLEXES
© 1983 PAWS, INC. All Rights Reserved.

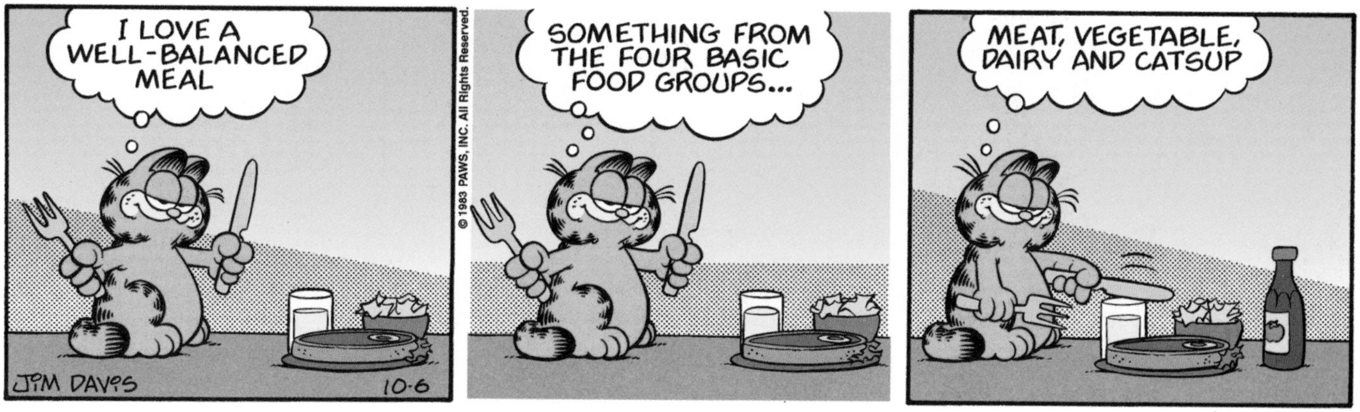
I LOVE A WELL-BALANCED MEAL
JIM DAVIS
10-6
© 1983 PAWS, INC. All Rights Reserved.
SOMETHING FROM THE FOUR BASIC FOOD GROUPS...
MEAT, VEGETABLE, DAIRY AND CATSUP

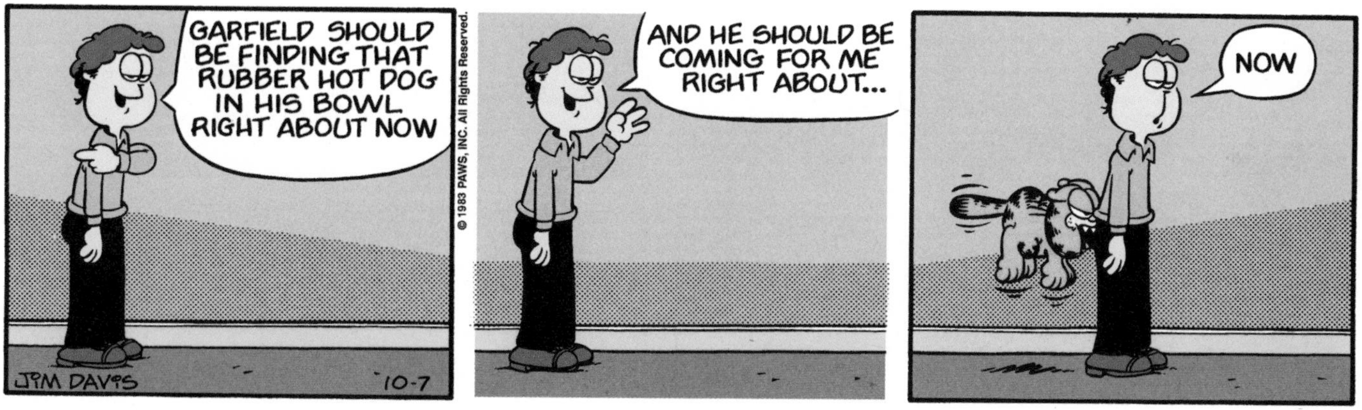
GARFIELD SHOULD BE FINDING THAT RUBBER HOT DOG IN HIS BOWL RIGHT ABOUT NOW
JIM DAVIS
10-7
© 1983 PAWS, INC. All Rights Reserved.
AND HE SHOULD BE COMING FOR ME RIGHT ABOUT...
NOW

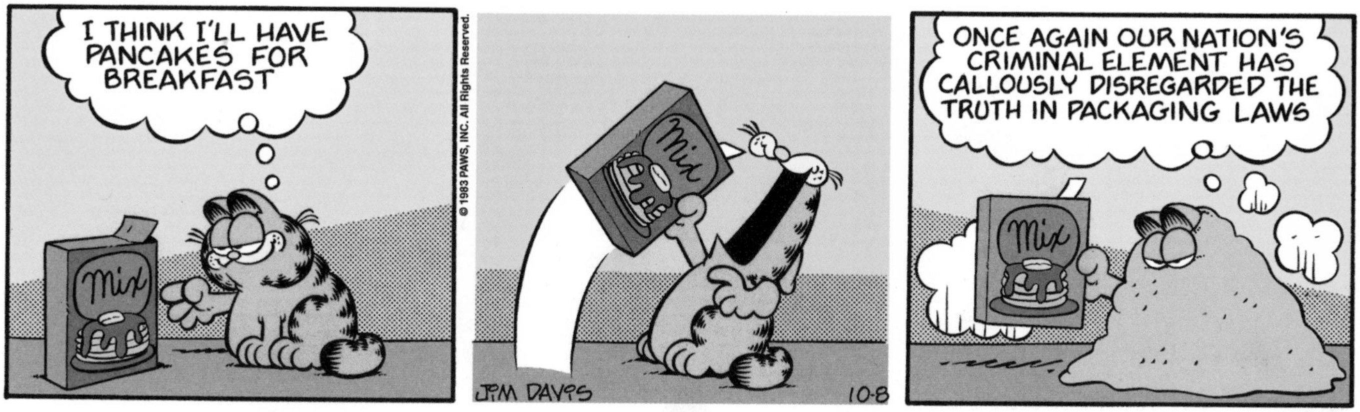
I THINK I'LL HAVE PANCAKES FOR BREAKFAST
Mix
© 1983 PAWS, INC. All Rights Reserved.
Mix
JIM DAVIS
10-8
ONCE AGAIN OUR NATION'S CRIMINAL ELEMENT HAS CALLOUSLY DISREGARDED THE TRUTH IN PACKAGING LAWS
Mix

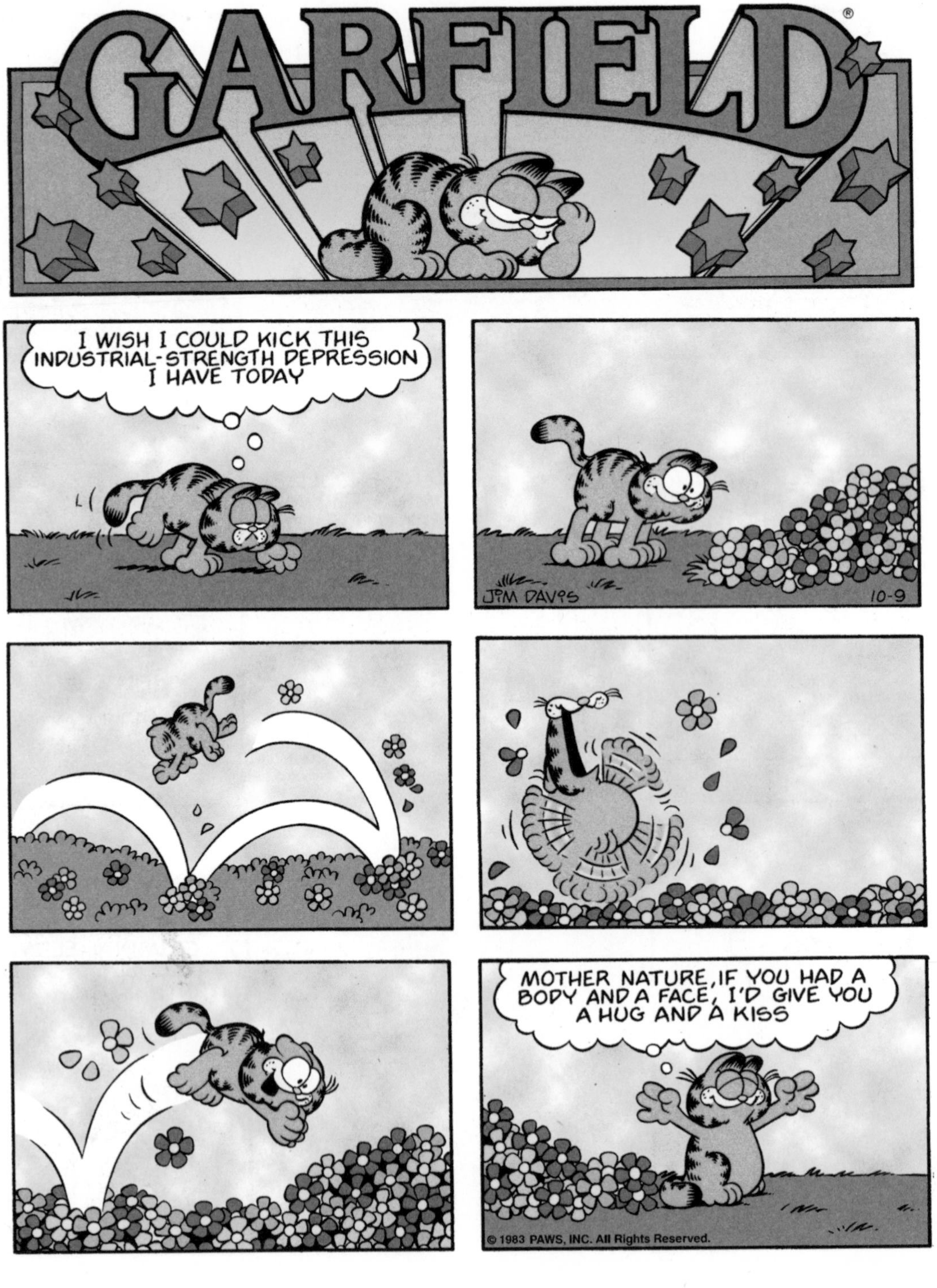
GARFIELD®
I WISH I COULD KICK THIS INDUSTRIAL-STRENGTH DEPRESSION I HAVE TODAY
JIM DAVIS
10-9
MOTHER NATURE, IF YOU HAD A BODY AND A FACE, I'D GIVE YOU A HUG AND A KISS
© 1983 PAWS, INC. All Rights Reserved.

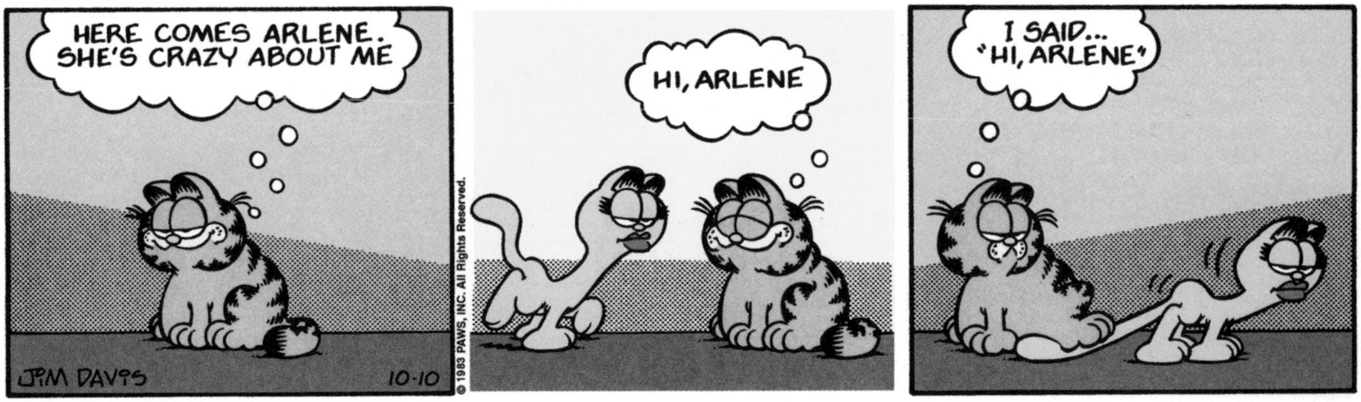
HERE COMES ARLENE. SHE'S CRAZY ABOUT ME
HI, ARLENE
I SAID... "HI, ARLENE"
JIM DAVIS
10-10

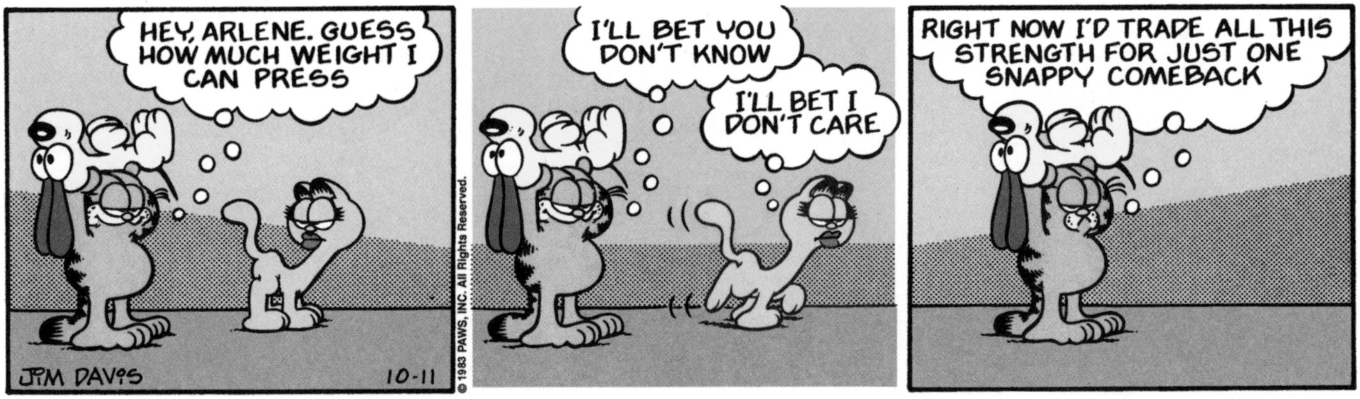
HEY, ARLENE. GUESS HOW MUCH WEIGHT I CAN PRESS
I'LL BET YOU DON'T KNOW
I'LL BET I DON'T CARE
RIGHT NOW I'D TRADE ALL THIS STRENGTH FOR JUST ONE SNAPPY COMEBACK
JIM DAVIS
10-11

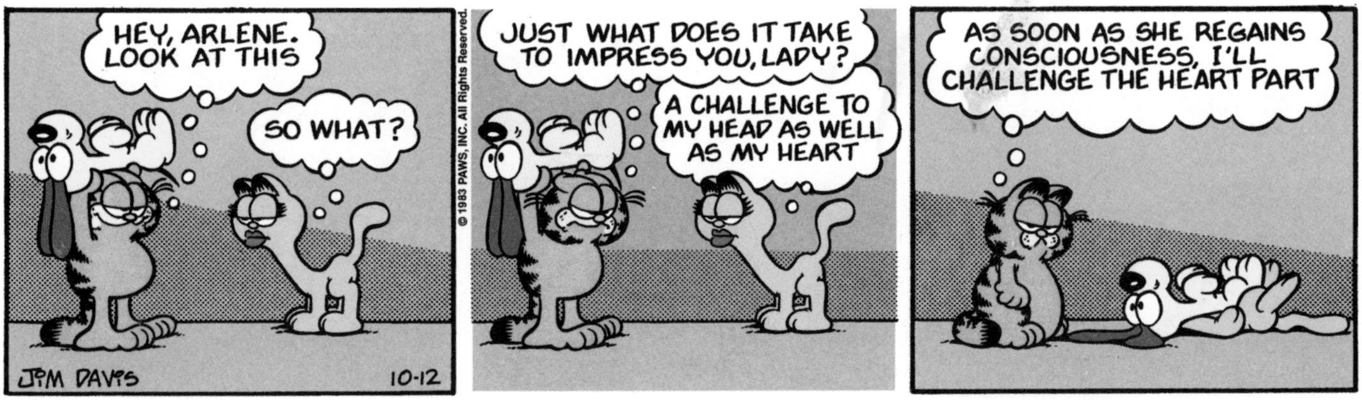
HEY, ARLENE. LOOK AT THIS
SO WHAT?
JUST WHAT DOES IT TAKE TO IMPRESS YOU, LADY?
A CHALLENGE TO MY HEAD AS WELL AS MY HEART
AS SOON AS SHE REGAINS CONSCIOUSNESS, I'LL CHALLENGE THE HEART PART
JIM DAVIS
10-12

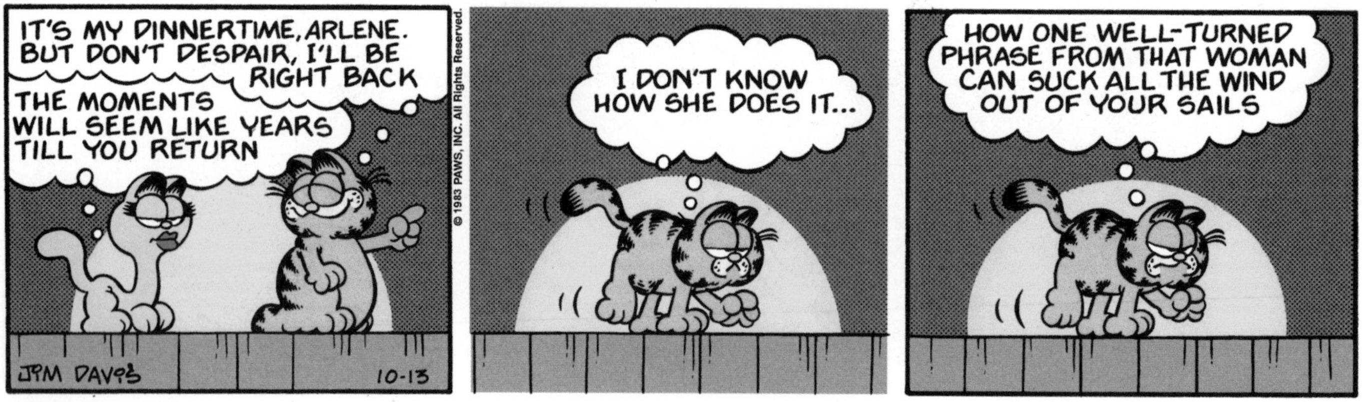
IT'S MY DINNERTIME, ARLENE. BUT DON'T DESPAIR, I'LL BE RIGHT BACK
THE MOMENTS WILL SEEM LIKE YEARS TILL YOU RETURN
JIM DAVIS
10-13
© 1983 PAWS, INC. All Rights Reserved.
I DON'T KNOW HOW SHE DOES IT...
HOW ONE WELL-TURNED PHRASE FROM THAT WOMAN CAN SUCK ALL THE WIND OUT OF YOUR SAILS

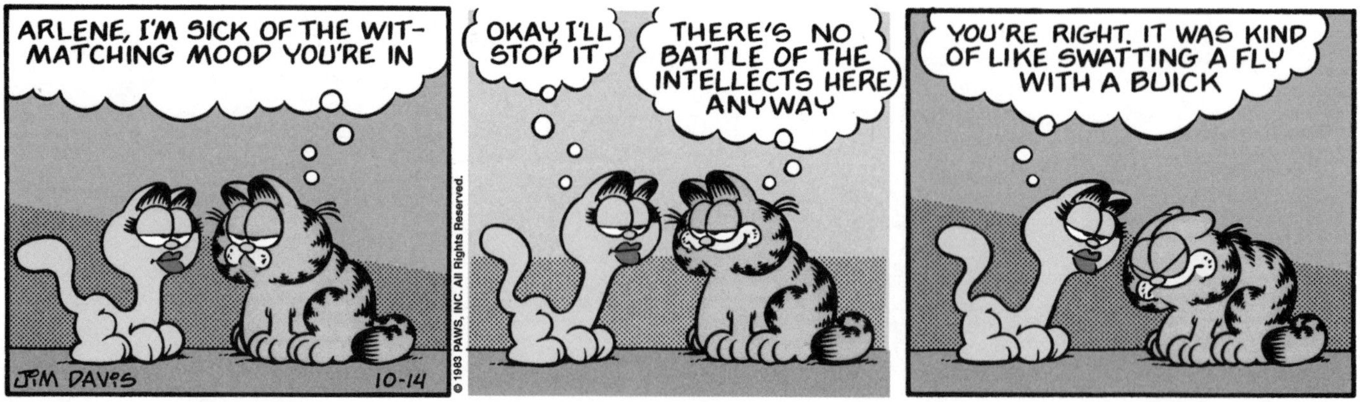
ARLENE, I'M SICK OF THE WIT-MATCHING MOOD YOU'RE IN
JIM DAVIS
10-14
© 1983 PAWS, INC. All Rights Reserved.
OKAY I'LL STOP IT
THERE'S NO BATTLE OF THE INTELLECTS HERE ANYWAY
YOU'RE RIGHT. IT WAS KIND OF LIKE SWATTING A FLY WITH A BUICK

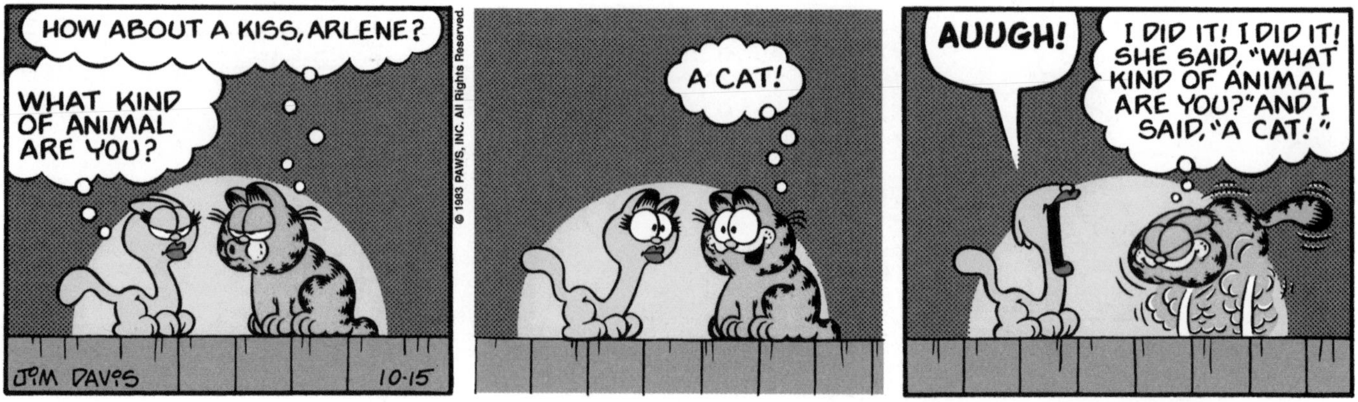
HOW ABOUT A KISS, ARLENE?
WHAT KIND OF ANIMAL ARE YOU?
JIM DAVIS
10-15
© 1983 PAWS, INC. All Rights Reserved.
A CAT!
AUUGH!
I DID IT! I DID IT! SHE SAID, "WHAT KIND OF ANIMAL ARE YOU?" AND I SAID, "A CAT!"

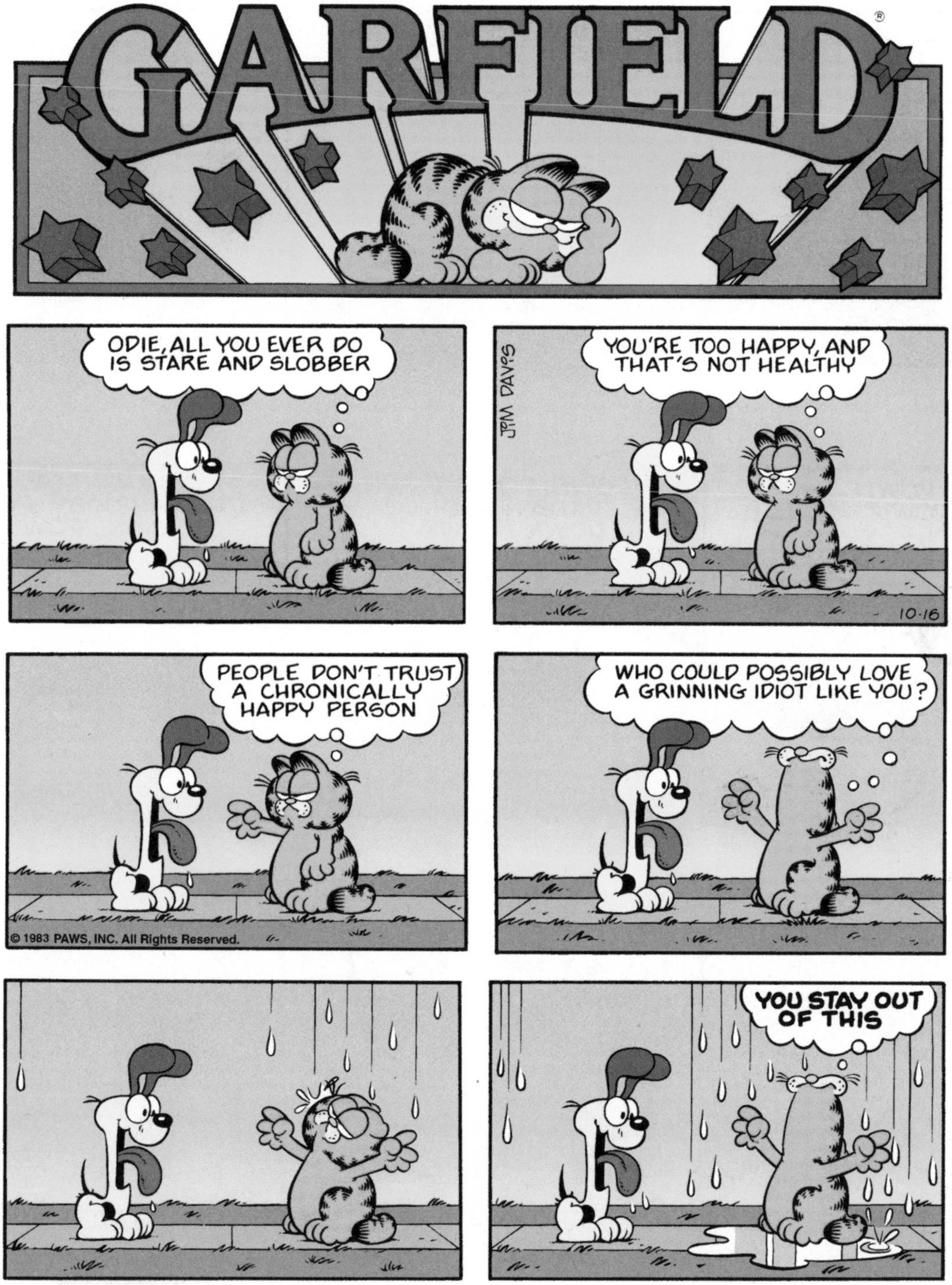
GARFIELD
ODIE, ALL YOU EVER DO IS STARE AND SLOBBER
JPM DAVIS
YOU'RE TOO HAPPY, AND THAT'S NOT HEALTHY
10-16
PEOPLE DON'T TRUST A CHRONICALLY HAPPY PERSON
WHO COULD POSSIBLY LOVE A GRINNING IDIOT LIKE YOU?
YOU STAY OUT OF THIS

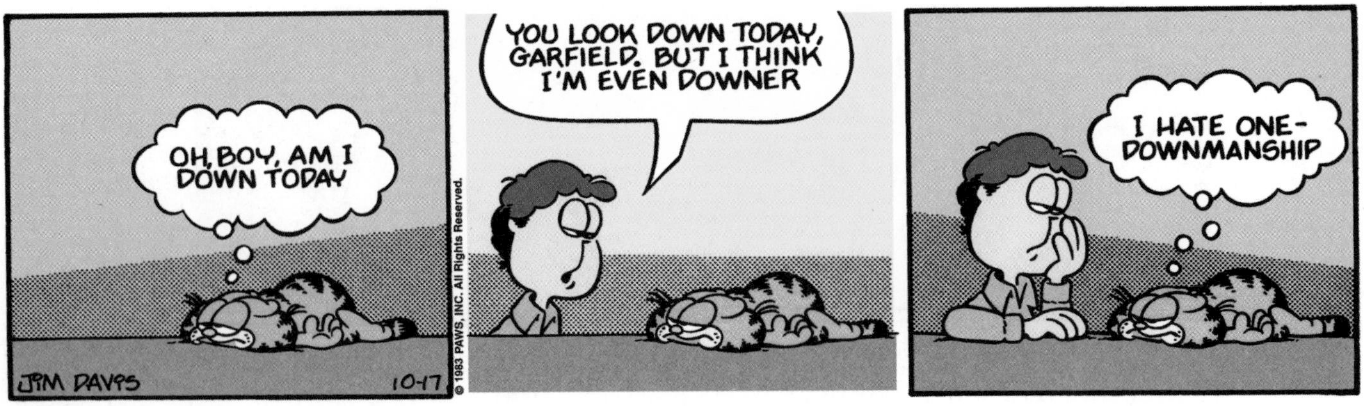
OH, BOY, AM I DOWN TODAY
JIM DAVIS
10-17
© 1983 PAWS, INC. All Rights Reserved.
YOU LOOK DOWN TODAY, GARFIELD. BUT I THINK I'M EVEN DOWNER
I HATE ONE-DOWNMANSHIP

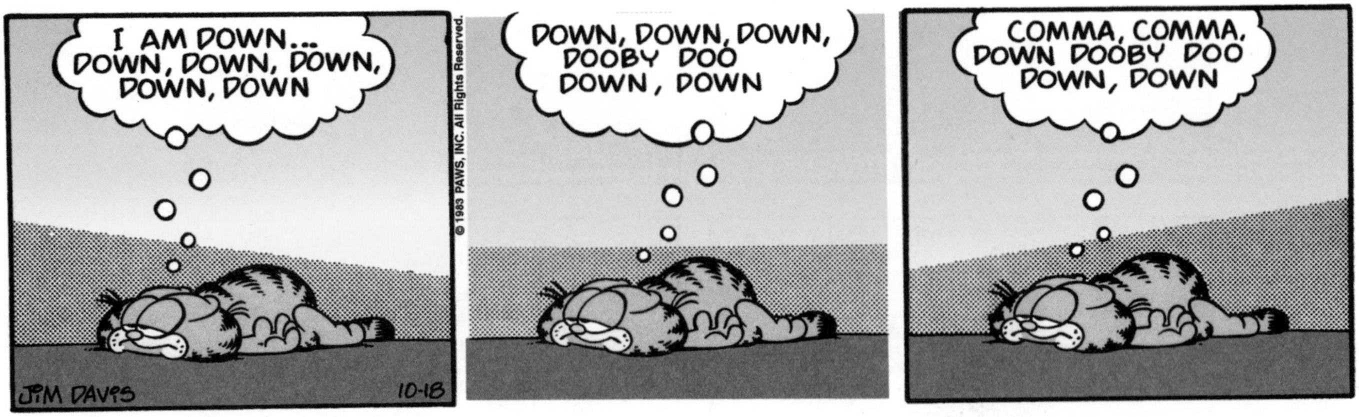
I AM DOWN... DOWN, DOWN, DOWN, DOWN, DOWN
JIM DAVIS
10-18
© 1983 PAWS, INC. All Rights Reserved.
DOWN, DOWN, DOWN, DOOBY DOO DOWN, DOWN
COMMA, COMMA, DOWN DOOBY DOO DOWN, DOWN

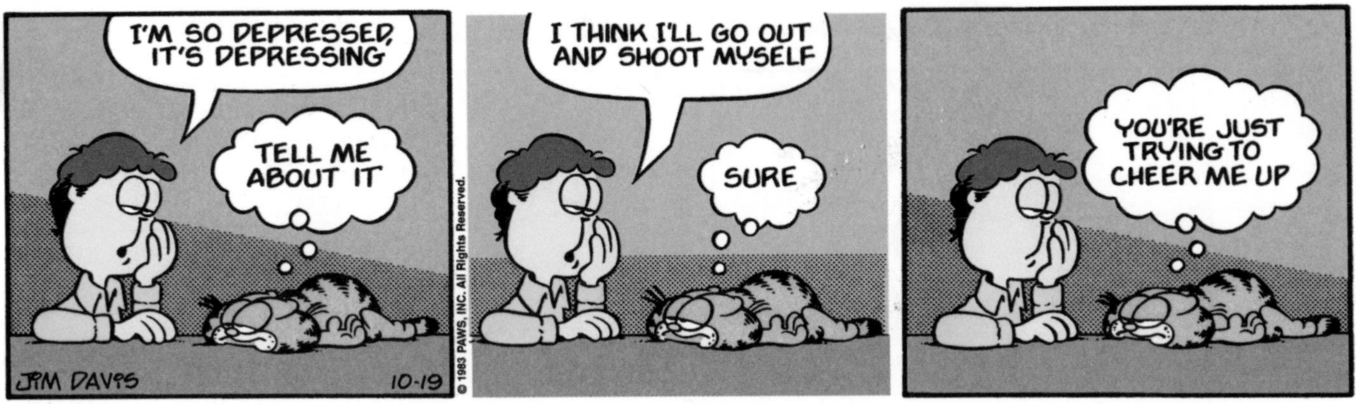
I'M SO DEPRESSED, IT'S DEPRESSING
TELL ME ABOUT IT
JIM DAVIS
10-19
© 1983 PAWS, INC. All Rights Reserved.
I THINK I'LL GO OUT AND SHOOT MYSELF
SURE
YOU'RE JUST TRYING TO CHEER ME UP

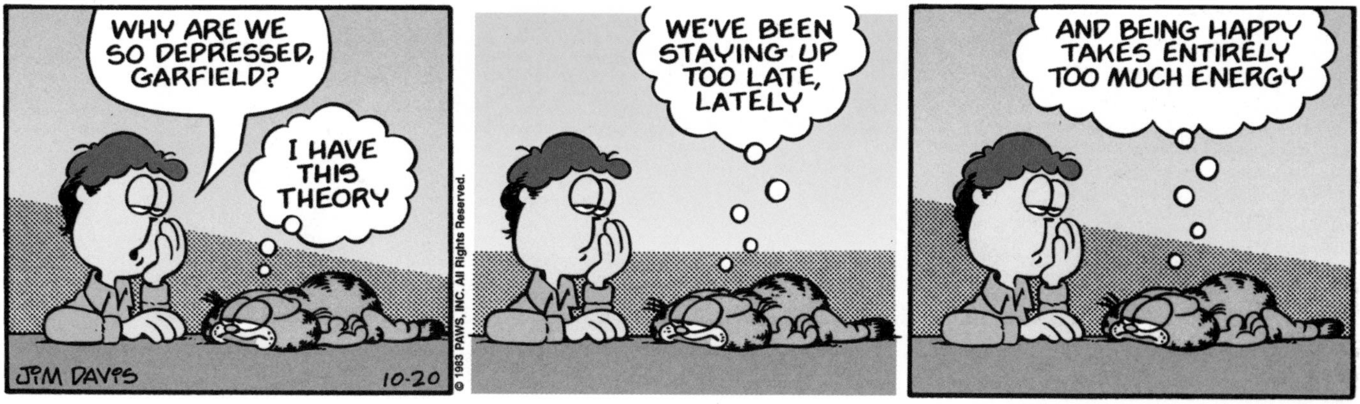
WHY ARE WE SO DEPRESSED, GARFIELD?
I HAVE THIS THEORY
JIM DAVIS
10-20
WE'VE BEEN STAYING UP TOO LATE, LATELY
AND BEING HAPPY TAKES ENTIRELY TOO MUCH ENERGY

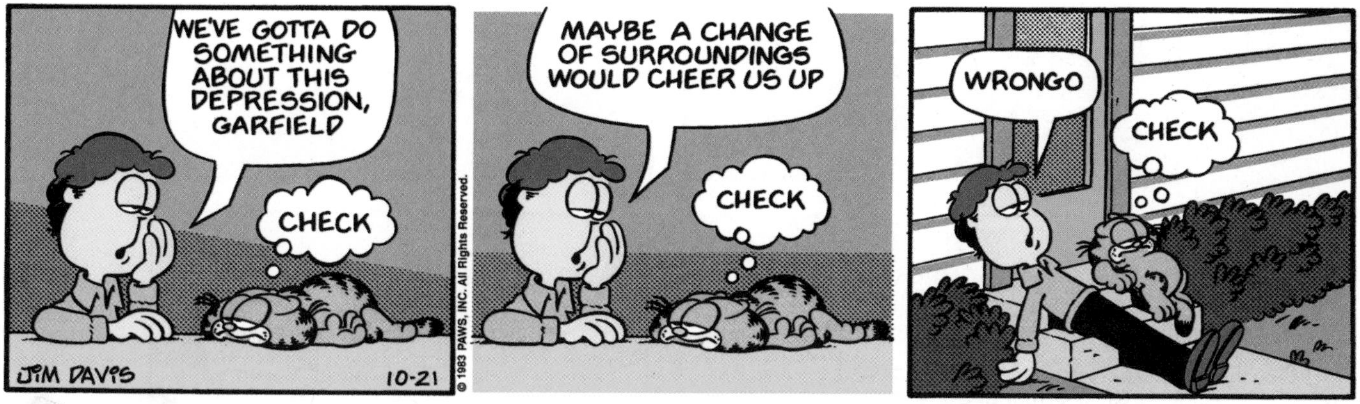
WE'VE GOTTA DO SOMETHING ABOUT THIS DEPRESSION, GARFIELD
CHECK
JIM DAVIS
10-21
MAYBE A CHANGE OF SURROUNDINGS WOULD CHEER US UP
CHECK
WRONGO
CHECK

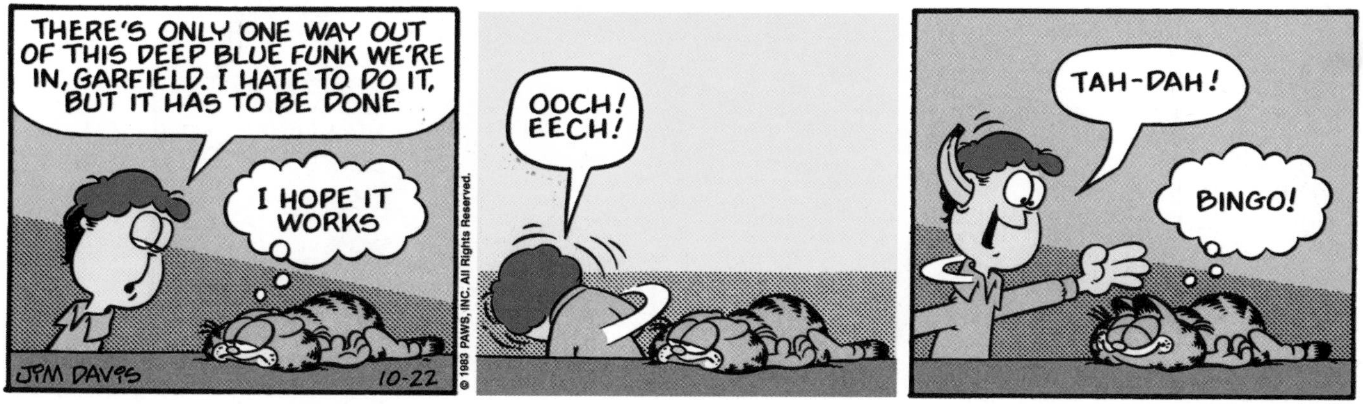
THERE'S ONLY ONE WAY OUT OF THIS DEEP BLUE FUNK WE'RE IN, GARFIELD. I HATE TO DO IT, BUT IT HAS TO BE DONE
I HOPE IT WORKS
JIM DAVIS
10-22
OOCH! EECH!
TAH-DAH!
BINGO!

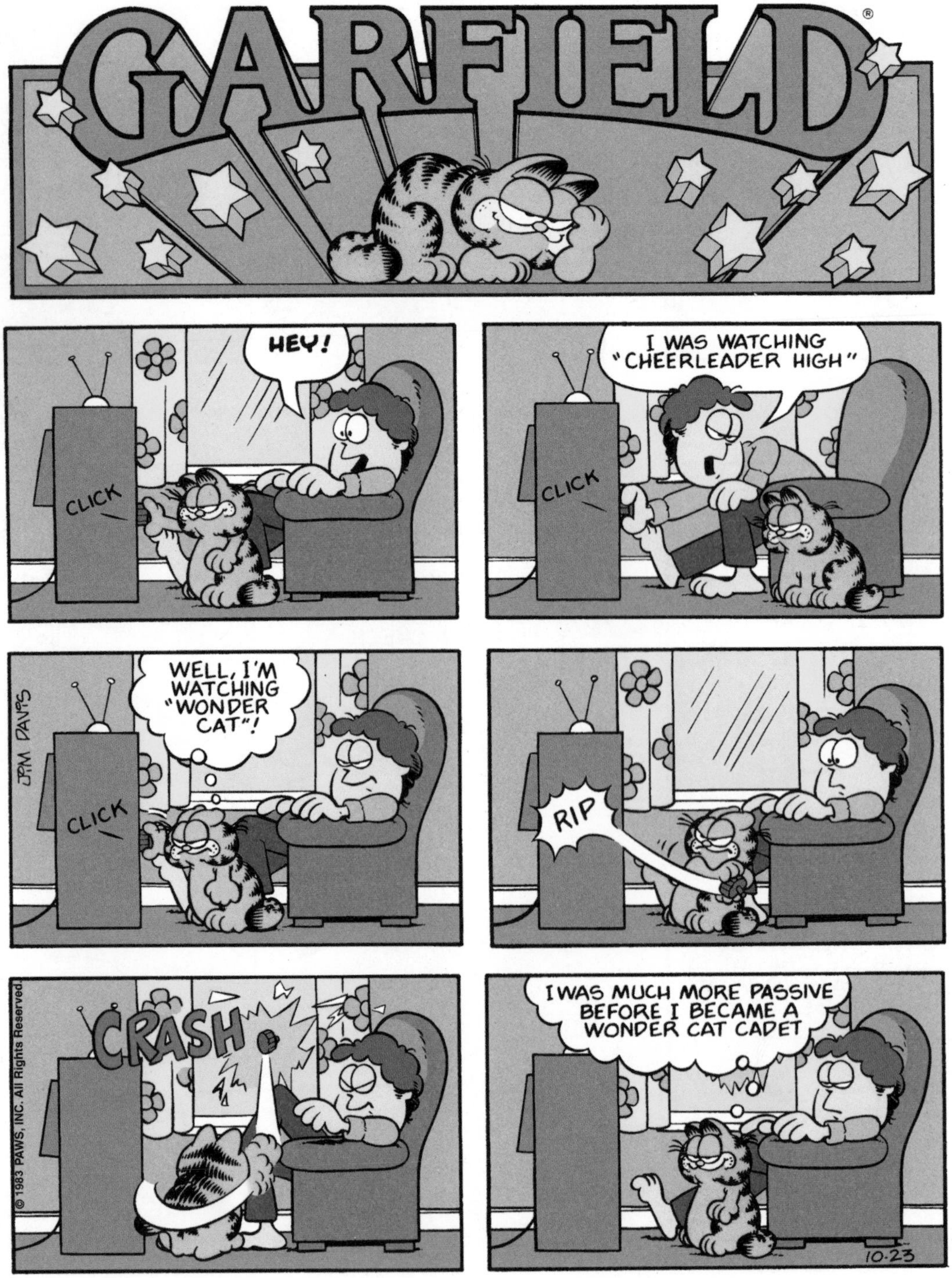
GARFIELD
CLICK
HEY!
CLICK
I WAS WATCHING "CHEERLEADER HIGH"
JIM DAVIS
CLICK
WELL, I'M WATCHING "WONDER CAT"!
RIP
© 1983 PAWS, INC. All Rights Reserved.
CRASH
I WAS MUCH MORE PASSIVE BEFORE I BECAME A WONDER CAT CADET
10-23